The Chilean Dictatorship Novel

The Chilean Dictatorship Novel

MEMORY,

POSTMEMORY,

AFFECT, AND

EMOTIONS

Helene Carol Weldt-Basson

© 2024 by the University of New Mexico Press
All rights reserved. Published 2024
Printed in the United States of America

ISBN 978-0-8263-6900-0 (paper)
ISBN 978-0-8263-6619-1 (cloth)
ISBN 978-0-8263-6620-7 (pdf)

Library of Congress Control Number: 2024937319

Founded in 1889, the University of New Mexico sits on the traditional homelands of the Pueblo of Sandia. The original peoples of New Mexico—Pueblo, Navajo, and Apache—since time immemorial have deep connections to the land and have made significant contributions to the broader community statewide. We honor the land itself and those who remain stewards of this land throughout the generations and also acknowledge our committed relationship to Indigenous peoples. We gratefully recognize our history.

Cover and interior designed by Isaac Morris
Composed in Bookmania, Garamond, and Transtat

To my grandmothers Regina Dorros (1902–1989) and Anna Weldt (1894–1973), in their memory, and to Marc—for the memories we have and the ones we will make.

The man with a good memory remembers
nothing because he forgets nothing.

—Augusto Roa Bastos, *I the Supreme*

Contents

ACKNOWLEDGMENTS   x

CHAPTER 1. Introduction: History, Memory, Postmemory, and Empathy
1

CHAPTER 2. Sins of the Fathers: Abandonment and Loss in Nona Fernández's Novels *Mapocho* and *Fuenzalida* and Álvaro Bisama's *El brujo*
23

CHAPTER 3. Expressions of Despair: Romance Plots and Affective Landscapes in José Donoso's *La desesperanza*, Carlos Franz's *Santiago Cero*, Álvaro Bisama's *Estrellas muertas*, and Germán Marín's *El palacio de la risa*
61

CHAPTER 4. Melancholic Allegories in Ariel Dorfman's *La última canción de Manuel Sendero* and Diamela Eltit's *Jamás el fuego nunca*
95

CHAPTER 5. Betrayal and Abjection in Luce Arce's *El infierno*, Arturo Fontaine's *La vida doble*, and Carlos Franz's *El desierto* and *Almuerzo de vampiros*
128

CHAPTER 6. Affect and Empathy in Nona Fernández's *La dimensión desconocida*, Alia Trabucco Zerán's *La resta*, and Fátima Sime's *Carne de perra*
157

CHAPTER 7. Conclusion: The Chilean Dictatorship Novel in Context
192

NOTES   217

WORKS CITED   224

INDEX   236

Acknowledgments

The completion of this book would not have been possible without the support of University of North Dakota, which granted me a research sabbatical during the 2021–2022 academic year. In addition, I would like to thank the dean of the College of Arts and Sciences, Dr. Bradley Rundquist, for his unfailing support of my research, as well as my former and current chairpersons, Dr. Thyra Knapp and Dr. Melissa Gjellstad, respectively, both of whom have granted me multiple course reductions to do research and write. Their support is deeply appreciated.

Part of chapter 5 was published as "The Concept of Abjection in *El infierno*, *La vida doble*, and *El desierto*," (*Inti*, vol. 91–92, 2020, pp. 252–267) and part of chapter 6 was published as "Affect and Emotions in Two Chilean Postmemory Narratives: *La dimensión desconocida* by Nona Fernández and *La resta* by Alia Trabucco Zerán" (*Revista Canadiense de Estudios Hispánicos*, vol. 45, no. 3, 2021, pp.161-187). Thanks to both of these journals for granting permission to use this material in my book.

Unless published English translations of the novels and other works I examine in this study already exist, all translations are mine. Such published translations frequently appear in parenthetical citations in the text and come after the original Spanish. When that happens, readers will find the published English translation indicated in brackets, shortened and printed in roman. In the endnotes, when the occasion demands it, I remind readers of those instances when translations are mine and when I rely on those of others.

I would also like to thank everyone at the University of New Mexico Press, especially my editor Elise McHugh, and my copyeditor James Cruise for their hard work.

CHAPTER 1

Introduction

History, Memory, Postmemory, and Empathy

IN DECEMBER 2021, CHILE HELD a presidential runoff between two candidates from opposite ends of the political spectrum: on the far right, José Antonio Kast and on the far left, Gabriel Boric. Although Kast had a slight edge over Boric in the initial election in November, Boric went on to defeat Kast having won about 54 percent of the vote. These election results illustrate how in many ways Chilean citizens continue to be sharply divided in terms of politics and the future of Chile, as well as how they continue to be influenced by the past. In fact, many of the citizens whose comments were published in newspaper articles cited memories of the Pinochet dictatorship (whether positive or negative) as the reason to support one candidate or the other. Those who voted for Kast backed how he embraced Pinochet's economic policies, while those supporting Boric recoiled from that embrace, fearing that Kast represented a threat to their freedom and a repudiation of any reform that would aid the poor.

To some degree, Chile's recent election confirms the ideas put forth by Tomás Moulián who in *Chile Actual* posits the origins of contemporary Chilean society in the Pinochet dictatorship and, in particular, its neoliberal economic policies. According to Moulián, the military justified its use of cruelty by proposing and achieving the transformation of Chile from an outmoded society to a modernized country through neocapitalism. This economic philosophy continued after the dictatorship's end in the democratic Concertación governments. For Moulián, the Concertación governments, built on a platform of consensus, assure "la arquitectura del dispositivo transformista. . . . Después de este siglo de enfrentamientos entre dos ideas de la modernidad, la capitalista y la socialista, la primera ha demostrado su viabilidad histórica. Según este razonamiento, bien ha comprobado su carácter de encarnación real de la razón" ([54] the architecture of the transformist mechanism. . . . After this century of confrontations between two ideas of modernity, the capitalist and the socialist, the former has demonstrated its historical viability. According to this reasoning, capitalism has proven itself to be right). In the recent election, Kast supporters clearly signaled their approbation of neoliberal economic policy, while Boric supporters talked about economic reforms to help the poor.

Juan Poblete takes the impact of neoliberalism in Chile one step further, illustrating how neoliberal economic policy contributed to a politics of forgetting past atrocities in Chile. According to Poblete,

> [a]s a memory apparatus neoliberalism depended on a dual evacuation of historical time. Individuals in constant pursuit of personal satisfaction in a market society were pushed to shed the past so that the present could persist unchanged (the developed future being just a radical and massive extension through consumption of the trickling-down successes of the present as currently enjoyed by a few). But this historical social past was also recreated [sic] as simultaneously irrelevant and dangerous for such an extension. By definition, any idea stemming from the social past (especially the socialist past) was deemed irrelevant for the present and future at the same time it was conceived as threatening them (at best as a negative counterexample). A future-as-extended present that could so decisively dispose of the past was then affirmed precisely on such radical erasure, always dependent on its radical newness. (105)

Poblete's comments refer both to the dictatorship and postdictatorship period in Chile and explain, to a degree, why some citizens remembered Pinochet positively during this most recent election.

Finally, neoliberalism also contributed to the discontent that led to the Chilean student movements of 2006 and 2011. According to Peter M. M. Cummings, although Chile's economy had grown because of neoliberalism, which meant greater access to education, these increased capabilities led to higher expectations among students who were still suffering from high tuition rates, unequal wealth distribution, and school segregation based on income (61). Whereas in the 1990s, many were simply content with the return to democracy and were thus afraid to "rock the boat," the students of the 2000s were known as "la generación sin miedo" (the generation without fear) and were more ready to protest. Cummings states that "the fearless generation" became a collective identity of the post-Pinochet era that united students and moved them to action (64). A second factor in the delaying of protests was related to the governments of the left-center coalition party La Concertación during the transition to democracy in the 1990s, which had "deliberately broken ties with social organizations and conducted an elite-centered form of politics focused on consensus-building and negotiation. . . . [K]ey leaders of the student movement of the 1980s [accordingly] found themselves boxed out of the new political scene" (59).

The election comments and results that coincided with the writing of this book reflect the ongoing importance of the topic of memory of the dictatorship in Chile. In this introduction, I explore four key intertwined concepts that ground the literary works I have chosen to study: history, memory, postmemory, and empathy. My fundamental proposition is that the majority of works written about the dictatorship, particularly those in the postdictatorship period, not only resurrect the emotions that people then experienced but also have done so in such striking ways that contemporary readers, stirred by empathy, have become new witnesses of past horrors and unimaginable suffering. After examining this hypothesis in numerous works, I demonstrate in the conclusion how the Chilean body of literary works on the Pinochet dictatorship, through its collective focus on emotions, is different from other national dictatorship literature that tends to seize on dictator profiles, collective psychology, and historical events.

Historical Overview

In 1970, the Socialist candidate Salvador Allende Gossens was democratically elected president of Chile. Allende advocated a peaceful and open road to socialism but met strong opposition from the Chilean upper classes, as well as from the United States, both fearing that Chile would become another Cuba as the Cold War dragged on. An economic blockade by the United States, the CIA-backed trucker strike, and other events led to severe product shortages in supermarkets and an eventual state of crisis by 1973. Allende, as Steve J. Stern argues, wanted the legislature to approve a state of emergency, but senators of the Center and Right feared that he could not control his party's hard-liners, which would lead to economic ruin and ultimately a left-wing dictatorship (*Battling* 21). This breakdown eventually led members of the Center (Christian Democrats), such as future president Patricio Aylwin, to support the military coup led by army general Augusto Pinochet on September 11, 1973.

Most Center and Right citizens who backed the dictatorship thought that it would be a temporary measure that would ensure the restoration of democracy. However, what followed was what Stern terms a systematic "policide" of the Left, which he likens to a smaller scale Holocaust:

> In the Chilean case, the scale of violent annihilation was far smaller than the extermination campaigns of Nazi Germany and Hutu Power Rwanda. In Chile, the main targets for systematic destruction were defined as political beings, not ethnically or racially. . . . If one moves away from a lawyerly discussion of historical taxonomy, however, one can see a family of similar historical phenomena. In Chile the project of policide—annihilating the Left and more broadly Center and Left cultural understandings of politics as a process of popular mobilization, via massive killing and abduction of real and alleged Left activists . . . —yielded issues of comprehensibility and representation similar to those in classic cases of genocide. (*Reckoning* 101–02)

In *Battling for Hearts and Minds* (2006), Stern cites the following credible estimates of the tortures, murders, and disappearances that the Pinochet government perpetrated: 3,500–4,500 deaths and disappearances; over 100,000 torture victims; 150,000–200,000 political arrests; and 400,000 political exiles (*Battling* xxi). These events were traumatic for the victims and their families, but both the government and Chilean citizens long denied they ever happened.

The Pinochet dictatorship endured until 1990. In 1988, a plebiscite was held in which the populace was to vote "yes" or "no" to his continuance as president. The anticipation of the plebiscite led to the formation of a strong Center-Left Coalition party known as La Concertación, which tirelessly worked toward the achievement of a "no" vote. Although Pinochet lost the plebiscite, and the Concertación candidate Patricio Aylwin won the 1990 presidential election, which restored democracy to Chile, Pinochet's influence did not end there. Through the rewriting of the Constitution during his tenure and the passing of various laws, he managed to incorporate numerous protections for himself, such as the 1978 Amnesty Law that forbade prosecution of the members of his government and the army for human rights abuses. In the difficult negotiations to assure his exit as president, Pinochet was able to remain an army commander until 1998 and to continue as senator for life after that.

Memory and postmemory of traumatic events such as the Pinochet dictatorship have been the subject of studies in many disciplines. Elizabeth Jelin's *Los trabajos de la memoria* (The Work of Memory) is a sociological reflection on the workings of memory in society that is highly applicable to Chilean history. She probes many aspects of memory and among them are how different social actors fight for different memories, how memory relates to gender, and how memories are transmitted to future generations. Of particular interest for this study are Jelin's reflections on the relationship between history and memory. Hers is a postmodern view of history and, as such, history itself is not a "'reconstrucción' de lo que 'realmente' ocurrió" (a reconstruction of what really happened) but a complex task that incorporates the subjectivity of social agents, interpretive processes, and narrative strategies. History and memory are different but intertwined processes. Jelin suggests three possible relationships between the two:

> En primer lugar, la memoria como recurso para la investigación, en el proceso de obtener y construir "datos" sobre el pasado; en segundo lugar, el papel que la investigación histórica puede tener para "corregir" memorias equivocadas o falsas; finalmente, la memoria como objeto de estudio o de investigación.... La construcción de memorias sobre el pasado se convierte, entonces, en un objeto de estudio de la propia historia, el estudio histórico de las memorias, que llama así a "historizar las memorias." (96–102)

First, memory as a resource for research, in the process of obtaining and constructing "facts" about the past; second, the role that historical research may have in "correcting" mistaken or false memories; finally, memory as an object of study or investigation.... The construction of memories of the past is converted, then, into an object of study of history itself, the historical study of those memories, that thus calls for "historizing memories."

Likewise, Stern's trilogy (*Remembering Pinochet's Chile* [2004], *Reckoning with Pinochet* [2010], and *Battling for Hearts and Minds* [2006]) on the Pinochet dictatorship also examines the history of Chile during the dictatorship and postdictatorship period through the lens of memory. He argues that interpreting Chile's history as a battle between "memory" and "forgetting" oversimplifies the matter and that, instead, we must view its history as a set of competing memory narratives that he describes accordingly:

> The metaphor I find useful ... is that of a giant, collectively built memory box.... The memory chest is a precious box to which people are drawn, to which they add or rearrange pictures and scripts, and about which they quarrel and even scuffle. This trilogy asks how Chileans built and struggled over the "memory box of Pinochet's Chile," understood as the holder of truths about a traumatic turning point in their collective lives. (*Battling* xxxviii)

Stern posits four main memory "stories" that were created at different time periods (and often overlapped) from the inception of the dictatorship through the death of Pinochet in 2006: memory as salvation; as cruel rupture; as persecution and awakening; and as a box containing the dirty past that must be closed (forgetting). The "memory as salvation" narrative was based on false "evidence" that the dictatorship created to justify the imposition of military rule and a purge of the leftist subversives. It included Plan Z, a forged list of individuals the Left intended to murder and spurious photographs of weapons it would use to enforce its own dictatorship. Pinochet "saved" the country from an even worse fate: a violent Marxist takeover that would have resulted in the murder of prominent individuals and led to economic ruin. The subsequent "counter" memories of cruel rupture and persecution/awakening to Chile's reality started to take hold around 1976–1977, reinforced by the creation of the *Vicaría de la Solidaridad* (The Vicariate of Solidarity) on January 1, 1976, by archbishop Raúl Henríquez Silva. The *Vicaría* housed the group known as the *Agrupación de Familiares de Detenidos-Desaparecidos* (The Family Members of the Detained-Disappeared) who embodied the concept of memory as cruel rupture. Memory as persecution and awakening, while similar, emerged a little later, between 1979–1982, and involved what Stern calls the "self-reflection" of the Christian Democrats who initially supported the dictatorship but now realized their mistake with a growing awareness of the human rights abuses that were being committed (Battling xix–xxxi). In this regard, the discovery of cadavers in the town of Lonquen in 1979 was the first physical proof of crimes committed by the dictatorship and aided in the "awakening" of many Chilean citizens who had previously turned a blind eye to the actions of the dictatorship. Finally, the narrative of the need to forget the dirty past and move on by defining the traumatic events "as inevitable tragedies and excesses of war" became dominant by the early 1980s when Pinochet sought to institutionalize the dictatorship through a new Constitution in 1980 (*Battling* 167).

Stern examines what he terms "memory knots," which are "strongly motivated human groups, symbolically powerful events and anniversary or commemoration dates, haunting remains and places ... [that] galvanize struggles to shape and project into the public cultural domain ways of remembering that capture an essential truth" (*Battling* 4). As we shall see subsequently, Stern's concept of "memory knots" constitutes the central axis of some of the novels dealing with dictatorship that I examine.

The memory question did not end when Pinochet eventually stepped down in 1990; it was, instead, only just beginning. Since Pinochet was still a threat to the budding democracy, the transition government had to walk a fine line between placating Pinochet and the Right and acknowledging and repairing the wrongs done to those who were tortured, disappeared, and murdered under him. Under the 1978 Amnesty Law, perpetrators could not be punished, but it was also the task of the new government to somehow provide recognition and repair to those who had been victimized and their families. In the end, the need for justice could not be permanently shelved. Stern calls the tensions of this moment a "memory impasse" (*Battling* xxviii). President Aylwin's government relied on "Convivencia" (coexistence) and reconciliation as its primary values. To recognize the trauma suffered by citizens and their families under Pinochet, Aylwin constituted the Truth Commission (known as the Rettig Commission) to research and examine cases that resulted in death. Although the Commission was limited in scope (it did not deal with surviving torture victims) and in its ability to bring about justice (the cases could not be prosecuted), it was an important first step in acknowledging and repairing the harm done to many Chileans. When Aylwin presented the results of the Rettig

Report to his country, he apologized to the victims and their families on behalf of the entire nation. In that presentation, Aylwin states:

> When it was agents of the State who caused so much suffering and the pertinent organs of the State could not or knew not to avoid it and punish it and there also was not the necessary social response to stop it, the State and the whole society are responsible, whether by action or by omission. It is Chilean society that is in debt to the victims of violations of human rights.
>
> That is why the suggestions for moral and material reparation that the Report formulates are shared by all sectors. [Voice turns emotional, eyes fill with tears]. That is why I venture, in my condition as President of the Republic, to assume representation of the entire nation in order, in its name, to apologize [pedir perdón] to the relatives of the victims.
>
> It was Aylwin's finest hour as president. (*Reckoning* 85)

The intertwining of history and emotion in Aylwin's speech is significant because subsequent Concertación governments (such as Eduardo Frei's, which followed Aylwin's) were far less concerned with remembering the past and, according to Stern, felt that "prudence dictated indifference to emotion" (*Reckoning* 155). In other words, although emotion was inextricably linked to the historical past and the perpetrated atrocities, the Concertación governments tended to divorce remembering from the emotions felt by victims and their families. Nonetheless, these emotions were directly associated with what had happened and became as important as the events themselves.

Stern traces the eventual evolution of this "memory impasse" in the final chapters of *Reckoning*, the third volume of his trilogy. Although the memory situation slowly evolved over time, numerous events from 1998–2000 contributed to an important memory shift. These included Pinochet's loss of influence over the military when he retired as army commander in 1998, his arrest in London that same year, and the *funas* or outings of former torturers that began to occur in Santiago. Despite the Frei government's indifference to memory work, in 1999 the Defense Minister Edmundo Pérez Yoma announced the formation of a "Dialogue Table," constituted by members from opposing memory sectors, to take up unfinished work on human rights abuses under Pinochet. The work of the Dialogue Table, however, was largely unsuccessful. Nonetheless, its participants "floated a new framework for collective memory—... as a shared tragedy" (*Reckoning* 264), a key concept to which I give additional attention.

In 2002–2006, "memory as unfinished work," took hold, helped by President Ricardo Lagos's (2000–2006) establishment of a second truth commission, the Valech Commission. According to Stern: "The Valech Commission's mandate was to identify persons who suffered imprisonment and torture for political reasons under military rule and to make recommendations for social repair. Its broader mission was awareness: the truth of torture, irrefutably documented and recognized by the state" (*Reckoning* 286).

The ability to obtain justice for the tortured and disappeared in Chile evolved over time. Aiding that cause were provisions in the Amnesty Law that allowed for the prosecution under current law of open disappearances as kidnappings (*Reckoning* 217). Eventually, old judges who were loyal to Pinochet retired and replacing them were more open-minded judges who were willing to prosecute previously untouchable cases. Judge Juan Guzmán investigated murders committed in the Caravan of Death and other famous cases, ultimately declaring Pinochet fit to stand trial, though the former dictator died before he could ever be brought to justice.

I have chosen to focus extensively here on Stern's trilogy on Chile because it is unique in the way Stern examines Chilean history through the lens of memory, which is the historical element most pertinent to the literary texts I study in this volume. Despite the eventual achievement of justice for the victims of Pinochet and their families, the question of how to remember and learn from the past looms large in Chile and to which the literary narratives about his dictatorship (its fiftieth anniversary in 2023) attest. Many of those who lived through the initial coup are now gone. However, subsequent generations have listened to stories about Pinochet and continue to be affected by him. They feel it is important to remember the dictatorship. The relationship of subsequent generations to the dictatorship brings us to the concept of postmemory and its relationship to memory.

Memory versus Postmemory

During the last decade, cultural criticism has focused extensively on the terms "memory" and "postmemory." The latter term became popular in the wake of Marianne Hirsch's *The Generation of Postmemory* (2012); in it, she discusses the effects of the Holocaust on the second generation who did not directly experience it but heard firsthand stories from their parents. Writes Hirsch, this second generation is the postmemory generation because even though its members do not have direct memories of the traumatic event, their experience of the Holocaust is almost as if their parents' memories were their own and are thus also traumatic for them: "these experiences were transmitted to them so deeply and affectively as to seem to constitute memories in their own right. Postmemory's connection to the past is thus actually moderated not by recall but by imaginative investment, projection and creation" (5). Ever since Hirsch's seminal work, other critics have expanded the term "postmemory" to include not only the second generation but also all subsequent generations. For example, Stephen Frosh indicates in *Those Who Came After* (2019) that the concept of postmemory is "a field of study concerned mainly with the 'transgenerational' impact of personal and social trauma" (8). He broadens the concept to refer not only to children of trauma victims but also to members of future generations who are haunted by past traumas:[1]

> How then do we deal with these shadowy "memories" passed on by those who have come before us, including unconscious sensations and echoes of a past that was not our own? What should we do with those memories, especially when they are disturbing or unsettling? The tendency to think that when we are haunted by ghostly figures and events from the past ... [then that] is because the issues they raise—mostly of maltreatment, violence, untimeliness, and trauma, have not been resolved and continue to fester, becoming a kind of poison in the bloodstream of the present. (28)

Ron Eyerman's *Cultural Trauma* (2002), in this vein, offers useful terminology for discussing the effects of trauma on subsequent generations. He defines three types of trauma: individual, cultural, and national. Individual trauma is self-explanatory: it refers to the physical or emotional trauma suffered by a particular person. Cultural trauma, in turn, refers to the "traumatic loss of identity and meaning, a tear in the social fabric, affecting a group of people" —as examples, Holocaust victims or enslaved African Americans. However, cultural trauma, which affects a specific group, can rise to the level of what he terms "national trauma" when it becomes part of the collective memory of an entire nation. To that end, Eyerman cites Arthur Neal's definition of "national trauma" as an event with "enduring effects... which cannot be easily dismissed, which will be played over again and again in individual consciousness... [as it is] ingrained in collective memory." The civil rights movement in the United States, by reopening "the wound of slavery," translated a past cultural trauma into a national trauma (2).

As Stern's analysis of Chile's memory box illustrates, in time the human rights abuses perpetrated under the Pinochet dictatorship rose to the level of national trauma in Chile. The memory narrative that emerged from the Dialogue Table established by the Lagos administration, that of "shared national tragedy," suggests that both the Right and the Left came to view the atrocities committed in this way, even though there are individuals who continue to see Pinochet in a positive light. Memorials such as the Museo de la Memoria Chilena, opened in 2010, and the Villa Grimaldi Peace Park, in 2014, suggest that what was once a left-wing cultural trauma, now constitutes a Chilean national trauma.

One of the many ways in which subsequent generations "remember" the Pinochet dictatorship is through the literature written by a traumatized generation, the postmemory generation, and beyond. According to Grínor Rojo, in *Las novelas de la dictadura y la postdictadura chilena* (2016), by 2016 Chilean authors had written 179 novels about the dictatorship. This number has undoubtedly grown given that every year new novels on the topic are published, several of which appear in this study. In this book, I argue that the majority of these novels, as a function of postmemory, capture the essence of the Pinochet dictatorship by seizing on the emotions of its victims. Although novelistic literature often depicts the emotions of characters and thereby seeks to evoke emotions in readers, the emphasis on emotions in these novels is unique for three reasons: first, the focus on feelings is unusual in the genre of dictatorship novels that typically feature other elements; second, emotions specifically fill a historical void in Chile's so-called "memory box"; and third, the emphasis on character and reader emotion constitutes a form of "witnessing" trauma within the context of national trauma to create empathy and prosocial behavior in the reader. In the remainder of this introduction, I focus only on the historical void and the concept of witnessing.

One of the major criticisms of the Concertación governments (the administrations of Aylwin,[2] Frei, Lagos, and Bachelet) was that they severed emotion from trauma—the kind Chilean citizens and their families had suffered—and reduced the question of memory to acknowledgment and reparations, that is, to the need for reconciliation and moving beyond the past. Stern notes that

> [t]he perils of the Contreras affair and the Frei administration's own priorities heightened desire, within Concertación sectors as well as the opposition, to close the memory box of Pinochet's Chile.... Prudence dictated polite indifference to emotion.... Could conflict and unbridled expressiveness unhinge Chile's transition? The culture of elite prudence, a kind of self-censorship within democracy, took especially sophisticated form in Concertación circles. (*Reckoning* 155)

The important cultural critic Nelly Richard in *Eruptions* similarly registers the lack of emotion that characterized the approach of La Concertación:

> During the Transition, the political meanings of memory were once again rendered inoffensive through the use of words stripped of both emotion and fear. Even if the Transition's discourse occasionally alluded to memory as conflict, it was not able to *express its agony*....
> The Transition-era administrations followed a consensus-oriented script that turned memory into a solemn yet almost painless citation. Their evocation of memory failed to mention all the material injury of the past: its psychic density, its experiential volume, its affective trace, and its scarred backgrounds, the pain of which is diminished neither by the merely compulsory method of the judicial process nor by official memory plaques. (3)

These citations underscore how the transition governments voided memory of its emotions. Yet, as Eva Hoffman, a second-generation postmemory writer, emphasizes in *After Such Knowledge* (2005), the trauma suffered by her parents

Introduction 13

during the Holocaust was communicated to her as pure emotion rather than coherent narrative:

> But in our small apartment, it was a chaos of emotion that emerged from their words rather than any coherent narration. Or rather, the emotion, direct and tormented, was enacted through the words, the forms of their utterances.... In my home, as in so many others, the past broke through in the sounds of nightmares, the idiom of signs and illness, of tears and the acute aches that were the legacy of the damp attic and of the conditions my parents endured during their hiding. (8)

In a like manner, the Chilean novel of dictatorship seeks to reinscribe emotion into the memory of the atrocities committed under Pinochet.

Hirsch emphasizes the connection between postmemory and imaginative re-creation of events. Although she focuses primarily on photography and images, much of what she says is equally applicable to literary works: "As the images repeat the trauma of looking, they disable, in themselves, any restorative attempts. It is only when they are redeployed, in new texts and new contexts, that they regain a capacity to enable a postmemorial working through. The aesthetic strategies of postmemory are specifically about such attempted, and yet always postponed, repositioning and reintegration" (122).

The Chilean writer Nona Fernández, who is considered a second-generation writer because she was two years old at the time of the military coup, emphasizes the important connection between memory and emotion, as well as the significance of literature in communicating the past to the future. In *Voyager* (2020), Fernández writes:

> La palabra recordar, como muy bien se sabe, viene del latín *recordari*, y está formada por el prefijo *re*, que señala una repetición, y por la palabra *cordis*, que quiere decir corazón. Recordar es entonces, etimológicamente hablando, volver a pasar por el corazón. Pero si cada vez que recordamos una constelación de neuronas se enciende en algún lugar de nuestro cerebro, habría que suponer entonces que el cerebro y el corazón, como dos peces amarrados de sus colas, están estrechamente vinculados. (81)

The word to remember [recordar], as it is well known, comes from the Latin word *recordari*, and is formed by the prefix *re*, which indicates repetition, and by the word *cordis*, which means heart. To remember is then, etymologically speaking, to go through the heart once again. But if each time that we remember a constellation of neurons lights up somewhere in our brain, one must then suppose that the brain and the heart, like two fish tethered by their tails, are closely connected.[3]

For Fernández, books are the principal vehicle for connecting the memory of the past to the future: "Un libro es una cápsula espacio temporal. Detiene el presente y lo lanza al mañana como un mensaje" ([152] A book is a time capsule. It freezes the present and launches it toward tomorrow like a message). The literary reworking of the emotions experienced by Chileans resulting from the dictatorship (whether during or after) can be critically judged, then, as a creative act that allows the reader to bear witness to trauma.

In *Literature in the Ashes of History* (2013), Cathy Caruth suggests that imaginative transformations of traumatic events offer a way to simultaneously memorialize and move forward from such events. Caruth offers the example from Freud's writings in which a child repeatedly makes a spool of thread appear (*da*, here) and disappear (*fort*, there):

> Yet the game of the child playing FORT and DA, gone and here, with his spool seems to become not less, but more, enigmatic when it is understood in relation to traumatic repetition. If the child's reenactment of his mother's departure repeats, ultimately, her loss and her death, the game remains, nonetheless, an act of creation that, unlike the dream of the war veterans, does not simply compulsively repeat a history it doesn't own but creates, in its repetition, something new. (7)

This concept is key to comprehending the Chilean dictatorship novel and its basis in emotive re-creation. Like the example from Freud in Caruth's book, the literary reimagining of emotions creates something new, namely, Fernández's "time capsule," which aims to promote empathy in the reader/witness and hence the avoidance of the repetition of similar atrocities in the future. The emotions of despair, fear, and abandonment that pervade the dictatorship novels result in the reader's identification and empathy with the characters. E. Ann Kaplan identifies three ways in which readers may respond empathically to images: empty empathy, vicarious trauma, and witnessing. Empty empathy occurs when empathy is "numbed" because the viewer is bombarded with numerous and successive catastrophes and vicarious trauma when the viewer identifies too strongly with the image and turns away because the empathic response is too painful to bear. Witnessing, on the other hand, refers to

> a response that may change the viewer in a positive pro-social manner, and that, more than the first two types of response, involves ethics.... It involves feeling so shocked by suffering that one is moved to act. One may feel vaguely responsible, but in any case, one is motivated to see that justice is done. In witnessing, we understand empathy's potential social impact, especially when it is deeply and enduringly felt. (256)

Kaplan's categories are equally applicable to literary works. The Chilean dictatorship novels studied here cause the reader to bear witness to the past atrocities and advocate for future social justice through an empathetic response. The ways in which literary texts inspire empathy are numerous and complex, meriting a separate overview.

Empathy

Although an extensive body of work exists on readerly emotions and reader-response, that is beyond the scope of this book. It is well-established, nonetheless, that readers experience emotions when reading novels even though they know that they are reading about fictional worlds, not reality. I would like to mention one of the more recent contributions, Mariano Longo's *Emotions through Literature* (2019). Longo subscribes to the idea that readers experience "quasi-emotions" in their reactions to fictitious worlds:

> Quasi-emotions emerge as a response to fictional situations ... which make the referential attitude no longer relevant. Quasi-emotions are

elicited by actions, situations, or characters which, rather than being untrue, are true only in the circumscribed reality of fictional worlds.... This means that we are not actually emotionally involved by fictional events or characters, but we take part in a representative game.... By make-believing, we simulate the belief in the reality of an utterly different, separated world, that is the fictional world of narrative art.... If the world of fiction and the real world are neatly separated, one has to explain why we nonetheless are empathetically moved by fictional characters. The solution is quasi-emotions.... For Walton [author of "Fearing Fictions"], to interact in any way with a fictional character we must 'enter' a fictional world. (66–68)

The existence of "quasi-emotions," however, does not actually explain the process whereby reader empathy is created. Theories from various disciplines (among them, psychology, philosophy, and neuroscience) attempt to explain this phenomenon. One of the principal psychological foundations of empathy is simulation theory. Amy Coplan bases her definition of empathy on it:

Empathy is a complex imaginative process in which an observer simulates another person's situated psychological states while maintaining clear self-other differentiation. To say that empathy is 'complex' is to say that it is simultaneously a cognitive and affective process. To say that empathy is 'imaginative' is to say that it involves the representation of a target's states [the target is the person or character experiencing an emotion] that are activated by, but not directly accessible through, the observer's perception. And to say that empathy is a simulation is to say that the observer replicates or reconstructs the target's experiences, while maintaining a clear sense of self-other differentiation. (5)

Simulation theory thus is one way of explaining how readers experience empathy for literary characters. A second major explanation of empathetic identification evolves from experiments conducted in neuroscience. Tania Singer and Claus Lamm cite Frédérique De Vignemont and Tania Singer's definition of empathy, but also acknowledge that empathy has been defined in numerous other ways:

Introduction   17

> We "empathize" with others when we have (1) an affective state,
> (2) which is isomorphic to another person's affective state,
> (3) which was elicited by observing or imagining another person's
> affective state, and (4) when we know that the other person's affective
> state is the source of our own affective state. (82)

Singer and Lamm also discuss neuroscientific experiments on empathy. They cite, among others, experiments conducted on the reactions of individuals observing pain in others:

> One common finding of these investigations is that vicariously experiencing pain activates part of the neural network that is also activated when we are in pain ourselves.... The results suggest that parts of the so-called pain matrix which consists of the brain areas involved in the processing of pain, were activated when participants experienced pain themselves as well as when they saw a signal indicating that their loved one would experience pain. These areas—in particular, bilateral anterior insula [central lobe], the dorsal anterior cingulate cortex, brain stem, and the cerebellum—are involved in the processing of the affective component of pain; in other words, they encode how unpleasant or aversive the subjectively felt pain is. Thus, both the firsthand experience of pain and the knowledge that a beloved partner is experiencing pain activates the same affective brain circuits—suggesting that our own neural response reflects our partner's negative affect. (85)[4]

Neuroscience studies on empathy are principally based on the concept of mirror neurons. The book that best explains how they function is Marco Iacoboni's *Mirroring People* (2008) in which he remarks,

> [w]e achieve our very subtle understanding of other people thanks
> to certain collections of special cells in the brain called mirror neurons.... They bind us with each other mentally and emotionally....
> Why do we give ourselves over to emotion during the ... heart-rending
> scenes in certain movies? Because mirror neurons in our brains
> re-create for us the distress we see on the screen. We have empathy

for the fictional characters—we know how they're feeling—because we literally experience the same feeling ourselves.... When we see someone else suffering or in pain, mirror neurons help us to read her or his facial expression and actually make us feel the suffering or the pain of the other person. These moments, I will argue, are the foundation of empathy and possibly morality, a morality that is deeply rooted in our biology. (4)

The existence of mirror neurons raises an interesting question regarding the impact of mental imagery, particularly in the act of reading. According to Nigel Thomas, images can be "constructed inventively or retrieved from memory" (6). Terri Pullen Guezzar, drawing on Rudolf Arnheim's work, states:

> Arnheim ... emphasized the visual aspect of readers' responses, associating imagery with literary texts because description and metaphor preserve the initial perceptual impact of the visual sense: "Words gain their meaning only through the past experience of the reader. There are those who visualize the person and places of a novel with photographic exactness." (51)

Many other critics, such as Wolfgang Iser and Louise Rosenblatt,[5] also agree that literary reading inspires the construction of mental imagery (Guezzar 49). When reading acquires a visual aspect through mental imagery, it is akin to watching a film, only this "film" unreels inside the reader's head. We can thus argue that mental images have the same effects on mirror neurons as when one views or looks at something external or beyond the self. Iacoboni conducted experiments on volunteers who viewed and/or imitated expressions of images of faces that represented emotions such as fear, anger, sadness, and disgust. fMRI (functional magnetic resonance imaging) technology showed the simultaneous activation of three areas of the volunteers' brains (mirror neurons, limbic system, and insula). According to Iacoboni,

> [r]esults confirmed my two predictions. Indeed, mirror neuron areas, the insula, and emotional brain areas in the limbic system ... were activated while subjects were observing the faces, and the activity

increased in those subjects who were also imitating what they saw. These results clearly supported the idea that mirror neuron areas help us understand the emotions of other people by some form of inner imitation. According to this mirror neuron hypothesis of empathy, our mirror neurons fire when we see others expressing their emotions, as if we were making those facial expressions ourselves. By means of this firing, the neurons also send signals to emotional brain centers in the limbic system to make us feel what other people feel.... This simulation process is not an effortful, deliberate pretense of being in somebody else's shoes. It is an effortless, automatic, and unconscious inner mirroring. (128)

Numerous other theories exist of how empathy is created and that can be applied to literary texts. The ones I detail, however, are the most convincing. The fact that novels aim to create reader empathy is particularly important because of the posited connections between empathy and prosocial behavior, which Iacobini also establishes above between empathy and morality.[6] Singer and Lamm, likewise, view empathy as a prerequisite to prosocial behavior:

Folk psychological accounts usually relate the occurrence of empathy to prosocial and altruistic, other-oriented motivations.... In general ... empathy is conceived to be a first necessary step in a chain that begins with affect sharing, followed by understanding the other person's feelings which then motivates other-related concern and finally engagement in helping behavior. Empathy and prosocial behavior are thus closely linked on a conceptual level. (84)

I posit that the novels written about the Pinochet dictatorship, particularly by postmemory writers and writers of all generations subsequent to the dictatorship, focus on conveying the feelings and emotions suffered by victims, precisely to inspire readers to action, even if this action means avoiding such actions that result in dictatorship and atrocities. This goal melds with the desire to fill in the memory gap of emotion that defined the government's position from 1990–2010 with its emphasis on "Convivencia." It is important to emphasize, as I show in my conclusion, that this focus differs from that expressed in the most typical dictatorship novels, which despite generally representing victims' emotions, especially that of fear, rarely present those emotions as the "purpose" or main message of the novels. Instead, these novels concentrate on humanization or criticism of the dictator, representation of the social psychology of a nation, or US imperialism, topics that contribute to the construction of different central messages.

Overview of the Book

Chapter 2 explores the manifestation of feelings of loss and abandonment suffered by children who were separated from their fathers during the dictatorship through an analysis of three important postmemory novels. Using Sabine Schlickers concept of "perturbatory narration," the chapter explores the roles of narrative indeterminacy (through intertextuality in Nona Fernández's *Mapocho*, the blurring of boundaries between reality and fiction in her *Fuenzalida*, and narrative ambiguity in Álvaro Bisama's *El brujo* [The Wizard]). This indeterminacy mimics the indeterminacy regarding what happened to the disappeared and is employed to help create the human environment of wrenching loss that resulted from the dictatorship. In addition to the emotional loss of family, these novels also contain feelings of loss articulated through the theme of spatial injustice (as defined by Edward Soja in *Seeking Spatial Justice* [2010]). The neoliberal reconfiguration of the city of Santiago initiated under the Pinochet dictatorship led to the loss of common spaces and the alteration of both the physical and natural environments. In turn, this resulted in feelings of loss of the landscape and the familiar architectural structures of Santiago. Spatial injustice is an important theme in both *Mapocho* and *Fuenzalida*, whereas the need for the total abandonment of Santiago, because of its association with torture and death, is a significant aspect of *El brujo*. Finally, I examine the role of images and photography in both *Fuenzalida* and *El brujo* in which these devices play an important role in articulating the feelings of the characters.

Chapter 3 examines how four important novels (José Donoso's *La desesperanza* [Curfew]; Carlos Franz's *Santiago Cero* [Santiago Zero]; Germán Marín's *El palacio de las risa* [The Palace of Laughter]; and Álvaro Bisama's *Estrellas muertas* [Dead Stars]) explore the despair Chileans felt under the

Introduction

dictatorship and, as a result of the politics of forgetting, how they prepared for moving beyond and living in the postdictatorship years. The chapter examines the concept of narrative tone, using Sianne Ngai's definition in *Ugly Feelings* (2007) to illustrate how these four novels convey the sense of hopelessness Chilean citizens experienced during these oppressive times. The chapter analyzes how these novels employ two major techniques to create a tone of despair. Instead of the traditional use of heroic plots (see Patrick Colm Hogan, *Affective Narratology* [2011]) typical of the dictatorship novels, these novels employ tragic romance plots to communicate the despair felt by Chilean citizens. In addition, I illustrate how landscape and architecture in these novels aid in the creation of the atmosphere of despair by focusing on those elements that Jacky Bowring defines as melancholic elements of landscape, such as ruins, fragments, silence, patina, weathering, and voids in *Melancholy and the Landscape* (2018).

Chapter 4 studies what Enzo Traverso calls "left-wing melancholia," which was one of the consequences of the end of socialist utopian projects after the fall of the Berlin Wall. It focuses on two allegorical novels (Dorfman's *La última canción de Manuel Sendero* [The Last Song of Manuel Sendero] and Eltit's *Jamás el fuego nunca* [Never Did the Fire]), which use allegory to express feelings of melancholia associated with the end of the Allende years. (Dorfman was Allende's Minister of Culture and went into exile, while Eltit remained in Chile during the dictatorship and was forced to use allegory to avoid censorship.) I show how Dorfman's novel, which focuses on the dictatorship era, constitutes what Gary Johnson terms a "strong allegory" in *The Vitality of Allegory* (2012) because most of its references are relatively clear, while Eltit's novel, which centers on the postdictatorship aftermath, constitutes a "weak allegory" because of its frequent indeterminacies. Narrative tone, myth, and symbols reconstruct the melancholia of the left-wing in both of these works.

Chapter 5 explores how Chilean citizens, as depicted in Carlos Franz's *El desierto* (The Absent Sea) and *Almuerzo de vampiros* (Vampire Lunch); and Arturo Fontaine's *La vida doble* (The Double Life), were made to feel abject through torture and that, to survive, often led them to betray their compatriots. Some of these citizens became collaborators with the government after their imprisonment and torture. I explore these feelings of abjection using Julia Kristeva's concept of the same in *Powers of Horror* (1980) and Mikhail Bakhtin's concept of the grotesque in *Rabelais and his World* (1965). All of the works in this chapter contain (to varying degrees) "gray-zone" characters (a term coined by Primo Levi in *Drowned and the Saved* [1988]), which are an important reflection of the human environment under dictatorship.

Chapter 6 examines how affect is stimulated and translated into emotions of shock, surprise, and fear in three important postdictatorship novels: *Carne de perra* (Dog Meat), *La resta* (The Remainder), and *La dimensión desconocida* (The Twilight Zone). The chapter will show how each novel employs a different technique to create a startle reaction in the readers: fetishistic sexual torture in *Carne*; children's violent games in *La resta*, and parallels with episodes of the famous television series *The Twilight Zone* in *La dimensión*. The chapter employs psychologist Silvan Tomkins's theory of affects that distinguishes affect from emotion by focusing in particular on how the startle affect helps to create reader identification and empathy in *La dimensión*. I also apply Stefano Ercolino's concept of "negative empathy" to *La resta* to show how despite exhibiting characteristics that may seem undesirable to the reader, the characters in the novel manage to inspire audience empathy. Finally, I use Tomkins's work on the affect of disgust/dissmell,[7] as well as William Ian Miller's work on disgust (*Anatomy of Disgust* [1997]), to explain how the creation of disgust in *Carne* is mirrored in the reader who is thus led to empathize with the main character María Rosa. These novels all re-create torture victims' experiences to inspire empathic identification in readers.

Chapter 7 compares the central topics and messages of the Chilean dictatorship novel to this genre in other countries to underscore how the Chilean focus on emotions differs from other novels of dictatorship. I examine four Argentine novels of the dictatorship/postdictatorship period because the history of Argentina most closely resembles that of Chile. Argentina suffered a military coup in 1976 that lasted until 1983; accompanying it was a purge of the left known as "the dirty war." The value in this comparative approach, despite the generic and thematic similarities I point to in Argentinian and Chilean novels, is that it highlights how the focus on emotion in the Chilean dictatorship novel is uniquely tailored to the country's historical circumstances.

CHAPTER 2

Sins of the Fathers

Abandonment and Loss in Nona Fernández's
Novels *Mapocho* and *Fuenzalida* and Álvaro
Bisama's *El brujo*

TWO OF THE MOST PERVASIVE feelings expressed in Chilean novels about the Pinochet dictatorship are those of loss and abandonment. Nan Zheng notes in her article on orphanhood and incest in *Mapocho* (2002) that Nona Fernández has stated that she comes from "una generación medio guacha" (a half-orphaned generation) because many fathers succumbed to torture or were "disappeared" by the government. That led to broken families and stood in stark contrast to the "mito de la nación armónica. En el Chile de la dictadura las equiparaciones ideológicas entre el amor a la familia y el amor a la patria fueron el sustento moral y justificativo del régimen" ([143] myth of the harmonious nation. In the Chilean dictatorship, the ideological equivalence between love of the family and love of the nation was the moral and justifying sustenance of the regime).

Of the many Chilean novels that focus on broken families, I have chosen three that best exemplify how memory of the dictatorship is captured in feelings of abandonment: Nona Fernández's *Mapocho* and *Fuenzalida* (2012); and Álvaro Bisama's *El brujo* (2016). In these novels, broken families are not merely a byproduct of the dictatorship but instead the central registers for remembering its effects. These novels capture abandonment (as well as other strong feelings, such as fear and emptiness) through numerous elements and techniques that include not only the focus on the father-child relationship but also the use of feelings of loss borne of neoliberalism's effects on Santiago, Chilean history itself, and the role of photography on narratives of remembrance.

Nona Fernández (1971–) is herself a Chilean actress and writer. She has published two plays, a collection of short stories, six novels, and an essay. *La dimensión desconocida* (The Twilight Zone), her most recent novel, won the Sor Juana Inés de la Cruz Prize for literature. *Mapocho*, the first of her novels, which was also critically acclaimed, was published in 2002. The novel relates the story of two siblings, Rucia and El Indio, who are now ghosts wandering through Santiago. The dead Rucia's narration alternates with that of a third-person omniscient narrator (and a brief narration by her brother, El Indio, at the end). The narration reveals that when Rucia and her brother were very young, their father was taken away by night by men working for the dictatorship. He never returned. The mother moves the children to a foreign country far from Chile. When pressed on the father's whereabouts, she tells them that he perished in a horrible fire that occurred in their town (the burning of the soccer stadium full of prisoners by the government). However, the reader later learns that the father chose to collaborate with the government (by writing its official history) and did not die in the fire. As a matter of fact, the father, Fausto, is the only main character alive throughout the novel, until his suicide at the end. The segments about Rucia's family and Rucia's return to Santiago as a ghost are mixed with segments about Chilean history: a brief narrative about Bernardo O'Higgins, considered Chile's founding father, an episode about Lautaro and Pedro de Valdivia during the Conquest, a narrative about the construction of the Cal y Canto bridge in the 1700s in La Chimba (Rucia's birthplace and where she grew up), and a segment about the dictatorship of Carlos Ibáñez.[1]

As I later show, most of the historical segments tie into the novel's spatial elements, which aid in articulating a sense of emotional loss and abandonment. However, it is worth noting that the narrative about Bernardo O'Higgins explicitly sets up the theme of abandonment in the novel when we learn that "Guacho es el que no tiene padres" ([168] Orphaned is he who has no parents)[2] and that O'Higgins was himself "guacho" because his father, an Irish colonel during the late eighteenth century, abandoned the family when he left Chile pursuant to military orders.

Rucia and El Indio "inherit" the status of "guachos" from that nation's founding father. In the absence of a father, one of the most significant elements in Rucia's family life is her relationship with her brother, referred to as El Indio (he has no other name in the book, a fact to which I will return). El Indio's relationship with Rucia is characterized by a strong incestuous desire that is mutual. Rucia's mother is aware of the sexual attraction between her children and strictly prohibits it. To avoid its consummation, she eventually sends El Indio away to live by himself in a separate dwelling. Even though the consummation appears not to occur while brother and sister are alive, it does occur after the two are dead. The imposed separation leads to extreme feelings of abandonment on El Indio's part, which grow even more intense when his mother confesses that his father did not actually die in a fire but remained in Chile to work for the government. Sometime afterward, El Indio gets drunk only to entice Rucia and the mother to come with him for a ride in his car. This leads to their fatal accident.

The role of incest in the novel is not immediately clear and has been interpreted variously in the commentary on *Mapocho*. Nan Zheng states that representations of incest "reterritorializan la inmundicia ilegítima del incesto para convertirla en una táctica de subversión" ([143] reterritorialize the idea of the filthy illegitimacy of incest to convert it into a subversive tactic) against patriarchal power, while Laura Senio Blair claims that "incest surfaces as a literary tool for writing about the transgressive violence experienced under Pinochet's rule" (184). The intertextuality of the novel leads to a third possibility, namely, that incest is a manifestation of the father's abandonment of his family and has been directly willed upon the children through the stories the father used to tell them.

There are two stories that Fausto, the family's father, tells his children and those of the neighborhood while they sit on the front steps of the house: one about a little man and woman who are constantly reborn, and a second about a little woman who is born "cracked" and the little man who attempts to "cure" her. Regarding the first story, the third-person narrator gives the reader a clue to its causal value in the following passage:

> Fausto no sabía lo que estaba diciendo cuando sentado en los escalones rojos de su casa inventó esa historia para los niños del barrio. Las palabras ... le salían como pájaros encantando a todos cada tarde. Fausto desconocía el poder de las palabras.... No sabía que bastaba enunciarlas para que ellas cobraran sentido ... Luz, pronunció el dios, y la luz se hizo. Las palabras salen al mundo y buscan su razón de ser, y trazan su futuro, lo amoldan, le dan el curso definitivo, arman la historia. Aquí nacen una mujer y un hombre. Y nunca dejarán de nacer porque la muerte es mentira.... *Fue su boca la que sentenció su propia condena.* (131; my emphasis)

> Fausto did not know what he was saying when seated on the red steps of his house he invented that story for the children of the neighborhood. The words . . . came out like birds enchanting everyone that afternoon. Fausto did not know the power of the words. . . . He didn't know that it was enough to enunciate them for them to make sense. . . . Light, the god pronounced, and light was made. The words come out into the world and look for their reason to be, and they trace their future, they mold it, they give it a definite course, they make up the story. Here a woman and a man are born. And they will never stop being born because death is a lie. . . . It was his mouth that sentenced his own condemnation.

In other words, the ghosts of Rucia and El Indio, as prophesized in his own tale, haunt Fausto. Although they die in a car accident, they are reborn as ghosts and haunt the streets of Santiago and their father. In this sense, death is a lie. However, what the narrator does not reveal in this passage is that Fausto's story about death and rebirth is not an original tale but one taken from volume 1 of Eduardo Galeano's collection of indigenous myths titled *Memorias del fuego* (Memories of the Fire). In the novel, Fausto tells this story in the following manner:

> Érase una vez, hace mucho tiempo, una mujer y un hombre pequeños. La mujer y el hombre . . . soñaban que un dios . . . los soñaba. En el sueño de la pareja el dios soñaba con una gran piñata de colores. . . . La mujer y el hombre pequeños soñaban que el dios, soñando, los creaba y mientras rompía la piñata . . . decía aquí nacen una mujer y un hombre. Y juntos van a vivir y morir. Pero nacerán otra vez y luego morirán. Y nunca dejarán de nacer porque la muerte es una mentira. (131)

> Once upon a time, a long time ago, a small woman and man. The woman and man dreamed that a god . . . dreamed them. In the couple's dream, the god was dreaming about a big, colorful piñata. . . . The small woman and man dreamt that the god, dreaming, created them and while he was breaking the piñata . . . he said here a man and a woman are born. Together they are going to live and die. But they will be born again and then will die again. And never will they stop being born because death is a lie.

A comparison to the myth "La creación" in Galeano's work illustrates that this is clearly the source of the tale:

La mujer y el hombre soñaban que Dios los estaba soñando... La mujer y el hombre soñaban que en el sueño de Dios aparecía un gran huevo brillante. Dentro del huevo, ellos cantaban y bailaban... Dios, soñando, los creaba y cantando decía:
—Rompo este huevo y nace la mujer y nace el hombre. Y juntos vivirán y morirán. Pero nacerán nuevamente. Nacerán y volverán a morir y otra vez nacerán y nunca dejarán de nacer porque la muerte es una mentira. (n.p.)

The woman and the man dreamt that God was dreaming them.... The woman and the man dreamt that in God's dream a big, shiny egg appeared. Within the egg, they sang and danced... God, dreaming, created them and while singing, said:
—I break this egg and the woman is born and the man is born. Together they will live and they will die. But they will be born again. They will be born again, and they will die again and be born again, and they will never stop being born because death is a lie.

In a similar fashion, there is a second story Fausto told the children before his disappearance, only this story remained unfinished:

Érase una vez un hombre y una mujer pequeños—dice. Un dios los lanzó al mundo desde una piñata... Ellos se miraron sus cuerpos desnudos, el uno al otro. ¿Te rajaron? preguntó el hombre al ver la entrepierna de su compañera. No creo, contestó ella. El hombre pequeño se empeñó en que la mujer pequeña estaba herida e inventó ungüentos de colores que aplicó con cuidado en la zona dañada... Un día cuando la mujer pequeña ya pensaba ponerle fin al juego, el hombre apareció loco de contento saltando de alegría gritando feliz ¡Lo tengo! Ya sé cuál es el remedio. (182)

Once upon a time a small woman and man—he says. A god launched them into the world from a piñata. They looked at their naked bodies and at each other. Did they crack you?, asked the man when he saw his companion's crotch. I don't think so, she answered. The little man insisted that the little woman was wounded and he invented colored ointments that he applied with care to the damaged area.... One day when the little woman was already thinking about ending the game, the man appeared over the moon jumping with happiness, gleefully shouting I have it! I know what the cure is.

Rucia always wondered about the ending to this story. When her ghost reencounters Fausto in Santiago, she requests that he finally finish it, but, in the end, he does not comply.

This story, just like the one about death being a lie, is not actually an original tale invented by Fernández for her character Fausto to tell. It is a slightly altered version of the myth titled "El amor" (also taken from volume 1 of Galeano's *Memoria*), its ending key to deciphering the role of incest in the novel:

La primera mujer y el primer hombre se miraron con curiosidad. Era raro lo que tenían entre las piernas.
¿—Te han cortado?—preguntó el hombre.
—No—dijo ella. Siempre he sido así.
Él la examinó de cerca.... allí había una llaga abierta. Dijo:
... Yo te curaré. Échate en la hamaca y descansa.
Ella obedeció.... se dejó aplicar las pomadas y los ungüentos....
El juego le gustaba, aunque ya empezaba a cansarse...
Una tarde, el hombre llegó corriendo...
—¡Lo encontré!
Acababa de ver al mono curando a la mona en la copa de un árbol.
—Es así—dijo el hombre, aproximándose a la mujer.
Cuando terminó el largo abrazo, un aroma espeso de flores y frutas invadió el aire. (n.p.)

The first woman and the first man looked at each other with curiosity. What they had between their legs was strange.
"Have they cut you?" asked the man.

> "No," she said. I have always been this way.
>
> He examined her closely.... There was an open wound there. He said:
>
> "I will cure you. Lay down on the hammock and rest."
>
> She obeyed.... She allowed him to apply the creams and ointments....
>
> She liked the game, although she was beginning to tire of it.
>
> One afternoon, the man came running...
>
> "I found it!"
>
> He had just seen a monkey curing a female monkey in the treetop.
>
> "It is this way," said the man approaching the woman.
>
> When the long embrace was over, a thick aroma of flowers and fruits invaded the air.

At the story's conclusion, the man and the women have sex, which is the "cure" for the woman's "open wound." Thus, if Rucia and El Indio are the "hombre y mujer pequeños" of the father's story (as children tend to identify themselves with the tales they are told), the two are essentially willed to have incestuous sex thanks to their father's story. For the fact is that every story the father tells in the novel comes true, which underscores what the narrator claims regarding the magical power of words to mold reality. Thus, the father is responsible for their incestuous love, which he "causes" through his storytelling. It is also significant that this story is left unfinished. Had Fausto not disappeared, then presumably he would have finished it in due course. Thus, the unfinished story that sanctions incest symbolizes the father's abandonment of his children.

Brendan MacCarthy has noted that "It is striking too how frequently it is found that prior to the first [incestuous] encounter there has been a significant loss, such as a breakup with a partner or a major family bereavement" (115). Argentieri additionally points out that Freud indicates that even if incest is just an unconsummated fantasy, its pathogenic effect remains (22). Since the incestuous desire between the siblings in *Mapocho* develops after their father has left the family, which the children ritualize by burying pictures of him (38), feelings of abandonment and loss tacitly account for the incestuous connection between the protagonists.

It is interesting that Fausto also suffers from feelings of abandonment. After the government releases him, he returns home to find that his family has left. The narrator describes him as being orphaned (172). Eventually, he receives a letter from his wife requesting money and that he not search for them. He continues to work for the government so that he can send them money, all the while hopeful that one day they can reunite and be happy again. That, however, never comes to pass.

Nor is it a coincidence that Fausto lives in a skyscraper that has been erected on the site of what used to be the town's soccer stadium. Both the skyscraper and the soccer stadium have symbolic value within the context of Chile's history. The soccer stadium evokes the Estadio Nacional de Santiago and also Estadio Chile, which were turned into concentration camps where prisoners were tortured and killed during the first few months of the dictatorship. This same trajectory occurs in the novel with this local stadium. In time, though the Estadio Nacional was reopened as a sporting arena, which, according to Johanna Lozoya, exists

> as a contested emotional landscape. A space of fear, sadness and rage for the leftist population; a place of forgetfulness, disbelief, resentment and annoyance for traditional conservatives and extreme right parties, the Estadio Nacional of Santiago ambiguously exists in the national consciousness. (56)

As critics of this novel have indicated, the modern skyscraper attempts to hide the past of torture and disappearances that occurred in the stadium (Cardone 7). Moreover, the skyscraper is a symbol of modern neoliberal development in Chile. In *Urban Design Under Neoliberalism* (2019), Francisco Vergara Perucich defines neoliberalism as "an extremist implementation of capitalist principles wherein the means of production are privately owned and run by a capitalist class for extracting value" (20). He also traces how Pinochet created a neoliberal state in Chile and its effects on urban development in Santiago.

According to Vergara Perucich, who cites an article by J. E. Vergara, one of the many effects of neoliberalism on urban planning in Santiago is verticalization. In other words, "the consumers of dwellings prefer to live within the limits of Americo Vespucio (a circular road that surrounds Santiago) in consolidated neighborhoods making the city grow skyward . . . [because they are] aiming to live nearer downtown and their workplace" (75). The skyscraper in which Fausto lives represents this neoliberal trend, which has profitability as its end and not what Vergara Perucich calls the creation of "good cities" (1).

Two other important aspects of neoliberal development on urban policy that Vergara Perucich examines are the elimination of public spaces and the segregation of the poor farther away from the city center. He states that

> [d]uring the times of Frei and Allende, the construction of housing in big cities was one of the most viable public policies. . . . An interesting strategy involved building social housing in central areas . . . aiming . . . to reduce residential segregation and increase access to amenities . . . for low-income communities. . . . Pinochet reshuffled the urban segments, moving people from one side to the other . . . in order to liberate areas for real estate investments. . . . Pinochet created 36 *comunas* segmented by social classes. . . . In the new areas of Santiago, the dictatorship allocated the urban poor space away from the centre . . . [as] spatial products (mostly housing) [were decided] according to people's purchasing capacity . . . . [Thus] an organization of the city by class [took hold]. . . . While the dictatorship set up the basis of neoliberalism, the outcomes of urban design under neoliberalism emerged during the transition to democracy. (46–68)

Vergara Perucich raises issues that Edward Soja categorizes under "spatial justice." According to Soja,

> [j]ustice has a consequential geography, a spatial expression that is more than just a background reflection or set of physical attributes to be descriptively mapped. . . . [T]he geography or "spatiality" of justice . . . is an integral and formative component of justice itself, a vital part of how justice and injustice are socially constructed and evolve over time. . . . Viewed this way, seeking spatial justice becomes fundamentally . . . a struggle over geography. (1)

Soja emphasizes how the right (or lack thereof) to public spaces is one of the ways in which spatial (in)justice becomes manifest:

> For some the essential starting point in the search for spatial justice is the vigilant defense of public space against the forces of commodification, privatization, and state interference.... For example, we can see public space as a localized urban expression of the notion of common property or... the commons. All the publicly maintained streets... crossroads, plazas, piazzas, and squares are part of the commons... the mass transit networks, buses, and trains. (45)

Frequently injustice in *Mapocho* is tied to physical spaces. This spatial injustice is not just a byproduct of neoliberalism during and after the dictatorship, but it also intertwines with historical themes in the novel that date back to the Conquest. Fernández maintains the constant presence of this original spatial injustice through the character El Indio. The fact that Rucia's brother has no other name in the novel and is constantly referred to as "El Indio" serves as a constant reminder to the reader of the spatial injustice committed during the conquest through the usurpation of indigenous lands by the Spanish. Moreover, Fernández includes an episode about the relationship between Lautaro and Pedro de Valdivia, the Spanish conqueror who fought the indigenous populations of Chile. In all three of the historical segments from the past included in the novel, Fernández counterposes a popular version of history to that of official history on the topic through the words "dicen que" (they say that).

In the historical segment set during the Conquest, the narrator relates a popular legend in the novel about Lautaro's rape. Lautaro was in fact captured by Valdivia and served as his page before his escaping and rejoining the indigenous fight against the Spanish. This popular tale about Lautaro expresses the sense of loss suffered by the indigenous tribes of Chile. The unofficial history that posits Valdivia's rape of Lautaro symbolizes the rape of Latin America by the Spaniards. Valdivia's own ambivalence here toward the colonized subject is the sort Homi Bhabha posits when he contends that the colonized individual is at once desired and scorned by the colonizer (109–18). Lautaro, to be sure, is made the object of sexual fetishism (as Bhabha uses that term) by Valdivia.

After being raped, Lautaro cuts off his hair, which may be symbolic of a feeling of loss, since in many indigenous cultures hair is only cut when one has experienced a death in the family or some other traumatic event (Densmore 77).

Another instance of spatial injustice pertains both to Chile's past and present and is associated with the La Chimba neighborhood of Santiago where Rucia's family has lived until she leaves Chile with her brother and mother. In the novel, we see La Chimba both in the present, through the wandering of Rucia's ghost through the area and, then again, in the historical segment that presents the construction of the Cal y Canto bridge. Katherine Trostel signals the importance of La Chimba, "a traditionally indigenous and working-class sector of Santiago," as a symbol of neoliberal spatial injustice (123):

> The restaurant owner warns her [Rucia] that not many homes like this exist anymore "but that buildings in Santiago are well-ordered" and have been organized by systems of numbering.... By insisting on a particular way of ordering space, the restaurant owner denies the power of Rucia's memories as a means of navigation.... La Rucia's ... paths through the city begin to chart for the reader a guide to a practice of walking through space that will uncover a counter-history of Santiago. She orients herself spatially in the city by finding "el poto de la Virgen." This unusual landmark refers to the twenty-two-meter statue of the Virgin Mary that sits atop the Cerro San Cristóbal ... The inhabitants of La Chimba, in its marginalized position across the river from the city's center, can only see the backside of the figure. (126–28)

Resha S. Cardone adds that the building of the Cal y Canto bridge in 1780 (which collapsed a century later) eventually transformed La Chimba into Bellavista, an affluent neighborhood, leading to a form of "environmental injustice" that, with increased urbanization, occurred with the paving of the local riverbed to protect human dwellings from nature (8). Katherine Karr-Cornejo also discusses injustice in La Chimba, focusing on the people who suffered while building the Cal y Canto bridge: "The disposable beings—criminals, the poor, indigenous persons—destroyed on the altar of progress—haunt the city ... as the disposable bodies of the men whose labor laid the foundation upon which national progress has been built" (15).

Space in *Mapocho* serves as another means of articulating feelings of loss and abandonment, not only for Rucia but also for Chileans as a populace. Various spatial elements encapsulate these feelings as well as the spatial injustice associated with them: the skyscraper (previously discussed), the soccer stadium and the mini soccer field, the train station (Estación Mapocho), the Mapocho River, and the cemetery. It is important to note that with the exception of the skyscraper, these are all public spaces.

When Rucia's ghost returns to Santiago to meet El Indio, she searches for her family's house, asking a woman whether she has seen the now-absent mini soccer field and streetlamp that used to exist near her home (21). The mini soccer field, of course, represents a public space that has disappeared from her neighborhood. Although Rucia eventually finds her family home, it is in extreme disrepair, in contrast to the modern skyscraper in which her father lives. The house is described as falling apart with a crack extending from the foundation of the house to its roof, which the narrator likens to Rucia's open wound after her car accident (29–30). Spaces, like the house, work symbolically as places of deep emotion and cruel abandonment.

The Mapocho Train Station brings this elimination or transformation of public space to the fore and figures prominently in the third historical episode about the dictator Carlos Ibáñez. In the present time of the novel, the narrator explains how the once-active station has been, after its long abandonment, repurposed as a cultural center (125). We can read that encapsulation blindly as simple reportage or a mark of progress. But that obscures the history it typifies. The demise of the station—its disrepair—begins with the military dictatorship's forsaking its duty to operate and maintain a public space by turning that space over to the private (neoliberal) sector. In fact, the Arts Center that replaced the station was the first public building in Chile to become privately run—and that thanks to the government's putting the management of the building out for bid in pursuit of its neoliberal platform and agenda ("Renaissance of the Train" n.p.).

Moreover, through the historical segment about Carlos Ibáñez, the Mapocho Train Station becomes symbolic of city dwellers who have been marginalized, discriminated against, and displaced from their housing space. Carlos Ibáñez del Campo was president of Chile from 1927–1931 and then again from 1952–1958. The novel portrays a popular tale about Ibáñez, a homophobe, who disposed of a group of transvestites by putting them on a boat and sending them out to sea. What is particularly interesting about Fernández's representation of this alleged incident is that she allegorizes Chile as a house in which the transvestites, referred to as "Las locas," are forced to live in a backroom separated from the other rooms of the house, which has Carlos Ibáñez as the father in charge: "Dicen que Chile era una casa vieja . . . que el Coronel era un mago . . . que podía hacer desaparecer a la gente . . . Apartadas de todo, en una pieza color rosa . . . se encontraban la locas de la casa" ([154–55] They say that Chile was an old house. . . . They say the Colonel was a magician . . . that he could make people disappear . . . . Separated from everything, in a pink room . . . the queens of the house were found.) The narrator explains that one day Ibáñez secretly enters the room and asks "Las locas" to dress him up as a woman. While he is parading around in feminine attire, his guards enter the room. As a result, Ibáñez orders the guards to take "las locas" away (164). This is why in a separate segment of the novel (166), when the narrator describes the Mapocho train station, echoes of the voices of "las locas" can still be heard in it.

The relegation of "Las locas" to a room in the house distinctly separate from the other rooms suggests the same use of space and spatial injustice common to a neoliberal Chile, whereby other marginalized groups, such as the poor and indigenous, were shunted off to less desirable areas of the city, far from the center of Santiago. Their eventual exile from the house and presumed death at sea represent Ibáñez's political fascism and despotism, exerted on many different liberal groups in Chile. "Las locas" have been abandoned by their "father" (Ibáñez), just as the Mapocho Train Station has been abandoned by the military dictatorship.

The Mapocho River is another public space that gives title to the novel. The river, just like La Chimba, is a natural social divider between the rich and the poor. Readers see it both in the present and in the past. As a river that runs throughout the city, it does not by itself constitute a form of spatial injustice. However, it becomes that through human interference in a manner that evokes and coalesces all the other injustices the novel depicts over its historical span. Thus, the Mapocho represents the feelings of loss and abandonment that pervade Rucia, El Indio, Lautaro, and "Las locas."

First and foremost, though never directly mentioned in the novel, dead bodies floating in the Mapocho River were a common sight during the Pinochet dictatorship. So common was this occurrence that for Chileans this association is implicit in the title of the novel and in any allusion to the river itself. Second, when Lautaro is murdered, he is thrown into the river (57). Similarly, the prisoners who are mandated to construct the Cal y Canto bridge in the second historical segment are found floating dead in the river (86). Hence loss, death, and social abandonment are associated with the space of the Mapocho River.

The last public space of importance in the novel, the only one spared from the grasping hand of neoliberal commercialization, is the cemetery, which stands in direct contrast to the previous four spaces. It is, as the narrator reveals, the only place Rucia experiences that is unchanged from how it was during her childhood. Because of that, it makes her feel at home (104).

And so all of the spaces in *Mapocho*—the skyscraper, stadium, Train Station, Mapocho River, and General Cemetery—play a critical role in articulating not only the spatial injustices that have permeated Santiago, especially due to neoliberalism since the dictatorship, but also the feelings of loss and abandonment engendered by and emanating from these spaces. In that way, these spaces in Santiago effectively map Rucia's feelings of loss and abandonment as her ghost wanders about the city.

The presence of ghosts throughout Santiago is the final element used to articulate feelings of loss and abandonment in the novel. As this element has already undergone extensive study, I only discuss it briefly here.[3] Rucia and El Indio are not the only ghosts who wander the city. Haunting it as well are the ghosts of the rest of those town members who were murdered in the soccer stadium, as well as the historical ghosts of those killed through past injustices, such as Lautaro and the prisoners who built the Cal y Canto bridge.

We have already seen in the father's story how his line "death is a lie" prefigures the presence of Rucia and El Indio's ghosts in Santiago. Another of his stories does exactly the same as well as accounts for the motif of navels that runs throughout the novel. When Rucia's ghost visits the cemetery, she recalls a story her father told them when they visited the tomb of family members there. This story, like the other two told by the father, comes from Galeano's *Memorias*. In the novel, the story appears thus:

> Érase una vez una mujer y un hombre pequeños ... dormían tranquilos cuando un dios ... les habló en sus sueños. Les dijo que se cuidaran de los muertos que ... por las noches se camuflaban entre los vivos. ...
> Antes de aceptar una buena mocha con alguien o de involucrarse con

una mujer linda, es indispensable que con disimulo le rocen el vientre con el dedo índice. Solo así pueden distinguirlos porque los muertos no tienen ombligo. (104–05)

Once upon a time a small woman and man... slept peacefully when a god... spoke to them in their dreams. He told them that they should be careful of the dead who... at night camouflaged themselves among the living.... Before accepting a good cup of coffee with someone or getting involved with a pretty woman, you must surreptitiously rub that person's belly with your index finger. Only in that way can you distinguish the living from the dead because the dead do not have a navel.

In Galeano's collection of myths, this story appears in a section titled "Los peligros" (the dangers) and is incorporated into a prophecy to the *taíno* Indians regarding the Spanish Conquest:

El que hizo al sol y a la luna avisó a los taínos que se cuidaran de los muertos. Durante el día los muertos se escondían y comían guayaba, pero por las noches salían a pasear y desafiaban a los vivos.... Antes de aceptar la lucha contra un hombre o de echarse junto a una mujer, era preciso rozarle el vientre con la mano, porque los muertos no tienen ombligo.... Los hombres vestidos llegarán, dominarán y matarán ("Los peligros").

He who made the sun and the moon warned the taínos that they be careful of the dead. During the day, the dead hid and ate guayabas, but at night they came out to walk around and challenge the living.... Before accept[ing] a fight against another man or lying down with a woman, a person had to rub the man or woman's belly with his hand, because the dead do not have a navel.... The dressed men will come, will dominate, and will kill.

Both passages suggest that the dead can become ghosts and that the only way to recognize them is through the absence of a navel. This story relates to El Indio's obsession with Rucia's navel. His mother forbids him from painting it (El Indio is an artist), but when Rucia's ghost returns to her family's house in Santiago, her navel is painted in murals on the wall:

> Ahora el ombligo de la Rucia cubre todos los muros descascarados de la pieza... Por fin te atreviste, Indio, me sacaste el ombligo y lo viniste a dejar acá.... La tripa hedionda que los une... que la hace atravesar el mundo entero para venir a terminar ahí... justo en el corazón de un Barrio lleno de quemados y suicidas, al borde de un río podrido en mierda... El hoyo negro en el que han caído. La trampa de la que no escaparán. (75–76)

> Now Rucia's navel covers all the peeling walls of the room.... You finally dared, Indio, you removed my navel,... the smelly belly that united them,... that made her cross the entire world to end up here ... precisely in the heart of a neighborhood full of burn victims and suicidal people, on the edge of a river rotten with shit... The black hole into which they have fallen. The trap from which they will not escape.

The symbolic removal of Rucia's navel (another symbol of loss and abandonment), which has been "taken" for use on the mural, confirms her fate to eternally wander Santiago as a ghost because of her father's abandonment due to the dictatorship. This passage connects the navel to the ghosts wandering about La Chimba (in the heart of a neighborhood full of people burned to death and killed by suicide). This is the "black pit" into which Rucia and El Indio have fallen and must inhabit forever. It is the black pit to which all the victims of dictatorship have been condemned. It embodies the place of loss and abandonment that the Pinochet dictatorship caused and made lastingly vivid.

Fernández's second novel about father-abandonment *Fuenzalida* (2012) establishes the connection between abandonment and the dictatorship in a more indirect manner. The title refers to the last name of the narrator's father and is the name by which the female narrator, Fuenzalida's daughter, chooses to refer to him throughout the novel. This automatically establishes a distance between Fuenzalida and the narrator, who has not seen him since she was twelve years old.

The narrative begins with a photograph that blows in front of the narrator on the street where she lives, presumably from somebody's garbage. The photo turns out to be a picture of her father, Fuenzalida, that she took of him when she was a child; on the back of the photo is an inscribed dedication. As we shall see, this photograph is followed by several others in the novel. One is a photo of the narrator as a child on a ski trip; others include the numerous photos originally possessed by the narrator's mother and from which Fuenzalida has been cut out; the narrator also has two photographs she has received from her half-brother upon Fuenzalida's death. Although the photographs picture Fuenzalida's face, the only other tidbit of information they provide is that he wore a martial arts gi. Although one ski-trip photo of the narrator shows her with cotton stuffed in her nose due to a nosebleed, it is a picture without a story, though her mother later fills her in on important details of that trip.[4] Obviously, the many photos of Fuenzalida from which he has been cut out fail to offer any information about his character. As Macarena García-Avello states in an article on *Fuenzalida*, the photos serve to question the testimonial power of photography. Since there is no context for the photos, they do not reveal anything about the narrator's past and simply serve as departure points for fantasies about Fuenzalida (257–58).

Olga Shevchenko, in *Double Exposure* (2014), notes that

[p]hotography ... is not merely one of many media of memory where workings have been questioned.... It is also a representational practice that, from the time of its emergence, was accorded a privileged status as an indexical sign.... Yet the issue of the relationship between memory and photography is far more complex, and this ambivalence haunts the literature on photography.... Not only is memory mediated, it is also ... inherently unstable, situational and intersubjective. We remember different aspects of the same experience when we recall them in different contexts, with different interlocutors and in different points in our lives. In this sense, to frame photographs as containers, vessels or expressions of memory is to misconstrue memory by imagining it as a static thing to be contained and transmitted rather than a practice to be enacted and performed variously in different settings. (3–5)

Thus, photographs give the false impression that they represent a fixed reality. In actuality, they must be contextualized and do not automatically capture the truth. Hence, the narrator of *Fuenzalida* counterposes different forms of narrative or storytelling to photography as an imaginative means of "remembering" or filling in the past. Fernández indicates this intention in one of the novel's introductory epigraphs: "inventa un cuento que te sirva de memoria" ([*Fuenzalida* 6] Invent a story that serves as a memory). This is a "hint" that the segment in which the narrator recounts Fuenzalida's heroic acts during the Pinochet dictatorship, including attempts to rescue his son Ernestito, who had been abducted by the authorities, is not a narration of something that Fuenzalida actually did, but just an episode imagined by the narrator.

Obviously, an imaginative story is not the same thing as remembering a concrete past, though there is often a creative or imaginative aspect to the re-creation of memories. There are so many details about Fuenzalida that are unknown to the narrator that she has no choice but to invent. That being said, there is another more significant reason why the narrator invents two stories about Fuenzalida (one a narration of his actions during the Pinochet dictatorship and the other a soap-opera script in which a doctor's estranged father is brought into the emergency room). What is important here is not Fuenzalida's actual past, but how the narrator *feels* about Fuenzalida. These feelings can be expressed by the narrator's invention of events that never happened better than by some documentary narration of historical reality or reference to actual events.

The narrator expresses her lack of memory of her father by constantly referring to his car as being different colors followed by a question mark. The only concrete information the reader receives regarding Fuenzalida is that he had three families and ultimately decided to remain with family number two. In that family, he had a son, Ernesto Jr. There are a few scattered memories, such as when her father took her for a ride to La Dehesa, a new neighborhood under construction. While there, they heard some disturbing news about a man who burned himself in front of the cathedral in Concepción. There is a vague memory of one evening the two were watching a martial arts movie on TV, a rare occasion when Fuenzalida was babysitting her, and another in which she, Fuenzalida, and her mother went to a restaurant. Finally, the most persistent memory is the last time that the narrator saw her father. She was twelve, and she and her mother had moved to a new house. Fuenzalida was very insistent that the tile floor of the patio needed to be waxed, and this was becoming a source of friction between Fuenzalida and her mother. The narrator told Fuenzalida that if he wanted the tiles waxed, he should do it himself. Fuenzalida, upset by the narrator's comments, abruptly left and never returned.

Throughout the novel, the narrator periodically returns to this episode of the "baldosas enceradas" (waxed tiles). She never comments directly about how she felt about this being the last time she saw her father. She never states that she felt abandoned and yet, I would argue, the all of *Fuenzalida* is about the narrator's feelings of abandonment. As it happens, the way the narrator expresses her feelings is through the juxtaposition of her memory about the "baldosas enceradas" to other stories about fathers throughout the novel. In contrast to Fuenzalida's abrupt departure from her life when she was twelve and because of a trivial matter, the other fathers in the novel, whether real or invented, are all excellent, self-sacrificing fathers who stand by their children.

Even though Gonzalo Maier sees *Fuenzalida* principally as a parody of Bruce Lee films, he hypothesizes that the invention of a heroic Fuenzalida, the one who battles dictatorship, stands in ironic contrast to the narrator's real father (40–45). But that implied and indirect deflation, however ironic, misses the critical feature of the depiction. The narrator writes about the father she wishes she had to underscore her feelings of loss at not having a close relationship with her father because he left the family. Abandonment, not irony, is the main point here.

Fuenzalida presents four fathers: Max, the narrator's ex-husband and father to their son Cosme; Fuenzalida (both "real" and invented); Raúl Emilio Fuentes Castro (another invented character in the fabricated story of Fuenzalida); and Sebastián Acevedo Becerra, who is based on a real person who lived and died during the Pinochet dictatorship. The stories about these different fathers are implicitly (and occasionally explicitly) counterposed throughout the novel.

The first father contrasted with Fuenzalida is Max, who is not a perfect father. When he leaves the family, he abandons his son for a year, but then returns and wants to be a father to him again. After that initial abandonment, Max develops an excellent relationship with his son Cosme, and he takes him to his house for visits where he interacts with his new family. The narrator explicitly contrasts Max's relationship with Cosme to her relationship with Fuenzalida:

> Cosme está con su padre, ejerciendo su minivida de una vez al mes.... Yo nunca tuve minividas con Fuenzalida. Solo tuve momentos, ratos. Y muy pocos. Casi siempre eran en la calle Nataniel Cox, en el barrio Matta, en medio de un Santiago viejo y sucio... Mis escasos momentos con él tienen la forma de una fotografía cortada con una tijera. Fuenzalida desapareció. Se borró del mapa, se echó al pollo, se fue, llevándose con el todos nuestros miniratos. (28–29)

> Cosme is with his father, performing his minilife of once a month.... I never had minilives with Fuenzalida. I only had moments, short times. And very few. They almost always were on Nataniel Cox Street, in the Matta neighborhood, in the middle of an old and dirty Santiago.... My scarce moments with him have the form of a photograph cut with a scissors. Fuenzalida disappeared. He was erased from the map, he packed up and went, went away, taking with him all our mini-times.

This is perhaps the first indication the reader has regarding the narrator's sense of abandonment, which the contrast between "minividas" and "miniratos" makes emphatic.

The second father who appears outside of the narrator's imagination is Sebastián Acevedo Becerra. In one of her rare visits with her father, the narrator hears over the car radio about a man whose children disappeared. When he was unable to obtain information about their whereabouts through the authorities, the father burned himself outside the cathedral in Concepción in a desperate attempt to draw attention to his plight. Although he died from his burns, his daughter was freed, and his son moved from a torture center to a public jail where he would receive due process. Sebastián Acevedo Becerra died in Concepción on November 11, 1983, an "indirect" consequence of the dictatorship (*Battling* 257). Becerra's story can be thought of as one of Stern's "memory knots."

Becerra's story is one of two historical episodes about the dictatorship that appear in *Fuenzalida*. It has been very carefully chosen to develop the novel's main theme.[5] Fernández includes this particular tragedy/memory knot, among hundreds of others, because it is ultimately the story about a father and his children. However, this father, unlike Fuenzalida who disappeared because of unwaxed tiles, was willing to sacrifice his life to help his children. This historical episode stands in direct contrast to the narrator's relationship with Fuenzalida.[6]

The remaining two fathers portrayed in the novel are inventions of the narrator. The first is the Fuenzalida constructed by the narrator's fantasy (who appears both in a narrative story and in a soap-opera script), and the second is an Air Force lieutenant who serves the dictatorship and is Fuenzalida's opponent in a martial arts duel. The reader is unaware that their story is invented until near the very end of the novel.[7]

The novel's narrator, like Fernández herself, grew up during the dictatorship and this may indeed be part of the reason that she chooses to situate her invented story of Fuenzalida within the context of Pinochet's government. However, I believe a more significant reason for this pairing exists. Under the dictatorship, many fathers were forced to "abandon" their families because they were exiled, murdered, or "disappeared." Their fathers faultless, children grew up feeling orphaned and abandoned during the Pinochet years (1973–1990). Thus, the narrator makes a "natural" association between Fuenzalida, a man who abandoned his daughter, and the abandonment caused by the dictatorship.

Despite the connection between dictatorship and abandonment, the Fuenzalida portrayed in the narrator's invented story is the opposite of the Fuenzalida who left the narrator's family when she was twelve. The Fuenzalida of the invented tale, like Sebastián Acevedo Becerra, does everything in his power to help his child Ernestito, whom members of the dictatorship kidnap. The reason for this kidnapping is that Fuenzalida refuses to cooperate with the dictatorship by training its men in martial arts. In his efforts to recover Ernestito, Fuenzalida suffers capture and must engage in hand-to-hand combat with another father named Fuentes Castro. If he wins, the dictatorship will free Ernestito.

It is highly significant that Fuenzalida is associated with martial arts in the novel. The fact that Fuenzalida is dressed in a gi in the photograph that opens the novel suggests his potential for moral virtue. Fuenzalida's position as a martial arts expert in the invented tale stands in direct contrast to the values of the dictatorship. The narrator underscores the violence and injustice of the dictatorship by contrasting it to the philosophical values martial arts embody. According to Joseph J. Lynch:

> Plato emphasizes that the training of the body is the training of the soul.... Plato sees martial training as a battle to cultivate moral virtues.... For him, the athlete-warrior represents the essence of what it is to be human. Plato thought that since having a rational soul defines us as human beings, the person with the just and rational soul is most fully human. The philosopher king epitomizes this human ideal.... True martial progress requires both reason and spirit and most importantly rational self-control.... Plato ... held that there are certain moral virtues that characterize what it is to live a good human life; in particular, wisdom, bravery, moderation and justice. A warrior especially must exhibit bravery.... Plato include(s) an intellectual dimension to the concept of bravery.... Bravery is not the absence of fear; instead, reason ... puts fear in its place. (36–38)

Thus, Fuenzalida becomes the hero-father who exhibits superior moral virtues in fighting against the corrupt dictatorship to rescue his son and who refuses to aid the dictatorship, incapable of moral virtue, by training its men in martial arts.

In this invented tale, Fuenzalida is the same type of self-sacrificing father as Sebastián Acevedo Becerra. This Fuenzalida is implicitly juxtaposed to the Fuenzalida who abandoned his family because of floor tiles. The narrator's tale expresses a wistful desire to have had this type of father. That emptiness in the narrator's reality makes all the more acute the feelings of loss and abandonment that she carries with her.

The invented tale contains another father who is a "bad guy," though I would argue he also qualifies as a "gray-zone" character. Fuentes Castro starts out in the tale as a heroic firefighter who is in the Air Force Reserves and gets drafted into service under the dictatorship. He is forced to commit many atrocities, which he believes he is doing in the name of the "noble" fight against communism, but eventually he falls into disfavor with the dictatorship allegedly for freeing prisoners. Because of that act, he must go into hiding without saying goodbye to his family and later winds up going underground to continue his fight against "subversives." Fuentes Castro deeply regrets not being able to say goodbye to his young daughter, who undoubtedly feels abandoned. Before his hand-to-hand combat with Fuenzalida, he requests that if he loses the battle, that Fuenzalida give a letter he has already written in anticipation of defeat to his daughter. Fuentes Castro tells Fuenzalida:

> Si cuando esto partió hubiera sabido que iba a terminar de matarife, no sé si habría dado el paso.... Yo también quisiera ver a mi hija... Cambiaría todo, volvería atrás sin pensarlo dos veces, si pudiera estar con ella unos minutos... conversar un par de temas que no le alcancé a explicar antes de dejarla. Pero ya no se puede. (183)

> If when all this began, I had known that I was going to end up a butcher, I don't know if I would have taken that step. I would also like to see my daughter.... I would change everything, go back without thinking twice, if I could be with her a few minutes... speak to her about a couple of things that I did not manage to explain to her before leaving her. But now I cannot.

Fuentes Castro may not be a good person, but he is a good father who only abandoned his family members to protect them. His knowledge of martial arts also speaks to his possession of some virtuous qualities, not least, loving his family. Fuentes Castro is another father who stands in stark contrast to the Fuenzalida who abandoned his family over a trivial dispute.[8]

Finally, the last invented father we see is also Fuenzalida, but this time he appears in a soap-opera script as a dying patient. His abandoned daughter is the doctor Genovena Urqueta, who is in the hospital when her dying father is brought into the emergency room. We later see Genovena attend his funeral, but she is off to the side as an observer and does not directly participate. The reader is never told the name of the patient but infers that he is the doctor's father whom she has not seen in years.

Unlike the narrator who, upon learning of her father's death, chooses not to attend his funeral, Genovena makes herself present at the event. Once again, the theme of abandonment surfaces, only this time it is the narrator who abandons her father. Is this retaliation in kind for her father's abandonment? Is it a statement of the fact that they did not really have a relationship? In the novel's final imagined scene, the narrator reencounters Fuenzalida at the garbage dump and imagines possible exchanges with him: "Quizás yo me excuse por no haber ido a su entierro. Quizás él me dice que no me preocupe, que le gustó mucho más el que le escribí en 'Unidad de Urgencias' el culebrón" ([219] Perhaps I apologize for not having gone to his burial. Perhaps he tells me not to worry, that he liked a lot more that I wrote about him in "Emergency Unit," the soap-opera script).

Finally, *Fuenzalida*, like *Mapocho*, is concerned with issues of spatial justice. In one of the few real memories that the narrator has of her father, he takes her on a trip to la Dehesa neighborhood because he has an errand to do there. This passage portrays the abandonment of public spaces useful for both rich and poor in favor of privatizing those spaces solely for the rich. The narrator describes the neoliberal transformation that the area has undergone thus:

> Fuenzalida debe entregar algo ... a un cliente que vive en el nuevo barrio de la Dehesa. Me lleva para que conozca este sector que se está armando en Santiago. ... Se trata de un sector de reciente urbanización, habitado por familias de altos ingresos. Su historia se remonta a la conquista de Chile. De acuerdo con las leyes de Indias, cada vez que se fundara una ciudad o ... una villa, era necesario dejar lugares para el pastoreo de los ganados de uso común de los habitantes. Con este motivo se estableció La Dehesa de Santiago ... Cada cual iba a pastar sus animales a este sector y aprovechaba de conversar y socializar con los vecinos. Todos los santiaguinos tenían derecho a entrar y permanecer ahí con su ganado ... Durante la década de los '80 el gobierno militar comenzó la reestructuración de la Dehesa. (160)

> Fuenzalida has to deliver something ... to a client who lives in the new neighborhood of la Dehesa. He takes me to get to know this new neighborhood that is being built in Santiago. It is a sector of recent urbanization, inhabited by high-income families. Its history goes back to the conquest of Chile. According to the laws of the Indies, each time a city or village was founded, it was necessary to leave places for livestock to graze for common use by the inhabitants. For this purpose, la Dehesa was established in Santiago. Each one came to graze his animals in this sector and took advantage of the opportunity to converse and socialize with his neighbors. All residents of Santiago had

the right to enter and remain there with their livestock.... During the decade of the eighties, the military government began the restructuring of la Dehesa.

It is significant that while on this trip to la Dehesa that the narrator hears the story of Sebastián Acevedo Becerra, the self-sacrificing father who, to draw public attention to the plight of his "disappeared" children, commits suicide. The narrative closely connects spatial injustice, abandonment, the dictatorship, and fathers with each other through this particular narrative, and Santiago's geography becomes a part of the sense of loss and abandonment experienced by the narrator. The poor people have suffered loss of their public spaces through neoliberal policy. They have been essentially abandoned by the dictatorship and, later on, by the Concertación governments that followed.

In summary, although *Fuenzalida*, on the surface, appears to be simply a novel about the narrator and her father, the story within a story of Fuenzalida's fight against the dictatorship and the narrator's years of contact with her father during it transform *Fuenzalida* into a postmemory novel of the Pinochet era. That is, the narrator's tormented feelings about her father's abandonment are rooted in the history of dictatorship. Recognizing how that history insinuates itself is the same as it is in *Mapocho*. I want to turn now to Álvaro Bisama's *El Brujo* for yet another representation.

Álvaro Bisama (1975–) was born in Valparaíso, but his family moved to Villa Alemana when he was young. He holds a PhD in literature from the Pontífica Universidad Católica de Chile and is a professor at the Universidad Alberto Hurtado. He has published six novels: *Caja negra* (2006; Black Box); *Postales urbanas* (2006; Urban Post Cards), *Música marciana* (2008; Martian Music), *Estrellas muertas* (2010; Dead Stars), *Ruido* (2012; Noise), and *El brujo* (2016; The Wizard) ("Álvaro Bisama" 295). *El brujo* (2016), his most recent novel, is the third book I examine that deals with father-abandonment. It is divided into three sections. The first two are narrated by the protagonist's son, and the third by the father himself. The son-narrator recounts his father's life story, from his birth in 1979, when his parents were graduating high school, to the present. His father, originally an art major, dropped out of the university and became a photographer. After taking an iconic photo of a police officer threatening a young woman with a revolver held to her face, the father is abducted and tortured—though, too, eventually released. To recover from this episode, he spends two months in a relative's cabin in the remote southern island of Chiloé. After he returns to Santiago, government agents burn to death one of his fellow photographers. This episode causes the father to have a complete breakdown. He decides to leave his family and move alone to Chiloé and spends the rest of his life there. While he is there, many strange and ambiguous events occur that in the end result in a total break between the father and son.

Although Bisama has himself described the novel as a variant of crime fiction ("El escritor Álvaro Bisama"), the synopsis provided above essentially illustrates how the novel traces a progressive separation between the father and his son and the hand of the Pinochet dictatorship in it. The crime elements of the novel that Bisama describes serve to develop the protagonist's gradual mental and moral decline; these elements are also highly ambiguous, but we can see that Bisama uses them to create conflicting versions of the father.

Bisama's highly complex narrative can, in turn, be broken down into three overlapping elements: the construction of the father's abandonment of the son, photography as a vehicle for communicating feeling, and crime fiction as an agent that imparts ambiguity and uncertainty to the narrative as a whole and the father in particular. It is important to note that the last third of the novel, which centers on criminal elements, follows from the father's forced abandonment of his family due to the mental and physical trauma the Pinochet dictatorship has caused.

The son, who narrates the first two sections of the novel, describes his father's photography as immersing him in a world of unrelenting and debilitating violence:

> Mi padre comenzó a trabajar como fotógrafo de prensa en 1984. . . . Le pegaron. Lo detuvieron. Le rompieron varias cámara. . . . [Registraba] el modo en que los cuerpos resistían antes de caer al suelo, lanzándose sobre ellos para quedarse con una fracción de su dolor porque su deber era atrapar las marcas físicas de la violencia. . . . Cambió. . . . Se acostumbró a la adrenalina, a la violencia. . . . Pero no podía dejar de darme cuenta también de que mi padre se alejaba, se volvía más hosco y callado, era devorado por dentro por algo. (19–22)

> My father began to work as a press photographer in 1984.... They beat him. They detained him. They broke various cameras.... [He captured how] bodies resisted before falling to the ground, throwing himself on them to remain with a fraction of their pain because his duty was to capture the physical marks of the violence.... He became used to the adrenaline, to the violence.... But I also couldn't help but realize that my father was distancing himself, he became sullener and more silent, he was devoured from within.

The first stage of the father's separation from his family is purely emotional. The father is still physically present in Santiago but becomes more distant from his son in terms of their relationship.

The second stage in the father's progressive abandonment is his first trip to Chiloé. Although he leaves only temporarily, his son, who is only about seven years old, is aware that this is a prelude to a future and more definitive separation:

> Terminó viajando a Chiloé.... Mientras él me decía que ... esa imagen que él había atrapado lo iba a sobrevivir, que yo debía estar orgulloso de él porque él había sido valiente y que esta imagen lo había cambiado ... algo me indicaba que esa conversación era el preludio de una despedida, que desde ahí solo podía comenzar a alejarse de mí, de mi madre, de Santiago, de todo lo que conocíamos. (26)

> He ended up traveling to Chiloé.... While he was telling me that ... that image that he had captured was going to outlive him, that I should be proud of him because he had been brave, and that this image had changed him ... something indicated to me that that conversation was the prelude to a farewell, that from here on he could only begin to distance himself from me, from my mother, from Santiago, from everything that we knew.

About two years later, the father completely separates from his family, moving permanently to Chiloé.

No me dio pena, había previsto ese abandono desde siempre. Sabía que se iba a ir, sabía que se iba a romper, había crecido con esa pérdida prefigurada como un presentimiento.... Hasta el día de hoy recuerdo sus ojos. Los ojos de un hombre que abandona todo. Los ojos de un hombre que renuncia. Los ojos de un hombre que se está quedando vacío. (41–42)

It didn't make me feel sad, [as] I had always foreseen this abandonment. I knew that he was going to leave, I knew that he was going to break down, I had grown up with that prefigured loss like a premonition.... To this day I recall his eyes. The eyes of a man who abandons everything. The eyes of a man who gives up. The eyes of a man who is winding up empty.

Once in Chiloé, even though the father is supposed to visit with the son every two or three months, they do not see each other for a year. As the son gets older, they only speak on rare occasions, such as when the son calls to tell him that he is about to get married or become a father. This progressive distancing culminates with a phone call that the son receives telling him that the bodies of two men were found at the father's house in Chiloé and that the father has disappeared. Years go by. In that interval, the father is believed to be dead, until one day Nora, an ex-girlfriend (the father has been long separated from the mother) contacts the son and shows him some photographs that the father sent to her with an address on the envelope. The son goes to visit the father, who is now living in an even remoter part of Chiloé, growing his own marijuana plants and living near a cave. The father admits to killing the two men in a story so full of strange and conflicting details, that it becomes difficult to make an ultimate judgment about his crimes. There are three possible ways to interpret the events: he committed the crimes because he became mentally ill as a result of the torture and trauma he endured under the dictatorship; he became a murderer because his immersion in violence turned him into a savage person; or he killed the men in self-defense because they were persecuting him for unstated reasons related to his past.

Such ambiguity is compelling. Craig Taylor examines its workings in Joseph Conrad's character of Jim in *Lord Jim*. Conflicting elements of the narrative suggest differing interpretations of Jim's morality. Taylor states:

> My concern in this paper, however, is with a deeper, more troubling kind of ambiguity that may occur when a writer . . . has put all the truth [he] can into a work, yet whose particular characters and events portrayed remain unresolved for the writer. . . . In such a situation . . . reader[s] . . . exercise [their] own judgment in making sense . . . of . . . potentially conflicting responses to those characters and events. I am interested in the kind of case where . . . our conflicting emotional responses to the narrative suggest different ways in which we might fill it in. . . . In this sense my argument goes beyond the general point that literature engages our capacities of emotional response leading to moral understanding. Specifically, my interest is with cases where we have a conflicting response to a work and with the particular moral understanding that might lead to. (79)

Taylor's reflections summarize precisely the type of ambiguity that occurs in *El brujo*. Since many events remain unexplained, different interpretations of these events will inevitably lead to disparate visions of the father.

One possible interpretation is that the father is mentally ill; that the trauma suffered through his work and experience of torture has led him to become paranoid and unhinged, thus leading to his murder of the two individuals, Urbina and García, who are allegedly members of an environmental protection agency. One day these two individuals call on him and leave him their card. Although the father does not contact them, they return and ask permission to install equipment on his property to observe the possible presence of a bird species in danger of extinction. The father agrees. These two individuals make subsequent visits to the forest. While there, they locate the father's home and spot the father's cat Copito, accusing the latter of having killed many birds. They want to put the cat down, but the father refuses. The father relates numerous episodes to the son in which the two forestry representatives harass him. He claims he sees them surveilling him from the window at the school where he works; they try to run him over in their car one night; two individuals in ski masks enter his house, tie him to a chair, and beat him. His house was also ransacked in his absence. Finally, because of these incidences, the father buys a gun. When Urbina and García show up for the cat, he shoots Urbina and then García, who points a rifle at him after he has killed Urbina. This last act can be interpreted as one of self-defense.

The first question the reader must ask is whether Urbina and García are in fact environmentalists. If so, why would they try to run the father over, send two men to beat him up, ransack his house, and show up with a rifle? In this interpretation, the reader questions these details, and perhaps attributes them to the father's paranoid imagination. In terms of moral judgment of the character, he cannot be totally condemned for his actions because he is a victim of mental illness caused by traumatic events. Supporting this interpretation is the testimony of the father's ex-girlfriend Nora, who describes his absences from work and his appearance—that he would later return pale and with bags under his eyes, looking as if he had just been sick. These absences occurred during the several months immediately prior to the father's disappearance (92–93).

In the second possible interpretation, the reader views the father as having become accustomed to violence through his experiences as a photographer during the Pinochet government. Details found in the novel can substantiate this interpretation as well. In the first section of the novel, the son tells us that his father "se empezó a excitar con el gas. . . . Empezó a detestar los momentos muertos" ([22] he began to get excited with the [tear?] gas . . . . He began to detest the down times). Toward the end of the novel, during the father's confession of his own crime to his son, he recounts a violent encounter he once had with a forestry worker, whom he had met in a bar. During their brawl, the father broke a bottle over the head of the worker, but he walked away from the scene missing two of his teeth (149–50).

This episode suggests that the father was indeed capable of violent behavior and that his experiences with violence during the dictatorship were a precipitating factor. From that profile, readers may conclude that he killed Urbina and García in a premeditated fashion because he purchased a gun with that end in mind. If so, then he has descended into becoming a cold-blooded murderer, no better than his torturers during the dictatorship. And so the father, now morally corrupt, lies to the reader to justify his murder of the agents.

In both the first and the second interpretations, the father fits the typology of what Wayne Booth calls an unreliable narrator because this father either unknowingly or knowingly lies to the reader. For that reason, his narration does not accord with the norms of the implied author (158–59).[9]

The final possible interpretation that ambiguous details in the novel lend themselves to is that Urbina and García are not really environmentalists, that the father's cat did not actually eat the birds, and that somehow these men arrive to persecute the father for some other unexplained motive, perhaps related to his photography work in the past. Numerous novelistic details support this interpretation. For example, the principal of the school where the father works tells him that Urbina had called his workplace and asked strange questions about him. As a consequence, the principal called the office known as "SAG" (Servicio Agrícola y Ganadero; The Agricultural and Livestock Service) whose representatives state that Urbina "era un funcionario pero que no estaba a cargo de nada. Pidió hablar con jefe o un superior pero no se lo pasaron" ([168] was a functionary but he wasn't in charge of anything. He asked to speak with the boss or a superior, but they didn't put him on the line with them). If Urbina weren't in charge of anything, what was he doing installing cameras at the father's house? Why would the office not allow the principal to speak to a superior? In another instance, two men entered the father's house, whom he claimed were not Urbina and García, and beat him repeatedly, asking whether he had gotten their message. He said he had (207). If Urbina and García were truly SAG agents, why would they have sent two other men to beat up the father? And what is the message they were sending to the father that he claimed to understand? It would not be credible that these men were sent to beat him up over his cat. Something else had to be going on here, though the reader is never told what. Consequently, the reader is led to believe that Urbina and García are not SAG agents. Rather, they harbor some other hidden identity and are pursuing the father for reasons unknown. This idea is supported by the blog the father uncovers about Urbina, in which he is seen embracing a fascist military man in the '80s.

Another of the many reasons that the reader might choose this interpretation relates to the eating habits of the cat Copito. Although the SAG agents show the narrator's father a video of his cat eating the birds, the figure of the cat is blurry in the video; in addition, the traps set to catch the culprit are much larger than traps for a domestic cat. There are many more details of this nature that do not make any sense. Altogether, then, such circumstances lead the reader to conclude that the father is a victim of an unexplained aggressor and that he has shot Urbina and García in self-defense. In this instance, the father remains morally pure, and his escape is justifiable.

Although these ambiguous elements appear to give a crime fiction turn to the story, in reality, all three possible interpretations lead back to the effects of the dictatorship on the father. The impact of having had to abandon his family and his life in Santiago to feel safe directly relates to the first two possible interpretations of the father as having descended into mental illness or violence.

Schlomith Rimmon-Kenan, in *The Concept of Ambiguity* (1977), defines ambiguity thus: "When the two hypotheses are mutually exclusive, and yet each equally coherent, equally consistent, equally plenary and convincing, so that we cannot choose between them, we are confronted with narrative ambiguity" (10). Ambiguity is an example of what Sabine Schlickers terms "strategies of empuzzlement" in *La narración perturbadora* (2017). She also identifies strategies of "deception" and "paradox." According to Schlickers, at least two of these three categories must be present in a text to create what she calls "perturbatory fiction," which is narration that intentionally produces "disturbing effects such as surprise, confusion, doubt and disappointment" (206). However, in *El brujo*, these categories cannot always be discretely identified. In other words, deception, which includes "false leads," may not always be determined as such, because the false leads may or may not be intentional or represent deception on the part of the narrator. For example, as we saw in the three possible interpretations of the character of the father, the fact that he looked up information about the SAG agents and found that one had a fascist affiliation may or may not constitute a false lead. If a connection exists between what is happening to the father and this information, then the lead is not false. Even so, no reader can make that determination because a valid solution explaining the circumstances of the father's crime is not spelled out in the novel, and this is one of the defining conditions of perturbatory fiction that Schlickers puts forth (212). Nonetheless, I would like to argue that *El brujo* is in fact a perturbatory fiction, even though it may only contain strategies of empuzzlement. Its strong reliance on ambiguity and indeterminacy produces the exact effect described by Schlickers as perturbatory, despite her insistence on the presence of at least two of the identified categories.

A third and final element that emphasizes feelings caused by the dictatorship is the photograph that the father takes of a woman (later identified as Mónica) having a revolver shoved into her face by a police officer.

Like *Fuenzalida*, *El brujo* pivots around a photographic image. However, in contrast to *Fuenzalida*, which from the beginning emphasizes the inability of the photograph to provide an accurate memory, the photograph in *El brujo* is initially touted as a direct capture of reality:

> Sus fotos... captaban la violencia, la congelaban.... Sus fotos eran claras... no tenían dobles lecturas.... Fue por esos años cuando él sacó su foto más famosa... un carabinero amenaza con un revólver a una muchacha que está en el suelo. La muchacha no se tapa la cara ... solo mira con los ojos abiertos el arma que está a centímetros de su rostro.... Lo importante es la línea recta que va desde los ojos de la muchacha hasta el arma, ahí todo se transforma en una tensión muda que anima los músculos del brazo, concentrado en la violencia detenida que aún no se desata. (23–24)

> His photos were effective, they captured the violence, they froze it. ... His photographs were clear, precise, they didn't admit double readings.... It was around those years when he took his most famous picture.... A police officer threatens a girl who is on the ground with his revolver. The girl does not cover her face, nor does she establish any kind of defense, she only looks at the weapon that is centimeters from her face with her eyes wide open.... The important thing is the straight line that goes from the girl's eyes to the weapon, there everything is transformed into a mute tension that animates the muscles of the policeman's arm, concentrated on the paused violence that has as yet not been unleased.

Although the photograph becomes famous and receives awards because it captures the violence of the era, it is not a static image of reality, a simple vessel of truth because its meaning is determined through its contextualization. Zeynep Devrine Gürsel posits the afterimage of photographs and defines it as "a visual image that persists after the visual stimulus causing it has ceased to act.... I want to argue that photographic images also produce afterimages on the metaphoric mind's eye, and thus, that after-images belong to the domain of visuality" (65). However, this lingering image, for reasons of interpretive contextualization, cannot and will not be the same for everyone. As Jeffrey Olick illustrates in his analysis of the photo of Willy Brandt kneeling before the Polish Holocaust memorial, the remembering that occurs when viewing or thinking about an iconic photograph will elicit different responses depending on the filter through which it passes, including international politics, domestic politics, and memory politics (21–34).

The afterimage of the photograph taken by the father in *El brujo* means different things to different people as it is contextualized in diverse manners in the novel. As we shall see shortly regarding other important photographs in the novel, the father sees himself and his deteriorating mental and emotional state in his photographs. Since he was abducted and tortured a week after the circulation of the iconic image of the police officer and woman, that photo and all the others he takes in Santiago represent his feelings of mental instability caused by the violence he suffered as a result of photographing the dictatorship.

> Trataba de encontrar a mi padre en la foto sin darme cuenta de que todo lo que estaba ahí era suyo, todo era él porque todo era su mirada, era su ojo, era el modo en que él capturaba el tiempo para dejarlo atrapado.... Buscaba a mi padre en la violencia callejera sin saber que él ya había sido colonizada por ella. (30)

> I tried to find my father in the photograph without realizing that everything that was there was his, everything was him because everything was his gaze, his eye, the way in which he captured time to render it captive.... I looked for my father in the street violence without knowing that he had already been colonized by it.

This idea is supported by other photographs that the father takes throughout the novel. Toward its end, he takes a series of photographs with a broken Polaroid camera. The pictures all look the same and are described as black rectangles in which the photographed objects have no borders and melt into each other, which creates a feeling of unreality (170–71).

The clear and direct photographs that the father used to take have been replaced by a series of indistinct, black, deformed images. This deformity is "the world behind the world" of the father by reflecting his mental instability. These are the photos he takes right before committing the two murders of Urbina and García and thus mirror his dark feelings and ultimate transformation.

Similarly, the woman Mónica, who was photographed by the father with the gun pointed at her face, has feelings associated with this picture of her. She searches for the father years later and, upon finding him, tells him that the photograph ruined her life:

> Después de que se publicara... alguien me la mostró en una revista.... Me costó verme. Mi rostro no era mi rostro. Mi rostro era una máscara. Gracias a la foto recordé la pistola y el miedo que me provocó. Mi rostro era ese miedo encorvado. Mi miedo era lo que me había quedado de la foto.... Estoy enferma... La enfermedad comenzó cuando sacaste la foto. Yo me convertí en esa imagen. (137–38)

> After it was published... someone showed it to me in a magazine.... It was difficult to see myself. My face was not my face. My face was a mask. Thanks to the photograph I remembered the pistol and the fear that it provoked in me. My face was that hunched over fear. My fear was what had remained with me from the photograph.... I am ill... The illness began when you took the photo of me. I became that image.

For Mónica, the photo and its afterimage capture fear rather than violence. This fear has overpowered her life causing severe depression. It is interesting that the woman does not blame the event itself, but the memory of the event that the photo embalms, for ruining her life and making the fear persist. Although both Mónica and the father identify with the photograph to a degree, they each interpret the photograph differently, extracting distinct elements and feelings from it within the different contexts of their lives.

What Mónica and the narrator's father share in their viewing of the photograph is a retrieving and reliving of the trauma that each one experienced because of the dictatorship. According to Jill Bennett in *Empathic Vision* (2005), there are two types of memory: common memory and sense memory. Common memory "is the memory connected with the thinking process and with words—the realm in which events are rendered intelligible, pegged to a common or established frame of reference, so that they can be communicated to, and readily understood by, a general audience" (25). Bennett uses the example of the artist and Auschwitz survivor Charlotte Delbo to explain the workings of sense memory:

> Seen from the outside, Delbo's Auschwitz experience is the property of another self.... Delbo experiences these two selves as segregated, yet she also speaks of being in the grip of sense memory for periods of several days, during which time the physical pain of her trauma returns. Thus, the Auschwitz self, for all that it is discrete, retains a capacity to touch and affect, to trigger emotion in the present. (25)

Bennett explains that visual art that depicts trauma evokes sense memory and makes those who have experienced trauma spectators of their own emotions. This is essentially what happens to both Mónica and the father in *El brujo*:

> Up until now, theorists of trauma and memory have paid relatively little attention to visual and performance art. Yet in those fields, we find a long tradition of engagement with affect and immediate experience, not just as sources of inspiration or objects of representation, but as fundamental components of a dynamic between the artwork and the spectator. In an almost concrete sense, much visual and performance art evokes the possibility—for both artist and viewer—of "being a spectator of one's own feelings." The kind of imagery that operates in this vein—mediating affects, sensations, and traumatic memory—cannot be reduced to a form of representation. And insofar as such imagery serves to register subjective processes that exceed our capacity to represent them, certain of its features might be understood as reflecting those of traumatic memory (23).

Another important point is that the photograph of the police officer threatening Mónica with his pistol captures the place where the traumatic event occurred. Diana Taylor points out that memory is invariably linked to place (*Feeling Photography* ch. 9) and that photography has the capacity of reproducing the site of torture. Reviewing the torture site triggers a reliving of fear and violence in the protagonists.

Yet Chilean memory politics offer still another context for interpreting the photograph. Years after the end of the dictatorship, the office of human rights contacts the father regarding the exhibition of his photograph in a museum in Santiago. They ask him for a copy of the negative. The father, who after his encounter with Mónica is horrified by the destructive power of his photograph, tells them not to exhibit the photo and promptly destroys the negative. Within the field of memory politics, the photograph encapsulates a historical era, that of the Pinochet dictatorship, and not as a vehicle of individual feelings such as fear or mental instability. It is an important way to remember the significance of the past.

Finally, the title of Bisama's work invites a brief discussion. The reader might wonder why the book is called "The Wizard." The title bears a direct relationship to a Chilean myth of witchcraft in Chilóe. According to Sergio Fritz Roa:

> el nombre [recta provincia] vendría del hecho que en Chile existiría un reino subterráneo que estaría conectado a través de cuevas de brujos.... Carlos Keller señala "La creencia en brujos está todavía muy arraigada en el país. Se sostiene que en las profundidades de la tierra hay a lo largo de todo el territorio una inmensa cueva conocida con el nombre de Salamanca" (517).... Uno de los elementos característicos de la Recta Provincia es la presencia de una cueva ubicada en Quicaví, la que constituirá el punto central de las actividades de los brujos. (loc. 243)

The name [Straight Province] probably comes from the fact that in Chile there existed a subterranean kingdom that was connected through witches' caves.... Carlos Keller indicates "The belief in witches is still very rooted in the country. People say that in the depths of the earth there is an immense cave throughout the territory known with the name of Salamanca.... One of the characteristic elements of the Straight Province is the presence of a cave located in Quicaví, which probably constitutes the central point of activities for the witches and warlocks.

On a purely literal level, the father becomes like the warlocks of Chiloé because he lives near a cave and grows hallucinogenic plants. On a symbolic level, the father becomes "el brujo" because he is transformed from a peaceful man into a murderer at the novel's end. Just as the warlocks killed their enemies through black magic, the father tells us that he has dispatched Urbina and García to the cave of the dead.

It is not a coincidence that *Mapocho*, *Fuenzalida*, and *El brujo* all employ narrative strategies characterized by indeterminacy. *Mapocho* presents unfinished stories that rely on the reader's ability to make intertextual connections to fill in the gaps; *Fuenzalida* invents multiple imaginative narrations to provide an identifiable past for Fuenzalida in the absence of a known one, blurring the boundaries between "reality" and fiction; and *El brujo* presents narrative indeterminacies that result in conflicting visions of the protagonist. To some degree, these strategies "mimic" the narrative void of what happened to the disappeared during the Pinochet dictatorship. In the absence of concrete evidence, families had to guess what might have happened to their loved ones, creating their own narratives of the past. Forcing the reader to fill in the gaps helps the reader to identify with the feelings of loss and abandonment experienced by Chileans in the dictatorship era.

CHAPTER 3

Expressions of Despair

Romance Plots and Affective Landscapes in José Donoso's *La desesperanza*, Carlos Franz's *Santiago Cero*, Álvaro Bisama's *Estrellas muertas*, and Germán Marín's *El palacio de la risa*

A KEY ASPECT OF COMPREHENDING how despair (or any emotion) is expressed in literature requires a discussion of narrative tone. Sianne Ngai dedicates a chapter of *Ugly Feelings* (2005) to this issue, indicating that tone is often defined as the attitude of the speaker. Yet, as she contends, such a definition proves insufficient because it does not factor in many other elements that contribute to the creation of tone. Drawing on Otto Baensch, she observes that the "feeling" of a work is not a "free-floating phantom," nor can it be "brought into explicit correlation with its component elements" (45). Rather, tone signifies

> a literary text's affective bearing, orientation or "set toward" its audience and world. In other words, [it is] the formal aspect of a work that has made it possible for critics of all affiliations (Marxist, feminist, postcolonial, historicist) to describe a work or class of works as "paranoid" ... "euphoric" ... or melancholic ... and ... the formal aspect that enables these affective values to become significant with regard to how each critic understands the work as a totality within an equally holistic matrix of social relations.... It is clear, however, that tone ... remains loosely fastened to signifying practices, even if it is not literally a sign itself. (43–46)

In other words, tone does not rely merely on what James Phelan terms "textual cues" (50) or stylistic aspects of a narrative for its expression but on an overarching atmosphere that pervades a text. Nonetheless, it is important to identify, when possible, textual elements that lead us to state that a text communicates a particular emotive tone.

This chapter examines four novels (two that were written during the Pinochet dictatorship and two postmemory novels) that center on the feeling of despair experienced both during and after the dictatorship in Chile. Ironically, with the exception of José Donoso's *La desesperanza* (1986), which includes the word despair in its title, these novels suggest that there is no hope for the future. Keeping Ngai's definition of tone in mind, I would like to suggest that these novels communicate a tone of despair through two main textual elements: the romance plot and narrative descriptions of affective architecture and landscape. Although chronologically *La desesperanza* was the first of the four novels to be published, I leave its discussion for last since the novel does something different with these elements than the other three.

In *Affective Narratology*, Hogan defines three types of fundamental plot structures, each based on distinct emotions: the romance plot, the heroic plot, and the sacrifice plot. For my purposes, only the romance plot and the heroic plot are relevant. Hogan defines the romance plot as one predicated on the goal of happiness, both physical (sexual union) and nonphysical (attachment). Two people fall in love, encounter obstacles (such as parental objections or a love triangle), and eventually these obstacles are overcome and normalcy is restored when the romance is a comedy or are not when the romance is a tragedy (see "Emotional Structure of Stories"). Either way, the important point is that romance plots are based on happiness goals.

In contrast, heroic plots, writes Hogan, are generally based on the emotions of pride and anger between an "in-group" and an "out-group."

> There is a legitimate social order in the in-group. Someone illegitimately takes over the leadership role.... The ruler commonly has a helper who is a strong and loyal warrior. In some cases, the warrior may become the hero of the story.... Indeed, in some cases it is the warrior who loses his/her position and is exiled, not the ruler.... The home society is threatened with domination by the enemy. Eventually the enemy is defeated.... (ch. 3)

The defeat of the enemy leads to a reestablishment of normalcy, an "idealized society," but may be accompanied by an "epilogue of suffering" ("Emotional Structure") in which the pain of loss and grief remains. That leads to mourning or the emotions of guilt and blame, which lead, in turn, to reparation and penance.

One would expect that novels that center on the Pinochet dictatorship, its memory and aftermath, would follow the heroic plot sequence Hogan sketches. A legitimate leader (Allende) was overthrown by the "out-group" (Pinochet and the military) and eventually the "out-group" was defeated. Only then was normalcy (democracy) restored in Chile. However, none of the four novels studied in this chapter follows a heroic plot structure, other than including the element of a lingering suffering or grief (leading to despair) that results from the dictatorship era. Instead, these novels essentially revolve around tragic romance plots and thus unfulfilled happiness goals.

The author of the first novel I consider, Carlos Franz, was born in Geneva, Switzerland in 1959 to Chilean parents. He returned to Chile after his parents separated in 1970 and enrolled in the University of Chile to study law. He participated in various literary workshops, including the one conducted by José Donoso upon his return to Chile in 1981. His first novel, *Santiago cero*, won the Premio Latinoamericano de Novelas CICLA in 1986, even though it was not published until 1989 toward the end of the dictatorship. His most famous works include *El lugar donde estuvo el paraíso* (1996; The Place Where Paradise Was), *El desierto* (2005), and *Almuerzo de vampiros* (2007) (Rodríguez Freire 335–36). These last two novels I discuss in chapter 5.

Carlos Franz's novel *Santiago Cero* (1989) is a good example of how the subversion of romantic happiness goals leads to an atmosphere of despair. The title itself, which includes a veiled allusion to Bob Dylan's "A Hard Rain's Gonna Fall," suggests despair. We know that because one of the song's lyrics, "When black is the color and none is the number ["cero"]," serves as the epigraph to part 2. The darkness and void suggested by the lyric, with its emphasis on "cero" (zero), create an atmospheric despair that is with readers even before they read the first sentence of the first paragraph. The action of the novel is itself a flashback narrated by an unnamed protagonist who is in jail at the onset of the novel. He narrates his story in the "tú" (second-person) form, as if he were talking to himself and writing a love story:

> Mi memoria se detuvo años antes, en lo que podría llamar mi educación sentimental; pero ésta no interesa en absoluto a los fiscales. Sin embargo, si existiera un juez que se ocupara de esos primeros móviles ... de las causas remotas, en lugar de sus tardíos efectos, ante él me

> gustaría testimoniar. Hasta que no me lleven a su presencia, callo y escribo lo que pudo ser una historia de amor. (5)

> My memory stopped years ago, stuck in what could be called my sentimental education, but this does not interest the prosecutors at all. However, if a judge existed who would consider those first motivations ... of remote causes, instead of their later effects, I would like to give testimony before him. Until they take me before him, I am silent and I write what perhaps was a love story.

At this point, the reader does not know why the protagonist is in jail or whether the character is a hero or a villain. Nonetheless, despite his being in jail (which could hint at a "heroic" plot), the protagonist states that his tale is likely a love story. With that deflection, he obscures the political events behind his incarceration.

The protagonist proceeds to narrate a romance plot. During his first days at the university, he meets and becomes friends with a woman named Raquel. They become inseparable, but the narrator fails to recognize that he has fallen in love with her because she does not meet the criteria of his "ideal woman." Their relationship maintains its ambiguous status until the arrival of Sebastián at the university, a student who constitutes the third element of the love triangle. Sebastián gradually usurps the narrator's position within his group of friends. As a result, the narrator spends most of his time spying on the developing relationship between Raquel and Sebastián as he tries to regain his former position in the group.

The turning point in Sebastián's relationship with Raquel follows from a series of letters from a friend living abroad. Sebastián brings these letters to the cafeteria table where the group gathers and reads them aloud. The author of the letters writes of his adventures traveling throughout Europe, which effectively document and capture a sense of freedom unexperienced by the students who are living under the repressive environment of the dictatorship. For Raquel especially, the letters become a symbol of hope and freedom, as she feels particularly oppressed by her environment. Only later, however, do readers learn that Sebastián actually authored the letters to give her hope for the future. This fact is revealed thanks to the narrator's betrayal of Sebastián to the character

Blanco, an informant of the dictatorship, and with whom the protagonist joins forces, ostensibly motivated by his efforts to break up the relationship between Sebastián and Raquel. Sebastián's description of his motivations in the following passage serves to communicate the despair felt by Raquel and others living under the dictatorship:

> Sí . . . yo escribí esas cartas todo este año . . . Yo las inventé todas. ¡Pero te juro que no son mentiras! . . . Traté de convencerla de eso. Peleé por mantener una esperanza. Habíamos llegado a esas calles podridas que hay detrás del mercado. Todo se oscureció. Debe haber sido la noche, pero a mí me pareció que era el cielo sucio de Santiago que nos caía encima. . . . Un humo negro fue envolviéndola [a Raquel] a medida que yo pescaba otra cosa en su cara. Algo más que desesperanza o desilusión. Era la cara que tienen las viudas, compadre. Tenía la muerte de un ser amado en la cara. . . . Yo le escribí esas cartas por darle una ilusión para vivir, pero ella fue más lejos, pasándose sus propias películas. (94–95)

> Yes . . . I wrote those letters during the entire year . . . I invented all of them. But I swear to you that they are not lies! . . . I tried to convince her of that. I fought to maintain hope. We had arrived at those decayed streets behind the market. Everything was dark. It must have been night, but for me it seemed that it was the dirty Santiago sky that was falling on top of us. . . . A black smoke was enveloping her [Raquel] while I was looking for something else in her face. Something more than despair and disappointment. It was the face that widows have, pal. She had the death of a loved one on her face. . . . I wrote those letters for her to give her hope for life, but she went even further, creating her own fantasies.

That no good deed goes unpunished applies here, and underscoring that is the despairing imagery of "a black smoke enveloped her" or "something more than despair or disillusionment. It was the face that widows have." The death of Raquel's dream of escape also leads to the death of her romance with Sebastián. That second death catapults her back into the narrator's arms, as he had hoped. Eventually, Raquel and the narrator marry. Sebastián continues to write to her, but she never receives the letters because the narrator intercepts them. Finally, however, she learns that Sebastián was trying to contact her. She ends up leaving the narrator but, as she states, not because of his interception of Sebastián's letters. The reason is that he has told lies about his job as a government agent and his double life: "¿Con quién he vivido? ¿A quién he amado, intuyendo sin querer ver...? Es lo otro que me ocultaste lo que me asquea. ¡Yo, la ingenua, prefiriendo incluso pensar que serían mujeres las que te atrasaban en la noche!" ([106] With whom have I lived? Whom have I loved, intuiting without wanting to see . . . ? It is the other thing that you hid from me that disgusts me. Me, the ingenuous one, preferring even to think that probably women delayed you at night!)

The happiness goals sought by all three characters (the narrator, Raquel, and Sebastián) are thwarted, as is the return to normalcy and happiness that Hogan posits for the "comedic" romance plot. Sebastián's love remains unrequited, the narrator ultimately loses Raquel, and Raquel ends up alone with a broken marriage that was a deception. A sense of general despair is created through the romance plot and its lack of fulfillment of its happiness goals. Although the focus is on romance, the despair felt by the characters is intertwined with the effects of the dictatorship through not only the role of the letters but also the narrator-protagonist's role as a CNI agent,[1] which leads to the breakup of his marriage. The most important point is that an atmosphere of despair, which communicates what Chileans felt during the dictatorship, is fundamentally achieved through the use of the romance plot. The despair felt by Raquel, Sebastián, and the narrator in their love triangle parallels and encapsulates the despair felt by Chileans under Pinochet.

Álvaro Bisama's *Estrellas muertas* (2010) also suggests despair through its title and like *Santiago Cero* is a story that revolves around romance plots (actually, two of them). The story is a framed narrative (a story within a story). The first story, about an unnamed man and an unnamed woman, is told by the man, as they sit in the Café Hesperia in Valparaíso waiting to sign divorce papers. While in the café, the woman sees an article in the newspaper about an old college friend named Javiera who has been arrested. She proceeds to tell Javiera's story, which is also fundamentally a tale about love. Although the protagonists of the first love story live out their romance during the postdictatorship, as do Javiera and Donoso, Javiera's prehistory involves her trajectory as a revolutionary against and resister of the dictatorship. Javiera's status as a victim of dictatorship is not incidental; it is, indeed, essential to her life of despair.

The female protagonist met Javiera, now in her forties, at the university in the early nineties. One of the first things she learns about her is that she had been tortured:

> La había torturado la CNI.... Nos ... dijo que la violaron, que la aplicaron electricidad en la vagina y los pechos, que la tuvieron por horas en la parrilla ... que el dolor era tanto ... que al cabo de una semana en esa celda era casi un cadáver, una masa de carne y llagas ... que su cuerpo se pudrió. (*Estrellas* ch. 10)

> She had been tortured by the CNI.... [S]he told us that they raped her, that they applied electricity to her vagina and her breasts, that they had her on the "grill" for hours.... She told us that the pain was so bad ... that by the end of a week in that cell she was practically a cadaver, a mass of flesh and sores. (Stars ch. 10)

Although this is one of the few concrete mentions of the dictatorship in the novel, it is a defining moment in Javiera's life, as well as a significant reason behind the negative feelings in the lives of the two divorcing protagonists of the first love story. While at the university, Javiera meets a young man named Donoso; they become lovers, and she gets pregnant. Javiera has an ex-husband and a son. On one occasion, she meets with her former husband and they have sex. When she returns to Donoso and confesses what she has done, he beats her so savagely that she loses the baby she is carrying. Javiera chooses to forgive Donoso and returns to him after her hospital stay. However, her reasons for doing so directly recur to the dictatorship:

> La Javiera tenía la cara destrozada, los ojos morados, los labios hinchados, dijo ella.... Había visto sangre, pero nunca un cuerpo roto, nunca un cuerpo en ese estado.... Me dijo que no quiso ponerle una denuncia. Me dijo que esto no era nada al lado de lo que le habían hecho los milicos.... Me dijo que ya tendrían más hijos, que esto era solo un accidente.... Sentí ... ganas de vomitar. (*Estrellas* ch. 48)

> Javiera's face was destroyed, with black eyes, swollen lips, she said. I'd seen blood before, but never a broken body, never a body in that

state.... She told me she didn't want to press charges. She told me it was nothing compared to what the army thugs had done to her.... She told me she would have more children, that this was just an accident.... I felt as if I needed to throw up. (Stars ch. 48)

Javiera's experience of torture under the dictatorship has somehow made her accept violence (cf. the father in *El brujo*) and, in short order, as both its victim and perpetrator. The reader gets the impression that her willingness to accept the abuse stems from the torture she experienced under the dictatorship which, rather than making her "tough," has caused her to become unhinged. In another section, we learn that she once became hysterical because she thought she saw one of her torturers on the street, another sign of the deteriorating effects of the trauma she has suffered. As Javiera's relationship with Donoso further disintegrates, she becomes more and more aggressive and hysterical. They eventually have a daughter, but Javiera's progressively erratic behavior leads Donoso to leave her, taking the daughter with him. The final pages of the novel reveal, in a newspaper account, that the reason for Javiera's arrest is that she has drowned her two-year-old daughter in the bathtub, which drives home both the violence and despair that compel her.

Although the love story between the male narrator and the female protagonist of the first love story frames the tale of Javiera and Donoso, in reality it is Javiera's life as emblem of the dictatorship era that frames the story of the couple. Theirs is a story of two fraught people whose eventual meeting and marriage temporarily suspends their despair. Nonetheless, as their relationship collapses, that lurking despair comes back to haunt them. While the female protagonist narrates Javiera's life and romance with Donoso, she also narrates her own, its emptiness and despair measured in the cough syrup she is addicted to. Needless to say, images of despair congest her life story, which is equally true of the glimpsed life of her spouse. In part, this despair is due to the fact that the characters feel they have lived unheroically in unheroic times—unlike Javiera who fought against the dictatorship:

Como si ... estuviéramos obligados a rendirle tributo al fuego, a escuchar las historias de guerra de los otros porque eso sería lo único que tendríamos y nos dejarían conservar: las historias de las batallas ajenas, dijo ella. . . . El pasado era una liturgia donde estábamos excluidos del milagro, dijo . . . Sentía que quedábamos fuera . . . lo nuestro era solo la marea y la resaca. La era de la sangre y el vértigo ya había pasado. (*Estrellas* ch. 19)

As if . . . we were forced to pay homage to the fire, to listen to other people's war stories because that was all we had that they'd let us keep: the stories of other people's battles, she said. . . . I felt as if we were left out . . . that our lot was only wooziness [from a] hangover. The time of blood and vertigo was over. (Stars ch. 19)

The protagonists' lives lack a fundamental meaning, which parallels and reflects the inertia of the Concertación government regarding past human rights abuses and its pure focus on the market economy inherited from the dictatorship. The consequence was a meaningless, hopeless existence for Chilean youth who were denied any sense of the future. Indeed, the female protagonist, reflecting upon the government of Frei junior and the continuing presence of Pinochet, states that she had no other recourse but to "dope herself up" (Stars ch. 35).

So many depressing episodes and bleak images contribute to this overarching despair. The depressing tales include the female narrator's friend who committed suicide by jumping from the eighth floor because his girlfriend wouldn't take his phone calls, the memory of Keith Cobain's suicide (ch. 42), the man crying in the café who threatens suicide and temporarily becomes the female narrator's boyfriend (ch. 56), and the male narrator's tale of the disappearance and death of his friend's sister (ch. 50). In addition, the text is filled with a series of bleak, scary, or sad images that contribute to an aura of hopelessness. For example, Donoso dreams about an army of Vietnamese men in flames who follow him through the streets of Antofagasta (ch. 14); the female narrator asks her husband: ¿No te ha pasado como me pasó a mí, que pierdes la memoria y cuando abres los ojos y la recuperas hay una mujer golpeada, un bebé muerto y una cantidad de mugre de todo tipo alrededor? ([ch. 41] Hasn't it happened to you, as it happened to me, that you lost your memory and when you opened your eyes and got it back, there was a battered woman and a dead baby, and everything had gone to shit? [Stars ch. 41]). And his response to life is similar, as seen when he answers her question about what he was doing at that time: "Nada. O todo. Bebí coñac... No fui a ninguna parte... Vi películas de terror. No esperaba nada porque yo mismo no era nada, dije" ([*Estrellas* ch. 36] Nothing. Or everything. I drank Tres Palos cognac.... I didn't go anywhere. I stayed right there.... I watched horror movies. I expected nothing because I myself was nothing, I said [Stars ch. 36]). These episodes and images suggest lives emptied of hope and a future. However, the evolution of the couple's romance, with the repetition of the phrase "veniste tú" (you came) or "llegaste tú" (you arrived) suggests a glimmer of hope (which the reader knows is only temporary because the novel begins with the divorce) in what is otherwise a vicious circle of despair: "Terminaron los días de ese mundo congelado, empezó el tiempo. Y luego lo nuestro se fue al diablo" ([*Estrellas* ch. 42] Those days in that frozen world came to an end and time started up again. And then what we had fell apart [Stars ch. 42]). The female protagonist expresses similar thoughts: "Yo deseaba haberme borrado así, pero no lo hice... Después ese deseo se me pasó. Llegaste tú" ([*Estrellas* ch. 51] I would've liked to disappear like that too, but I didn't... Then that desire passed. You came along [Stars ch. 51]).

The role of salvation that each protagonist played for the other makes their breakup even more poignant. They compare the dissolution of their marriage to the images of shipwrecks in the paintings on the walls of the café Hesperia. The images of shipwrecks and black seas project the feelings of hopelessness that surround the protagonists and the novel as a whole. Bisama employs the frustration of the happiness goals implicit in the romance plot to reflect the general feelings of despair about life during the postdictatorship period and as a result of the dictatorship itself: "Después el siglo terminó... nos metimos a este café y nos convertimos en esos reflejos, en las fotos de eso que se hunde.... Dijo ella: ... Somos el mar negro de las fotos. La superficie sucia del océano donde todo se hunde ([*Estrellas* chs. 73–75] The century ended.... [W]e walked into this café and we turned into those reflections, those photos of something sinking.... She said: ... We're the black sea in those photos. The dirty surface of the ocean that everything sinks into. That's what we are [Stars chs. 73–75]).

Despite the temporary relief brought by their relationship, in these last three citations, the male and the female protagonist specifically tie their despair to the (political) times they were living in with locutions such as "the century ended." Those times, the 1990s, marked the immediate postdictatorship period and, in the context of the novel, signify an empty and hopeless era. It is not a coincidence that the male protagonist likens the decade to "a hangover full of black holes, of memory loss," which alludes to the Chilean memory battle over acknowledgement and reparation for the past atrocities of the dictatorship and the long reach of Pinochet even after he stepped down from power in 1990.

Germán Marín (1934–2019) was a Chilean journalist and writer. *Fuegos artificiales* (1973; Fireworks), his first novel, was burned by the military junta. *El palacio de la risa* (1995) is his only published novel. He also published a book of short stories titled *Un oscuro pedazo de la vida* (A Dark Piece of Life) shortly before his death in 2019.

El Palacio has a first-person narrator who has returned to Chile from a seventeen-year exile during the dictatorship. Almost the entire novel consists of his visit to what was the former site of imprisonment and torture, Villa Grimaldi, a site that constitutes an important memory knot. As Marín recounts in his novel, Villa Grimaldi was an estate that was purchased by the military government in 1973 and converted into a concentration camp known as Cuartel Villanova. In 1989, the military had the site bulldozed and its buildings razed. Nonetheless, a group of survivors managed to obtain the property and convert it into the Villa Grimaldi Peace Park. As Macarena Gómez-Barris explains, the Peace Park has become an important memory site of what she terms "witness citizenship." Witness citizenship is an active form of

> [p]articipation that structures political imaginations and creates civic networks and shared social experience through memory. As such, symbolic and cultural repertoires are used as meaningful bridges between the past and present-day forms of political activities. At the Villa Grimaldi Peace Park, the active participation of memorial artists, human rights workers, relatives of the disappeared and torture survivors revolves around stories that both clash and contend with official memory in the public sphere. These forms of mnemonic political action constitute spaces for the practice of democracy. Rather than force closure over the past, as transitional states are often conditioned to do, witness citizenship opens a window onto the shadow aspects of history and offers a means of putting vernacular memory at the center of an analysis of democratization. (44)

The protagonist's visit to the Villa Grimaldi site occurs prior to its conversion into a park and memorial site. The site is now mainly ruins, but the unnamed narrator recalls the history of the mansion that used to exist on the property, its different owners, and uses throughout the years. He knew the mansion as a boy, because his friend lived there with his family. Eventually, in the 1960s, it was transformed into a discotheque called El Paraíso and, as already noted, it was later appropriated by the dictatorship in the 1970s and made into its principal torture site. The narrator traces its history. The property itself also serves as a springboard for his memories of his life in Chile.

The narrator fuses Villa Grimaldi with his memories of his love affair with a young woman named Mónica. Using Villa Grimaldi as the landscape associated with a romance plot is inherently hopeless from the start, given its history as a place of torture. Although the narrator's reflections on the changes to the property serve many purposes in the novel, central to those reflections is his association of the place with Mónica, because, when he was younger, it was a discotheque to which he had brought her. That particular date cemented their relationship, but, more than that, he could show her the changes that the house had undergone from a residence to a disco, and how this transformation cheapened the mansion. The connection between Mónica and Villa Grimaldi is also significant because we later learn that Mónica was arrested by the military and tortured at Cuatro Álamos before switching sides and becoming an agent for the military dictatorship. At the end of the novel, it turns out she worked at Villa Grimaldi and was living with a military officer with whom she fled to Buenos Aires after the dictatorship ended.

The fact that Mónica is fused with the Villa Grimaldi site can be seen in the following passages:

> Villa Grimaldi había sido transformada después del año 1973 en el principal centro de torturas de la dictadura.... Me asediaba en la casa ... la sombra de la presencia de Mónica. (61)
>
> ...
>
> Proseguía sin una respuesta ante el enigma que me despertaba la hipotética presencia de Mónica en el lugar. Significaba que cedía a la sospecha de que algo suyo, innominado para mí, permanecía adherido a esos restos dispersos en el sitio hoy desierto donde se levantara la antigua casa. (89)

Villa Grimaldi had been transformed after 1973 into the main torture center of the dictatorship.... The shadow of the presence of Mónica besieged me in the house.

...

I continued without an answer before the enigma that the hypothetical presence of Mónica in that place awakened in me. It meant that I yielded to the suspicion that something of her, unnamed to me, remained stuck to those disperse remains in the place now deserted where the old house had been built.

In terms of the romance plot, the narrator is committed to finding out what happened to Mónica, last seen at Villa Grimaldi, after he returns from exile (90). As Grínor Rojo states: "En la figura de Mónica se metaforiza una posibilidad simbólica en favor de la reincorporación. Encontrar a Mónica, reanudar su relación con ella, equivaldría para él a una doble operación de reclamo de mundo y de reclamo de sí mismo" ([192] Mónica's figure symbolizes the possibility of reincorporation. Finding Mónica, resuming his relationship with her, would be the equivalent of a double reclaiming of the world and himself"). Mónica represents both the narrator's life in Chile before exile and the devastating effects of the dictatorship (once a victim of it, only to become one of its agents), as well as (before he learns her fate) the possibility of reintegrating into life in Chile. In Hogan's words, Mónica is the "happiness goal" that the narrator seeks.

Chapters 4–6 of the novel are dedicated to the narrator's search for information about Mónica. This process leads him to a psychologist who worked at Villa Grimaldi helping the dictatorship assess the psychological state of its torture victims. The woman, María de Carmen Posadas, is a damaged individual, an alcoholic riddled with guilt for her participation in the activities of the military government who fears retribution. Although she becomes the narrator's lover, the narrator only speaks of her with contempt. Their affair represents a degradation of his romance with Mónica.[2] Once again, the happiness goal of reuniting with Mónica and resuming their relationship is thwarted in the novel, filling the narrator with despair. This despair can be seen as the protagonist looks out over the landscape ("Todo era desolación al mirar el páramo" ([103] Everything was desolate as he looked out over the barren plain). In confessing that, he suspects Mónica of being a collaborator, his memory of her suddenly spoiled. He also sees his desire to resurrect the old house before it became Villa Grimaldi as "químerico" ([144] chimerical), which applies equally to returning Mónica to her former life.

As Rojo indicates, failure to reunite with Mónica means a failure to reintegrate into life in Chile, another devastating result of the dictatorship, leading the protagonist to hold no hope for the future:

> Era un extranjero en mi propio país ... todo esfuerzo de huir de mí mismo era una condena escrita. Tal vez lo mejor podía ser arranchar aquí al margen de las circunstancias sin ninguna clase de espera que significara una creencia en el futuro, dedicado a gozar las caminatas en los atardeceres púrpuras de Santiago ... bajo la repetición engañosa de los días, avanzar ojalá sin dolor hacia la muerte. (144)

> I was a foreigner in my own country ... any effort to flee from myself was a written condemnation. Perhaps the best thing was to settle in here on the margin of the circumstances without any kind of hope that would mean a belief in the future, dedicated to enjoying walks during the purple sunsets of Santiago ... with the deceitful repetition of the days, advancing hopefully without pain toward death.

Just as in *Estrellas*, the hopelessness associated with the dictatorship (and in the case, with a life in exile and the problem of reintegration) has its parallel in a romance that ends in despair, which thereby captures the feelings experienced under dictatorship and brought back to life in the romance plot.

José Donoso (1924–1996) is one of Chile's most famous writers. Donoso is considered one of the main contributors to the Latin American Boom, along with Julio Cortázar, Carlos Fuentes, Gabriel García Márquez, and Mario Vargas Llosa. He traces the trajectory of Boom fiction in his *Historia personal del boom* (1972). *Coronación*, his first novel, was published in 1957, followed by numerous others, the most important of which are *Casa de campo* (1978; Country House) and *El obsceno pájaro de la noche* (1970; The Obscene Bird of the Night). *Casa de campo* is considered an allegory of the Pinochet dictatorship. Between 1967 and 1981, Donoso lived in Spain. He returned to Chile in 1981 and began to conduct writer workshops. In *La desesperanza*, he reflects on the role of the artist vis-à-vis politics in the wake of the Chilean dictatorship.

Although the title of José Donoso's *La desesperanza* (1986) was changed to "Curfew" in the English translation, the title actually means "despair," cuing the reader toward an analysis of the novel in terms of this emotion. However, as noted earlier, although despair is a major and explicit theme in the novel, this is the only one of the four under discussion that presents the possibility of some hope for the future in Chile. This hope is based on two elements. First, the romance between the protagonists, Mañungo Vera and Judit Torre, even though it does not end in a happily-ever-after, is sufficiently open-ended to dangle the possibility of a positive resolution. Second, unlike the other three novels in which happiness goals were solely romantic, *La desesperanza* presents happiness goals that are also related to artistic creation and political commitment. Thus, the romance plot, while important, is not the only significant element in the novel. I will examine each of these elements in turn.

The novel opens with the return of the protagonist, Mañungo Vera, a famous singer, to Chile, after he lived in France for a number of years. Mañungo was living outside of Chile when the coup occurred and was advised not to return. His career was based on singing revolutionary songs, but his work eventually lost popularity as the public's interest in the Chilean cause waned. More important, he suffered an existential crisis that forced him to confront the lack of authenticity in his music and political commitment. This realization made him want to sing about other things and find a more genuine voice. His nostalgia for Chiloé, his birthplace, leads to his return to Chile, then under the dictatorship; there he hopes to find himself and define his political commitment. He arrives in Chile on the same day as the wake of Matilde Neruda, wife of the famous poet Pablo Neruda. During her wake and funeral, he rencounters a former girlfriend and revolutionary, Judit Torre. They resume the relationship that dissolved thirteen years ago. Despite their strong sexual attraction, they do not love each other, as readers are told repeatedly. This incomplete emotional connection may create certain expectations about a romance plot in the works—the possibility of a strong, loving relationship—though that never happens. For example, after Judit performs oral sex on Mañungo, he recognizes that he does not love her. Or, in another instance, we get this exchange:

—¿No me quieres?—[preguntó Mañungo]
—No sé, respondió Judit un rato después...
—¿Y tú?...
—Creo que no.
—Pero quieres que hagamos el amor, ¿no es cierto? (*La desesperanza* 213)

"Don't you love me?" [Mañungo asked]
...
"I don't know," answered Judit, a while later....
... "And you?" ... "I don't think so."
"But you want to make love, isn't that so?
(Curfew 186)

Toward the end of the novel, Mañungo plans to return to Paris with Judit to see whether their relationship will develop into something more there, but this plan is unrealized when their friend Lopito dies at the hands of the police. Thus, Mañungo's relationship with Judit remains static and incomplete. Happiness goals grow faint, yet they do not vanish entirely. That exception makes Curfew different from the three previous novels I have examined.

Despair comes to the fore again with the second set of happiness goals, those dealing with an authentic political commitment and its expression in Mañungo's music. As mentioned above, Mañungo returns to Chile in crisis over his music and his lack of political commitment. The character is initially portrayed as extremely indecisive.[3] His lack of political commitment dates all the way to his beginnings as an artist. Despite singing revolutionary songs and participating in the peñas,[4] he refused to join the Communist party, even though he supported the Unidad Popular, Allende's socialist party, because he was too confused to commit (112). This indeterminateness continues when he returns to Chile thirteen years later and remains a major source of his unhappiness. When asked in an interview "¿Te piensas definir?" ([*La desesperanza* 124] Do you think you'll ever take a stand? [Curfew 65]), he responds, "Tal vez. Denme tiempo para ver y pensar" ([*La desesperanza* 124] "Could be. Give me some time to see things and to think" [Curfew 65]). Later, during Matilde Neruda's funeral, he is asked to sing "Yo pisaré las calles de nuevo" (I will tread on these streets again), a revolutionary song by the Cuban Pablo Milanés. He agrees, but then stops in the middle when Fausta asks him not to sing it because she doesn't want the funeral to turn into a political event. In complying, he incurs the wrath and distain of the leftist revolutionaries. Four-hundred pages of reflections on the topic follow. But it is only at the very end of the novel, when the police force Lopito to do hard labor in the heat without first taking his heart medication, causing his death, that Mañungo realizes he must be committed to the revolution and the ousting of the dictator. That purpose, he realizes, must be the sole aim of his music. His second interview with a journalist is thus the complete opposite of his first. In the second, he affirms his political commitment and explicitly verbalizes the theme of despair—though he does not justify the use of violence: "¿qué se puede hacer si nos fuerzan a la violencia quitándonos toda esperanza? ([*La desesperanza* 456] Because what can we do when they force us into violence by taking away all our hope? [Curfew 304]).

It is important to note that Mañungo's trajectory from uncommitted artist to authentic voice of the revolution is that of the intellectual Trotsky traces in *Art and Revolution*. The intertextual connection between Trotsky's ideas and Mañungo's transformation is alluded to in the novel by the explicit mentions of Trotsky. Freddy Fox, Judit Torre's cousin and a member of the dictatorial government, obsessively collects Trotsky's letters to Neruda. That Mañungo undergoes the exact transformation discussed by Trotsky can be no coincidence:

> The wider, more popular, anonymous character of the rising bourgeoisie led, on the whole, to the theory of "pure art", though there were many deviations from this.... [T]he tendentious literature of the "populist" intelligentsia was imbued with a class interest; the intelligentsia could not strengthen itself and could not conquer for itself a right to play a part in history without the support of the people. That is why the intelligentsia not only did not conceal art with a tendency,[5] but proclaimed it, thus sacrificing art, just as it sacrificed many other things.... [Art] is not a disembodied element feeding on itself, but a function of social man indissolubly tied to his life and environment.... The effort to set art free from life, to declare it a craft sufficient unto itself, devitalizes and kills art. The very need of such an operation is an unmistakable symptom of intellectual decline. (Trotsky 37–45)

Mañungo begins his career as a bourgeois intellectual, who, though he may sing about the revolution, is not totally committed to it in his heart. He claims he must first read and travel and then perhaps later can define himself, "Pero no hubo después para Mañungo Vera: se fue a Europa a triunfar con la palabra 'revolución,' aunque sin participar en ella como los exiliados de veras" ([*La desesperanza* 112] But there was no "later on" for Mañungo Vera. He went off to Europe and cashed in on the word "revolution" [Curfew 56]).

Mañungo's identity as an uncommitted bourgeois intellectual is developed throughout the novel through not only his political indecisiveness but also his dedication to tokens of material status. We are told on several occasions that he owns a Rolex (159, 293) and is upset when it is stolen; we are also told he wore Gucci clothing (172). Finally, when Mañungo first returns to Chile and attends Matilde Neruda's wake, a left-wing member of la Jota comments that Mañungo is a disappointing and decadent bourgeois individual (125).[6]

It is not a coincidence that Mañungo Vera's transformation from bourgeois intellectual to authentic voice of the revolution is paired with the explicit theme of despair—or that this connection paradoxically opens up a path to hope in the end, as Hortensia Morel and Mary Lusky Friedman have argued.[7] Despair is both explicit and recurring throughout (*La desesperanza* 49, 150, 223, 372, 419, 440) and thus captures the principal emotional response to the dictatorship. Nonetheless, it is precisely this feeling of despair that leads Mañungo to finally decide his future, his political commitment, and the music he will pursue, all of which create a feeling of hope. It is interesting that the novel employs the Chilote myth of the "Caleuche" to symbolize transformation. Friedman has discussed Donoso's use of this myth extensively (13–21), illustrating how the phantom ship of witches and warlocks, the ship of black magic, is converted into a ship not of magic art, but of creative arts (music, poetry, dance) in Mañungo's imagination. "Caleuche," as the novel itself cites, comes from the Araucanian language of the Mapuche, which signifies change or transformation. What is particularly interesting about the connection between the ship and Mañungo is that the former can undergo physical transformation and that parallels Mañungo's emotional transformation. David Petremen holds that the Caleuche

> has the power to transform itself. First, in the form of a ship, it becomes a submarine or just lights or luminous spheres. . . . The music

that accompanies a Caleuche sighting is particularly interesting. . . .
Narciso García Barría states: "A very interesting peculiarity of the
archipelago of Chiloé is that sonority predominates in the atmosphere
as if a permanent symphony, presided over the course of the days. . . .
The crew of the Caleuche is made up of sorcerers and witches. . . . .
The crew celebrates magnificent parties on deck . . . all to the sound
of the orchestra whose music enchants and delights, while they drink
rum or gin brought from exotic lands. The sailors of the Caleuche can
transform themselves into seals, fish, dolphins, algae, even islands. The
ship itself can [be] transform[ed] into a rock or log, especially if it is
sighted by someone who is not a witch. (207–08)

In addition to transformation, the Caleuche also maintains a second relationship to Mañungo Vera—it is also associated with music. In other words, what might seem like a random association bears a concrete relationship to the character's development.

In summary, although despair is a theme and feeling developed in Donoso's novel, it is used paradoxically to create the possibility of hope in the future. Despair is more of an explicit theme than the pervasive overarching tone of the work, and Vera's final transformation suggests the possibility that Chile, too, may be transformed in the future.

The second way in which this group of novels re-creates the feeling of despair experienced under the Pinochet dictatorship is through what critics have called affective landscape. In *Melancholy*, Bowring offers an expanded definition of the term landscape: "The word [landscape] carries with it, then, both a pictorial appreciation of that which is beheld in the outdoors, as well as a holistic sense of the landscape as a place of dwelling where culture inscribes itself. This expansive etymology means that 'landscape' also encompasses architecture, as a contiguous element of the lived-in world" (3). Bowring also clarifies what it means for a landscape to be "affective" by drawing from Avril Maddrell who "writes of emotional geographies, how they are 'particular spaces [which] become emotion-laden places, both those we choose to identify and those affective spaces which unexpectedly interpolate us.' . . . The significant point is the shift towards acknowledging the subjective dimension of space" (30). To this, Juhani Pallasmaa adds,

[i]n addition to being memory devices, landscapes and buildings are also amplifiers of emotion; they reinforce sensations of belonging or alienation, invitation or rejection, tranquility or despair. A landscape or work of architecture cannot, however, create feelings. Through their authority and aura, they evoke and strengthen our own emotions and project them back to us as if these feelings of ours had an external source. (30)

The descriptions of landscapes and architecture presented in all four novels under discussion in this chapter reflect, in varying degrees, the feelings of despair as experienced by the characters. I begin again with *Santiago Cero* to show how affective landscape is employed. In it, three landscape descriptions reflect despair: the statue at the university where the greater part of the novel takes place; doña Yolita Manzur's boarding house, and the general description of Santiago.

The statue of the "Dama Verde" in the center of the patio, described as cold, indifferent, and cynical, produces feelings of impotence in the unnamed protagonist. These words relate to the despair he feels at losing Raquel to Sebastián, as well as his decision (cold, hard) to become a traitor. The protagonist's feelings are both inspired by and reflected back onto this element of the university's architecture:

> En el centro de su pileta, semidesnuda, la Dama Verde sonreía indiferente a tu desgracia y al frío. Nada la alteraría jamás. . . . Siempre te sentiste inseguro frente a esta estatua. El cinismo de sus invitaciones te producía un efecto inverso: de impotencia. Ahora estaba a su merced en el vasto desierto embaldosado del patio. . . . Supiste que harías cualquier cosa por recuperarla [a Raquel]. Y algo dentro de ti cambió en ese instante; algo se hizo de hierro, de un hierro verde y frío como el de la estatua que sonreía en medio de su fuente. (8)

> In the center of her pool, the Green Dame smiled indifferently at your misfortune and the cold. Nothing would ever upset her. . . . You always felt insecure in front of this statue. The cynicism of her invitations produced in you an inverse effect: one of impotence. Now you were at her mercy in the vast tiled desert of the patio. . . . You knew that you

would do anything to recover her [Raquel]. And something within
you changed at that moment; something became iron, a cold and green
iron like that of the statue that smiled in the middle of her fountain.

Other parts of the university are described as disintegrating—things falling apart and, for the observer, this results in a sense of hopelessness. When the unnamed protagonist searches for Sebastián in the attic above the university clocktower, all the images presented are of things falling apart: "muebles caducos" ([34] worn out furniture), "banderas apolilladas" ([34] moth-eaten flags), and "Una gran desconchadura mohosa" ([37] a large moldy, peeling section). Similarly, doña Yolita's boarding house, which is half boarding house and half old-age home, is characterized thus:

> En un afán de arquitectura lucrativa, el dueño de ese palacete *tambaleante* escamoteado a los equipos de demolición que eran la industria más floreciente en Santiago, abatió tabiques y paredes hasta unir el B con el A, los bajos con los altos.... Las batallas entre ambas dueñas de casa se libraban en el corredor del tercer piso, tierra de nadie y frontera entre ambas pensiones. Un *agusanado* pasamanos de escalera separaba a los viejos de los estudiantes. (53; my emphases)

> In an effort at lucrative architecture, the owner of that *tottering* palace that escaped the demolition teams that constituted the most flourishing industry in Santiago, knocked down partitions and walls until she united B with A, the lower with the higher.... The battles between both owners of the house were conducted in the hallway of the third floor, no-man's-land and border between both boarding houses. *A worm-filled* stair rail separated the elderly people from the students.

Buildings that are being demolished suggest an atmosphere of transience, destruction, and despair. This is further reinforced by the general description of Santiago: "Y siguió [Sebastián] diciendo que le daba vértigo pensar que todo Santiago es así. Como un *pozo*. Un agujero perdido en las cordilleras, tajeado por una acequia.... ¿Te podís figurar lo que era el aterrizaje después de eso? ¿La mierda en las paredes de Santiago? ¿El humo negro?" ([60, my emphasis] And [Sebastian] continued saying that it made him dizzy to think that all of

Santiago was that way. Like a *well*. A hole lost in the mountain ranges, slashed by a stream.... Can you imagine what the landing was like after that? The shit on the walls of Santiago? The black smoke?). Santiago is described as a well (in other words, a dark hole) filled with black smoke. These are clearly dark, negative images that suggest the despairing state of mind of the characters.

The despair implied in these architectural descriptions stands in direct contrast to the hope suggested by the poster that hangs above the cafeteria table where a group of students—the narrator, Sebastián, Raquel, and their friends—sit. This Lufthansa poster depicts the luxurious Neuschwanstein Castle, built by Ludwig II of Bavaria, and promises an escape from the reality of dictatorship in the same way that the letters from Sebastián's "friend" has done. The constant reference to the poster and the architectural wonder depicted on it in the end enhances the despair felt by the characters, as it represents an impossible goal.

This same connection to affective architecture is apparent to an even greater degree in *Estrellas*. Macarena Urzúa Opazo points out this relationship between emotions and architectural ruins: "Estas cartografías emocionales de la ruina y el desengaño podemos leerlas en este caso a partir de los recorridos por los espacios de Santiago y Valparaíso.... Valparaíso es escrita y revivida desde un mapa emocional" ([220] These emotional cartographies of ruins and disillusion can be read in this case using the walks through the spaces of Santiago and Valparaíso as a departure point.... Valparaíso is written and relived through an emotional map). Juhani Pallasmaa makes a similar point in emphasizing how ruins trigger emotions:

> Ruins stimulate us to think of lives that have already disappeared and to imagine the fate of their deceased occupants. Ruins and eroded settings have an especially evocative and emotional power. They force us to reminisce and imagine. Incompleteness and fragmentation possess a special evocative power. (21)

Buildings in ruin turn up a number of times in *Estrellas*. It is no coincidence that the principal building described is the hotel where Javiera and Donoso live. Its crumbling state reflects their crumbling relationship and the despair that has taken hold of not only it but also the two unnamed protagonists and all of Chile:

Como la ciudad, *como el país que vivía en un tiempo congelado*, ese hotel estaba en ruinas.... Siempre miraba esa fachada que alguna vez había sido blanca y que estaba llena de grafitis, descascarada. (*Estrellas* chs. 59–60; my emphasis).

Just like the city, *like the whole country frozen in time*, that hotel was in ruins.... I always noticed the hotel's facade, which had once been white but was now cracked and crumbling and covered in graffiti. (Stars chs. 59–60)

The female narrator repeats the information given to her by an architect sent to inspect the hotel:

Los gatos tenían los pasillos llenos de olor a mierda. Sucedió de todo ahí: asesinatos, suicidios, robos, violaciones... las cornisas y los ornamentos se habían desprendido con el paso de tiempo, el viento y la humedad... los muebles art deco de la recepción estaban destripados o parchados o llenos de manchas de grasa.... Ahí vivía gente que aspiraba pegamento.... No era un hotel, era una estación terminal, me dijo él. Los Kennedys sonaban perfecto ahí, dijo. La banda de música del desfile de la ruina, dijo ella. (*Estrellas* ch. 63)

The cats filled the hallways with the stink of shit. Everything you can think of happened there: murder, suicide, robbery, rape.... [T]he cornices and ornaments had crumbled off over time with the wind and humidity.... The art deco furniture in the reception area had the stuffing coming out of it, or was patched, or covered in grease stains.... There were people living there who huffed glue.... It wasn't a hotel, it was an end station, he told me. (Stars ch. 63)

In addition to ruins, like *Santiago Cero*, *Estrellas* presents numerous images of disintegration including rotting fruit and broken toys sold at the street fairs, those pairing with or juxtaposed to a reference to the "horrible" Congress building built by Pinochet (ch. 62). The reference to the Congress building, erected under Pinochet, directly associates ruins and their atmospheric despair to the erstwhile dictator himself. Moreover, Valparaíso, like Santiago in *Santiago Cero*, is covered in black smoke, which the male narrator compares to that of the concentration camp ovens in Nazi Germany or the aftermath of an atomic bomb explosion (ch. 1). These analogies clearly typify the despair that pervades the novel. There are many more examples, but these suffice to show the unhealthy symbiosis between landscape and character emotions in *Estrellas*.

The novel that perhaps best illustrates the notion of affective landscape and the emotive value of ruins is Germán Marín's *El palacio de la risa*. Indeed, as already discussed, most of the novel is the unnamed protagonist's contemplation of the ruins of the Villa Grimaldi torture site. There is, however, a fundamental difference between the role of landscape in Marín's novel and its role in the other works. Whereas the previously examined novels focus primarily on personal memories, landscape in *El palacio* unavoidably seizes on public memory because Villa Grimaldi is a public memory site. Thus, the narrator has both specific personal childhood memories attached to the property, as well as the public memories of the dictatorship associated with the property. This adds even more depth to the role landscape plays.

Many critics who study affective architecture have reflected on the role of landscape in memory. Marc Treib states that "Memory haunts built worlds that have fallen to natural disasters or to changes in political regime. In each case, the built form operates in a milieu propelled by memory though tempered by contemporary norms for living and building" (iv). Such is the case of Villa Grimaldi, which, as the novel shows, has been transformed in ways to suit its different owners. Under one owner, the government, it becomes a torture site, and, under the same owner, it is burnt to the ground to destroy evidence of atrocities. Donlon Lyndon comments upon the simultaneous role of personal and public memory in architectural sites:

> Places bring things to mind.... The experience of place is infused by memory; echoes of previous visits, expectations and recollections invoked by similar places, as well as images and descriptions in ads and books and on the internet. The memories lodged in places range from incidents of personal biography to highly refined and extensively interpreted segments of cultural lore, vested in the forms and the elements of ornament with

which the place is made.... The experience of place within architecture landscape and cities is in some sense made of memories. (63)

Again, this passage perfectly describes the unnamed protagonist's experiences at the Villa Grimaldi site as he remembers both his youth there, the transformations it has historically undergone, and its final role as torture site, which he has extensively researched. This results in a fusion of both personal and public memories that suffuses the property.

The Villa Grimaldi ruin site, in that regard, becomes what Pallasmaa terms an "existential space" for the unnamed protagonist, which he defines as a combination of a material space and the memories and fantasies that space evokes:

> We do not live in an objective world of matter and fact, as commonplace naïve realism tends to assume.... We live in mental worlds in which the material and the spiritual, as well as the experienced, the remembered, and the imagined, constantly fuse into each other. As a consequence, the lived reality does not follow the rules of space and time as defined and measured by the criteria of Western empirical science. In fact, the lived world is closer to the reality of a dream.... To distinguish the lived space from physical and geometrical space, we can call it "existential space." Lived space is structured on the basis of meanings, intentions and values reflected upon it by an individual either consciously or unconsciously, existential space is a unique quality interpreted through the memory and the experience of the individual. (26)

The ways in which the unnamed protagonist in *El palacio* describes the Villa Grimaldi site also illustrates many of the categories that Bowring describes as "melancholic" in *Melancholy*. There is an inherent connection between melancholia and despair. Melancholia is a pervasive sadness that successful mourning does not resolve, as Idelber Avelar, citing Freud, indicates in his study on allegory and postdictatorial fiction:

> Mourning designates a process of overcoming loss in which the separation between the ego and the lost object can still be effected,

> whereas in melancholia, the identification with the lost object reaches an extreme in which the ego is engulfed and becomes itself part of the loss. Cutting across this distinction, Abraham and Torok differentiate between introjection and incorporation as two modalities of internalization of loss. Introjection designates the horizon of a successful completion of mourning work, whereby the lost object is dialectically absorbed and expelled, internalized in such a way that the libido can now be discharged into a surrogate object.... In incorporation, on the other hand, the traumatic object remains lodged within the ego as a foreign body "invisible yet omnipresent," unnamable except through partial synonyms.... For Freud art and literature constitute ... a privileged mode of manifestation of this unresolved trauma and loss. (8)

Consequently, it can be argued that when melancholic elements are presented in certain contexts that suggest stagnation or lack of future possibilities, melancholia can be equated with despair.

Bowring in fact dedicates each chapter of her book to a different melancholic landscape element. These include: the void, silence, the uncanny, aura, liminality, fragments, leavings, submersion, weathering, and patina. Below I show how these different elements connect to despair in *El palacio*.

According to Bowring, weathering and patination are "traces of time's passage ... [as they] register on surfaces as a cumulative process.... Erosion wipes away the layers of utility ... and pushes the structure into the realm of uselessness" (143). In *El palacio*, the following passage is one of several that describe the weathering of the Villa Grimaldi property:

> Faltaban los álamos grises que circundaban aquel espacio, donde tampoco se destacaba de afuera la bóveda semi esférica de la cúpula principal.... me di cuenta de que la tranquera de antes ... había sido reemplazada por un portalón de hierro de dos hojas cuyas rejas oxidadas estaban tapiadas con una gruesa plancha de acero de color negro.... pero al empujar el portalón ... tuve una vez ante los ojos, en una vista que me sobrecogió, la desolación en que se había convertido el lugar. (22–23)

The gray poplar trees that used to surround that space were missing, as was the semi-spheric dome of the main cupola that used to stand out on the outside.... I realized that the old door from before... had been replaced with an iron door with two door leaves whose rusty grilles were covered with a thick, black-colored plate of steel... but when I pushed the door... I had before my eyes, in a vision that startled me, the desolation into which the place had been transformed.

Weathering also characterizes the pool, which is the only structure left from the original mansion: "El tanque se veía oxidado por completo, cubierto de verdín en la profundidad de su interior" ([27] The tank was completely rusted, covered with moss in the depth of its interior). The uselessness implied by weathering suggests the uselessness of the protagonist's life. In a later passage, only one tree remains, its starkness a reminder of all the other trees that once stood: "Al perderse en los escombros dispersos sobre la tierra, flotaba... un silencio pétreo congelado en el aire en el que saltan a los ojos casi como una interrupción, el esqueleto de un árbol defoliado. Su corteza yacía carbonizada. Si bien estaba muerto como un inmolado más, era el único vástago que permanecía en pie en los dos mil especies forestales" ([23] When one loses oneself in the scattered rubble, a stony silence floated over the earth, frozen in the air in which the skeleton of a defoliated tree jumped before one's eyes almost like an interruption. Its bark lay carbonized. Although it was dead like one more sacrificed being, it was the only shoot that remained intact from the two thousand forestry species.) The lone tree is an excellent example of what Bowring calls the void: "The void is both an absence of things and an absence of meaning ... The void is vividly involved in the presence of an empty chair, something which is at once so directly a sign of presence, a place for sitting, when empty becomes a vessel of loss" (58). The leafless tree skeleton with a burnt bark evokes the absence of the lush full forest of the past, which the unnamed protagonist recalls from his boyhood. This lack of meaning suggested by the void reflects the lack of meaning felt by the protagonist regarding his own life. Parting from an enactivist-embodied theory of cognition,[8] Andrea Jelić and Aleksandar Stanićić suggest that there is a reciprocal relationship between architecture and emotion/affect:

> In short, what this means for architecture is that our experience of spaces is inherently affective, and that, accordingly, all our perceptions, actions and behaviors within built spaces depend on the workings of our emotional system, which in turn is influenced by and continuously adjusting to changes within the environment. (192)

Thus, the protagonist projects the meaninglessness of his life onto the architectural space, at the same time that this space mirrors these emotions in the protagonist.

Another of Bowring's categories relevant to the protagonist is the silence he experiences in his visit to Villa Grimaldi; this is the kind of silence he associates with cemeteries, churches, and monasteries. The protagonist describes the place's silence on several occasions and contrasts it with the memory of Antonio's brother leading a full orchestra there (83). The old marble pool, "agrietada por los ales y fríos de años" ([109] cracked by the salt and cold of years) is also described as surrounded by silence. The silence exists in stark contrast with the music and lively sounds of the mansion when it was the protagonist's friend's residence—the difference between the animation and happiness of distant times and the lifelessness of now.

Finally, Bowring speaks of the melancholic value of ruins and fragments, which is perhaps the most prominent characteristic of Villa Grimaldi. The narrator constantly contrasts the glorious past of the place with its present state of ruin, creating an atmosphere of despair. Says Bowring:

> [t]he fragment engages the mind in imaginative reconstruction of ruins, which are a species of fragments. Tim Edensor writes how they "function . . . allowing the viewer to see the intact object and its disappearance at the same time. . . . The fragment provokes melancholic contemplation, as the beholder mentally reconstructs that which is no longer whole. (109)

Essentially, all of *El palacio* is the protagonist's observation of the fragments left of the Villa Grimaldi property, once his friend's home, which enables him to imaginatively reconstruct the mansion and its various transformations over time. Other passages also focus on fragments, such as the following: "De la presencia del kiosco solo quedaba la losa del piso donde descubrí, cubierto de polvo, el trozo de un mosaico verde. El fragmento lucía, aunque borroso, el dibujo heráldico de la flor de lis" ([31] From the presence of the kiosk, the only thing that remained was the slab of the tile floor where I discovered, covered in dust, a piece of a green mosaic. The fragment shone, though blurred, the heraldic drawing of the fleur-de-lis). The fleur-de-lis is an emblem dating back to French royalty that here represents the nobility of spirit that no longer exists in Chile, which leads the protagonist, returned from exile, to despair over the likely success of his repatriation. His visit to Villa Grimaldi brims with references to the sorry and hopeless state in which he now finds his country. He looks, for example, at the garbage littering the property with repulsion and senses that the country to which he returned "ya no parecía ser el mío" (no longer seemed to be his). In other instances, the narrator laments Chile's conscious amnesia about the past:

> El país había terminado de embromarse después de aceptar que la infamia ya era asunto enterrado en que solo cabía por parte de los justos y tibios luego de restañar las heridas, trasladar lo sucedido al desván de la Historia. Una paz sin justicia, si es que podía haber paz en los espíritus, pues una generación de ofendidos le transmitiría a la siguiente los hechos perpetrados. (142–43)

> The country ended up fooling itself after accepting that the infamy was now a buried affair and that it was only fitting that those who were right and the lukewarm ones after licking their wounds, transfer what happened to the basement of History. A peace without justice, if it is possible that there could be peace in people's spirits, since a generation of offended people transmitted the perpetrated acts to the following generation.

This vision of Chile's future is hopeless because, as the narrator points out, there can be no future without coming to terms with what happened in the past.

Despair and landscape are also connected in Donoso's *La desesperanza* in a variety of ways and contexts. Several instances of affective landscape appear, too, in Mañungo Vera's birthplace of Chiloé. Although, as we have seen, the myth of the Caleuche is generally viewed as a positive symbol of transformation, for a despairing Mañungo, in at least one instance, the image of the ship and its surrounding nature are transformed in his mind into a negative landscape:

> ¿Era simplemente la desdichada historia contemporánea, y en ella, inseparable ... su propia historia, lo que había llegado a ensombrecer para Mañungo la imagen gentilicia del Caleuche ... porque ... en el destierro el buque de arte reflotaba alguna vez en los sueños de Mañungo transformado en un Caleuche cruel, depredador, tripulado por forasteros ... llevándoselos a todos no a la bella ciudad prometida por la leyenda, sino acarreándolos como a bestias para faenarlos ... [el] barco que crujía al avanzar por el huracán de olas colosales, el espinazo de los volcanes albos enrojeciendo el cielo con su lava ... en estos tiempos que corren el Caleuche solo lleva a sus pasajeros al extermino. (*La desesperanza* 190)

> Was this simply another chapter in the wretched history of our times? His own personal history, which had managed to darken for him the familiar image of the *Caleuche* ... because even when he had lost all hope of being carried to immortality, the ship of art in exile would surface from time to time in Mañungo's dreams, transformed into a cruel, piratical *Caleuche*, its crew made up of foreigners ... carrying everyone off, not to the beautiful city promised in the legend, but herding them like animals to slaughter. ... [T]he ship as it crossed through a hurricane with colossal waves, the spines of the white volcanoes reddening the sky with their lava ... these days, when the *Caleuche* is out, it only carries its passengers to death. (Curfew 114)

The ship is seen as sailing on a hostile sea with a "hurricane" of waves suggesting danger and volcanos threatening lives with eruptions of lava. Mañungo's fantasy about the Caleuche sailing in this environment, where it tortures people instead of lifting them up and redeeming them, is directly related to the despair he feels because of the "wretched history" dictatorship has wrought.

Chiloé, his birthplace, is also where Mañungo's mother died shortly after his birth. She was swept away by the tsunami that hit the islands. "Inundation," Bowring argues, is an ephemeral condition where culture and nature melt together, not necessarily ruined, nor complete. Submersion confounds boundaries, inverting, eroding, and removing datum. The condition of submersion is ambivalent and poignant. Volcanic eruptions, sand, silt, water ... all of these incursions erode the edges, blurring thresholds of containment. The drowning of culture by nature disturbs the certainty of existence.... The vision of architecture engulfed by flowing sand or water is mysterious, evocative, melancholy. (133)

Mañungo's secondhand "memories" of the event help to create an atmosphere of melancholy and despair in the novel.

Mañungo recordaba a través de la memoria de don Manuel el cadáver cosmogónico de su madre, fosforescente de lampreas y coronado de cochayuyos y huiros, como lo sacaron de la ensenada la noche después del cataclismo.... En ese pueblo de madera cana que Mañungo no conoció porque había desaparecido en el incendio después del maremoto, comenzaba él. (*La desesperanza* 179–80)

Mañungo relived through the memory of don Manuel his mother's cadaver, glowing with lampreys and crowned with algae and kelp, and the way they pulled it out of the cove the night after the disaster.... In that village of weathered shingles, which he had never known because it had disappeared in the fire after the tidal wave, Mañungo began. (Curfew 107)

Chiloé consists of numerous islands, of which Castro is one of the larger more inhabited ones. It stands as an excellent example of what Bowring terms "liminality":

Liminality is a potent zone for the evocation of memory.... Some of the most potent exemplars of the melancholy of liminality are islands and geographical threshold spaces.... Their condition as an edge zone, a threshold state, casts islands as an ultimate *terrains vagues* ... [which] are spatially and socially marginalized landscapes. (106)

Bowring also speaks of temporal liminality as potentially creating an air of melancholy. It is interesting that *La desesperanza* is divided into three sections marked by time: Twilight, Night, and Morning. Twilight (section 1) is an example of temporal liminality, while section 3, morning, begins at dawn, which is also a moment of temporal liminality. During the section marked "Night" and the following section "Morning," Mañungo and Judit share numerous adventures that include, among others, hiding out in an abandoned garden because Judit shot at someone and a second episode in which Judit visits her family's graves.. The first of these episodes uses temporal liminality along with ruins and fragments to create a tone of sadness and despair:

> En la niebla convocada por la proximidad del alba, el idílico jardín de thuyas piramidales, de bolas de boj, de tejos negros, de obeliscos de laurel tan desgreñados que ya era difícil adivinar la forma que originalmente se les destinó, cobró vida. . . . Se sentaron a hablar con las piernas colgando hacia el hoyo de la piscina en escombros. . . .—Cuando era chica vivía en ese barrio. Pero ya casi no quedan casas de las de entonces. . . . Era muy bonito—. (*La desesperanza* 287–88)

> In the fog drawn in by the coming dawn, the idyllic garden—pyramid-shaped thuyas, boxwood shrubs cut into balls, black yews, laurel obelisks, all so overgrown that it was difficult to guess the forms into which the bushes had originally been cut—began to take on life. . . . They sat down to talk, their legs hanging into the ruined pool. . . . "When I was a kid I lived in this neighborhood. But almost none of the houses from those days is left. . . . It was very pretty. (Curfew 182–83)

The use of the word "idyllic" here is somewhat ironic since the description of the garden reveals that its laurels are disheveled, and the pool is a pile of debris. Judit indicates that it used to be very pretty, which obliquely underscores its present decay.

After Matilde Neruda's burial, Judit visits her family's tomb at the cemetery. Cemeteries, as previously mentioned, are associated with melancholic silence. The sight of the graves, particularly a space for her future interment, creates despair in her, and so she begs Mañungo to get her out of the cemetery (403).

Finally, toward the end of the novel, the descriptions of the statue of the Virgin and the police commissary, once a country house, exist as decaying fragments. The architecture of the building and the statue reflect the feelings of despair experienced by Judit as she awaits news of Lopito who has been arrested by the police:

> A sus espaldas se iba empinando poco a poco la ladera de secano y abrojos hasta conducir mucho más arriba, pasados los bosques a la Virgen monumental que con el amplio gesto irónico de su manto, seguía bendiciendo la ciudad a pesar de que ahora la sabía condenada. Pero su bendición no era para ese sector de la ciudad, al que le daba la espalda ... desconsoladamente, Judit y don César ... escudriñaban la comisaría: el fragmento de una modesta quinta decimonónica con su ... frontón de madera descascarada. ... Reducida y transformada ahora, ... quedaba solo parte de la U de la estructura original abierta hacia atrás, hacia el secarral que antes debió formar parte de la exigua quinta. (*La desesperanza* 439)

> Behind them, the parched, bramble-covered hill slowly but surely grew steeper until it reached, much higher up, beyond the forests, the monumental Virgin who, with her generous, ironic gesture, went on blessing the city, even though she knew it was doomed.
> But her blessing was not for this sector of the city, to which she turned her back. ... Judit and don César disconsolately scrutinized the station. ... It was a fragment of a modest nineteenth-century villa, with its rear patio in the form of a U and a glass-enclosed gallery, and a zinc roof, with a wooden pediment. ... Reduced and transformed now, militarized, painted by the police, only part of the original structure's U remained open toward the dry patch in the back, which must have been part of the small orchard. (Curfew 292–93)

The statue of the Virgin encapsulates the despair of those living in Santiago, those who are "condemned," and particularly those on whom she has turned her back: the poor. The commissary itself is an example of a building that has been altered, that is a fragment of a larger and more beautiful structure that no longer exists. Its state of disrepair is signaled by the peeling wood. All of these elements come together to reflect the despair that characters living under the dictatorship confront with Lopito's arrest.

Returning to Ngai's definition of tone that opened this chapter, the use of romance plots and affective landscapes can be understood as two of the "signifying practices" that "loosely fasten" tone to the formal aspects of a narrative. Although the tone of the novels studied here cannot be reduced to these two elements or any others, tone is clearly a carefully constructed element of narrative fiction that relies on concrete structures for its comprehension.

CHAPTER 4

Melancholic Allegories in Ariel Dorfman's *La última canción de Manuel Sendero* and Diamela Eltit's *Jamás el fuego nunca*

A PROFOUND CONNECTION EXISTS BETWEEN two important Chilean novels: Ariel Dorfman's *La última canción de Manuel Sendero* (1982) and Diamela Eltit's *Jamás el fuego nunca* (2007). As their dates of publication show, these two works were written at very different moments in Chilean history. Dorfman's novel was written during the Pinochet dictatorship, while Eltit's novel was written after the transition to democracy in the postdictatorship period. Despite the fact that twenty-five years separate the publication of these two novels, they share a remarkable number of characteristics. In addition to the use of allegory, both novels are narrated from a distant point in the future and share a melancholic, nostalgic tone. Moreover, they have common motifs, such as the repeated mentions of the cold. Finally, and perhaps most important, both novels use as their departure point the same poem written by the famous socialist Peruvian poet César Vallejo, "Los nueve monstruos" (The Nine Monsters).

César Vallejo unites several motifs and intertextual references that appear in both novels, but particularly in *La última*. The fusion of a Marxist ideology with Christian imagery is characteristic of Vallejo's poetry, which, despite the contradiction between Marxism and religious piety, he adhered to both during his lifetime.

According to André Coyne, Vallejo grew up in "un hogar modesto, pero sin estrecheces; de ambiente quieto, religioso, en la vecindad de la iglesia y del 'blanco panteón'" ([18] a modest home, but without economic hardships, in a quiet, religious environment, near the church and the 'white cemetery.'" Owing to his family's economic difficulties, in 1911 he worked briefly in the Quiruvilca mines where he was able to view firsthand the misery in which the miners lived. This identification with the struggle of the workers, however, did not yet take the form of a political commitment. Vallejo continued to believe in the independence of art from politics until he fell seriously ill in 1928. His illness hastened a spiritual crisis that led to his desire to find a solution to social injustice. After recovering, he traveled to the Soviet Union, where he finally adhered to the Marxist cause and declared himself officially "comprometido" (40–41).

Dorfman begins his novel with an epigraph from Vallejo's poem "Los nueve monstruos" in which the poet contemplates death and birth: "Pues de resultas del dolor, hay algunos que nacen . . . otros mueren, . . . y otros que no nacen ni mueren" (Well as a result of pain, there are some who are born . . . others die . . . and others are not born nor do they die). Dorfman employs this citation of Vallejo to introduce the fundamental situation presented in his novel: a rebellion of the unborn children who refuse to be born into a world of violence and injustice. Similarly, the very title of Eltit's novel is a verse from that same poem: "Jamás, hombres humanos, hubo tanto dolor en el pecho . . . Jamás tanto cariño doloroso . . . jamás el fuego nunca jugó mejor su rol de frío muerto!" ([*Obras completas* 34] Never, human men, was there so much pain in the chest . . . Never so much painful affection . . . never did the fire ever play better its role of dead cold" [Complete Poetry 513]). The poem evokes pain, hunger, disease, and the general suffering of the populace. Thus, the departure point for each novel is a collective societal pain that failed to be eradicated because of the fall of the Allende government, as well as the subsequent period of dictatorship and neoliberal economic policy.

Although there is no clear-cut evidence that Eltit read and was influenced by Dorfman's novel, *Jamás* can be read as a postdictatorial version of *La última*. While *La última* projects its narration thirty thousand years in the future with a series of sociological footnotes and variable narrators located at distinct future points (among the narrators is the son of Manuel Sendero (Senderito); his favorite grandchild; and members of the second fetal rebellion), *Jamás* is narrated from an imprecise future point, sometimes referred to as a century later and at other times a millennium later. The principal narrator is an unnamed former revolutionary woman, who, though dead, constantly tries to remember the past. The fact that the narrators in both books reflect on the same past—the Chilean path to socialism under Salvador Allende—helps to create a tone and feeling of melancholia and nostalgia in each work. Monika Tuszewicka states that

[t]hree conditions have to be met in order for nostalgia to occur as a cultural phenomenon. First ... a society has to see continuity in its history. The second condition is crisis and disillusionment with the present. Finally, since it is a particular item from the past that triggers nostalgia, such objects have to be available. Nostalgia is much stronger when it is triggered by pictures and things that used to surround us in the past. (176)

The novels by Dorfman and Eltit fulfill the conditions set out by Tuszewicka for a nostalgic vision: the narrators see continuity in social history, both experience profound disillusionment with present circumstances (the dictatorship in Dorfman's novel and the neoliberal postdictatorship government in Eltit's), and each focuses on different "objects" that trigger nostalgia and melancholia, notably Sendero's song in *La última* and the dead son and the single photograph of him in *Jamás*, among others. This chapter will demonstrate how allegorical elements are employed in both novels to create these feelings of melancholy and nostalgia.

Both novels also rely on allegory, which Gary Johnson distinguishes and classifies as a "family" of individual texts in which

> the author's intention [is] to transform something... into something else.... I suggest we define allegory as that class of works that fulfills its rhetorical purpose ... by means of the transformation of some phenomenon into a figural narrative. Allegory metamorphoses a real (possibly historical) phenomenon into a narrative structure. (7–9)

Three factors, Johnson contends, lead one to interpret a text allegorically: 1.) intentions explicitly expressed by the author or the (historical) context within which the text was produced; 2.) textual phenomena, and 3.) readerly concerns or response to the text (16). Johnson identifies language, plot, theme, point of view, and characters as textual phenomena. To these one might add narrative voice and tone (perhaps subsets of language), which have been emphasized by Phelan and Ngai in their work on narrative. Tzvetan Todorov adds that syntagmatic (contextual) indices based on excess (repetition) or lack (contradiction) are also signals to the reader that textual elements should be interpreted symbolically, or allegorically, within a text (30).

Finally, Johnson defines four major types of allegory: strong, weak, embedded, and thematic allegory. Strong allegory (*La última* is a good example) is defined in these terms:

> In strong allegories, the reader has the overriding sense that the author both intends and does the work of the transformation and this intuition activates... the "intrinsic genre".... [W]hen the reader senses that the whole is allegorical, he/she will adopt a reading strategy that attempts to uncover the phenomenon that has been transformed into narrative structure, or, if the author has made it clear what the phenomenon is, to verify its transformation by a process of reconciling the text and the phenomenon.... Authors consciously construct strong allegories so that the hermeneutic feedback loop amplifies the thematic value of such phenomena as names, dates, and so forth, ultimately producing a work whose intended meaning emerges clearly. (37–49)

By contrast, weak allegories, such as Eltit's novel, transform a phenomenon "poorly or distractedly or with some or much irrelevance and indeterminacy into a narrative structure. The result is a narrative that evokes allegory while at the same time withholding commitment to it and undermining confidence in it" (53). Embedded allegory Johnson sees as a separate narrative within the larger narrative that can point to the allegorical nature of the larger narrative (79–80). Finally, thematic allegory occurs when allegory is an explicit topic or theme within a narrative.

With this set of definitions in mind, this chapter also demonstrates the ways in which *La última* and *Jamás* constitute strong and weak allegories, respectively, and how each novel uses its allegorical structure to communicate the feelings of nostalgia and melancholy experienced by those who participated in the socialist project in Chile during the 1970s.

In *Left-Wing Melancholia* (2021), Enzo Traverso examines at length the idea that the defeat of socialist project in most parts of the world resulted in a state of pathological mourning on the part of former left-wing revolutionaries:

> In our secular age... the culture of defeat takes the form of a melancholic retreat into meditation and introspection.... Differently from

the mourner who prevails over his sorrow, the melancholic remains narcissistically identified with his lost beloved object, transferring his suffering into an introspective isolation that cuts him off from the external world. In other words, melancholy ... is a pathological mourning. (42)

Traverso also indicates that the nature of memory, which is key to this pathological mourning, changed during the 1980s:

During these "street fighting years" of utopian strains, memory was not a cult object, it was rather incorporated into these struggles.... Memory was mobilized in order to fight the executioners of the present, not to commemorate the victims of the past. Nevertheless, a big change occurred during the 1980s. The revolutionary wave had its epilogue in Managua in July 1979.... In Europe, the Holocaust became the core of collective memory ... the victims began to occupy a new memorial landscape. (13)

Memory changed from an integral part of the socialist and other sociopolitical struggles into what Traverso calls a "cult object" (13). This focus on memory and the concomitant feeling of mourning, according to Fernando Cardoso, expresses: "The sadness and the fear born from the wounds of oppression and exile.... This crepuscular melancholy of a lost past took a nostalgic taste.... Left-wing melancholy is what remains after the shipwreck; its spirit shapes the writings of many of its survivors, drafted from their lifeboats, after the storm" (qtd. in Traverso 25).

Traverso specifically mentions the case of Chile and Carmen Castillo's video "Santa-Fe Street" with regard to this overwhelming feeling of melancholia:

It is in Latin America that this cycle of "glorious" defeats—celebrated as tragic, historical moments, that instead of putting into question the belief in socialism, strongly reinforce it—comes to an end. On Sept 11, 1973, a military putsch destroyed the Popular Union government in Chile establishing a brutal dictatorship that lasted twenty

> years and changed the political landscape of the continent. The last speech of President Salvador Allende, recorded that morning in the Moneda Palace just before he committed suicide, perpetuated—and completed—this long tradition of socialist martyrdom. Pronounced without lyricism, his last words and images . . . immediately transferred him into the pantheon of socialism beside Che Guevara, giving to his sacrifice an almost mythical dimension. (38)

Traverso signals the key relationship between melancholic, nostalgic memory and myth. There is no book that better illustrates this connection than Dorfman's *La última*.

Before turning to the elements in *La última* that aid in the creation of mythical structure and characters, it is important to note how Marxism might be thought to contain within its own philosophy a mythic or messianic foundation. According to George Steiner, Marxism, psychoanalysis, and structural anthropology constitute "mythologies" that arose to replace the void created by the gradual decline of the influence of formal religions in Western societies. Steiner defines "mythology" according to the following conditions:

> Now in order to qualify for the status of a mythology . . . a social, a psychological, or a spiritual doctrine or body of thought must fulfill certain conditions. The body of thought must make a claim of totality. . . . [A] mythology in this sense is a complete picture of "man in the world." . . . Secondly, a mythology in the sense in which I am using the word, will have certain very easily recognizable forms of beginning and development. There will have been a moment of crucial revelation or diagnostic insight from which the entire system springs. This moment and the history of the founding prophetic vision will be preserved in a series of canonic texts. . . . The third criterion of a true mythology . . . [is it] will develop its own language . . . its own set of emblematic images, flags, metaphors. (4)

Steiner goes on to specify the "messianic character" of Marxism (7) and, like Traverso, specifically mentions the case of Allende's Chile as an example of "visionary messianic character" and of idealistic sacrifice:

> But there can be no doubt about the visionary messianic character of what it [Marxism] says about the future.... It is just because the millenarian scenario of the redemption of man and of the establishment of the kingdom of justice on earth continues to grip the human spirit ... that every experiment in hope fires the imagination.... What do I mean by experiments in hope?... [t]he Prague Spring... Chile and the Allende government. (7–8)

I mention Steiner's ideas here about Marxism only to illustrate how Marxism as a philosophy inherently possesses an idealistic, prophetic nature and thus already carries within it the seeds of myth and idealization that Dorfman uses in his novel to create a nostalgic, melancholic allegory of the Allende government in Chile.

A biographical prelude is necessary, though, before considering *La última*. Dorfman himself (1942–) was Minister of Culture during the Allende government. A dedicated Marxist, he was born in Argentina, not Chile, and, as a youth, subsequently took up residence with his family in Chile, where he was educated. He eventually married a Chilean woman and became a Chilean citizen. After the military coup by Augusto Pinochet in 1973, Dorfman, who miraculously survived—having not been called to the Moneda Palace—went into exile in various countries (France, Amsterdam, and eventually the United States). A harsh critic of the Pinochet dictatorship, he has dedicated many of his works to the memory of the Allende government and has studied the question of remembrance during the postdictatorial period in Chile.

A brief summary of *La última*, a novel with an otherwise complex structure, will help in understanding my analysis of it. The novel itself has multiple narrators, of which the main ones are Manuel Sendero's son (referred to as the grandfather or Senderito), Senderito's favorite grandchild, and the unborn fetuses of the second fetal rebellion. As I intend to show, the narrative, developed in the sections marked "Adentro" (Inside), is an allegory of the Allende defeat and subsequent Pinochet government. These sections also contain two fetal rebellions. During the first, Manuel Sendero's son, as well as other fetuses from that era, refuse to be born into a world of violence and suffering. The rebellion fails, and thirty-three years later, there is a second fetal rebellion, for which Senderito/the grandfather is the spokesperson. These "Adentro" sections alternate with sections titled "Afuera" (Outside). The "Afuera" sections present a dialogue between David and Felipe. David's life trajectory is similar to that of Dorfman himself. A series of footnotes written thirty thousand years in the future analyze and comment upon this dialogue, which, as readers learn at the end of the novel, is a soap-opera script. Embedded within the dialogue is a third type of section, the comic strip written by David, which allegorizes Chile during the dictatorship.

Before I can illustrate how allegory is employed to create melancholy and nostalgia, it is important to examine how allegory is constructed in the novel. As previously noted, *La última* is what Johnson would term a strong allegory. Readers familiar with Dorfman and his historical time period will easily make the connection between the figure of Manuel Sendero and Salvador Allende. Although the literary criticism on the novel has also suggested that Manuel Sendero represents the famous Chilean singer Víctor Jara, who died in Estadio Chile,[1] tortured and killed by the military, I believe ample narrative clues exist to indicate that Sendero is either Allende or possibly a composite of Jara and Allende. Manuel Sendero evokes Jara because he is a singer who becomes mute after his imprisonment, but the singing itself functions metaphorically in the novel to refer to Allende's political philosophy (more on this below). Salvador Allende was an inspirational speaker, and his photographs frequently show him with his hands raised in the air: "levantar los brazos hacia las montañas como un predicador. ¿Pero y después, Manuel Sendero? ([*La última* 34] lifting your hands up to the mountains like a preacher. But afterward, Manuel Sendero? [Last 31]). In addition to this passage, the following further suggests the way in which Salvador Allende inspired his followers: "Manuel . . . que comprimía el tiempo en sus manos y se lo ofrecía de regalo a los menesterosos . . . Manuel creyéndose una divinidad ([280] Manuel . . . before he compressed time in his hands and offered it as a gift to the needy . . . Manuel believing himself to be a divinity).[2]

Moreover, just as Johnson suggests that names can indicate and reinforce allegorical interpretations, the name "Manuel Sendero" surely points the reader in this direction. Lucille V. Braun notes: "The surname Sendero clearly has the meaning of 'way' or 'path' and calls to mind Christ's phrase 'I am the way, the truth and the light.' His given name, moreover, derives from Emmanuel (God is with us)" (410). The "god" or leader of the Chilean path to socialism was not Víctor Jara, but Salvador Allende. Thus, the title character's name guides the reader toward the allegorical connection between Manuel Sendero and Chile's former president.

The novel presents another allegorical figure, that of the Caballero who is the nemesis of Manuel Sendero. Although some critics have identified the Caballero with Pinochet, this is true only insofar as this figure represents capitalism and neoliberalism, which Pinochet imposed after the coup. The connection between the Caballero and the neoliberal state is stronger because of his association with the cold (which I examine later) and economics. He first appears when he offers pills to Sendero's wife, Doralisa, so that she can sleep through the pains of her overdue pregnancy (caused by her fetus that refuses birth). Compassion, however, has nothing to do with the Caballero's act; rather, his company wants to test the efficaciousness of a new drug (*La última* 31). This immediately establishes the Caballero as a capitalist businessman. Later on, he offers the unemployed Manuel Sendero a job as "un encuestado" (a professional survey-taker). When Manuel is caught lying in his survey responses, the Caballero evicts him and his family from their house to live in an elevator. This incident pits capitalism against socialism. The Caballero has Sendero's house deconstructed, its boards and beams carted away by two carpenters (230). Yet the real import of this incident requires turning to Engels's "The Housing Question" in which he decries capitalist greed as the cause of the housing shortage—better shops and warehouses in high-value real-estate areas rather than homes for those of lower economic status:

> The growth of the big modern cities gives the land in certain areas, particularly in those which are centrally situated, an artificial and often colossally increasing value; the buildings erected on these areas depress this value ... because they no longer correspond to the changed circumstances. They are pulled down and replaced by others. This takes place above all with workers' houses which are situated centrally.... They are pulled down and in their stead shops, warehouses and public buildings are erected. (23)

For anyone familiar with Chile after the coup, this scene clearly evokes how neoliberal policy took hold there and created housing problems for the poor. It is hard to imagine that Dorfman did not have Engels in mind in crafting the scene. Still, living in an elevator carries other symbolic significance. As Andreas Bernard explains in *Lifted* (2014), elevators have a key role in defining spaces. Prior to the installation of elevators in buildings, the lower floors were considered superior to the higher floors, and affluent people tended to live lower down and stay on the lower floors of hotels. However, once elevators were constructed, higher floors—the "superior" parts of buildings— became associated with the rich, while servants and poorer people occupied the lower floors. Bernard states: "At the same time, it [the elevator] resolved the old symbolic dissonance between vertical hierarchy and social hierarchy.... Once the elevator established itself, the pyramid of society could be accurately reflected in the structure of multistory buildings as well" (70). Thus, in addition to reflecting the Chilean housing shortage, the elevator stands as a symbol for social division, an idea supported by the fact that there is a subterranean prison below the basement floor of the building in which Sendero occupies the elevator and performs building inspections.

The second characteristic consistently attributed to the Caballero is that of coldness. Every time he is mentioned, an adjective or epithet related to the cold materializes (Braun 412–13). This characterization is that of the stereotypical businessperson, who is cold and hard-hearted. More important, though, the "Adentro" sections about Manuel Sendero are set in a spring that is either described as cold, and thus not typical, or as false (*La última* 18, 21, 242; *Last* 10, 15, 305). These passages indicate that technically it is spring, but it is a false spring. It is not warm, and it doesn't smell like spring; indeed, only the meteorologists seem to think it is actually spring. Dorfman undoubtedly had Pinochet in mind, as the dictator's coup occurred on September 11th, the beginning of spring in Chile.

We can take the cold/winterlike analogy one step further by suggesting that the insistence on cold and a false spring qualifies as an independent embedded allegory. Johnson defines one as a narrative device that employs an intertextual reference outside the text to construct the allegory embedded in the work. In this case, cold references hearken back to the novel's epigraph and the poem "Los nueve monstruos" by Vallejo, which references the "frío muerto" previously discussed. In addition, it is possible that there is an intertextual connection with a second poem by Vallejo titled "El pan nuestro" (Our

Bread). This second verse in the first stanza reads: "Ciudad de invierno... La mordaz cruzada / de una carreta que arrastrar parece / una emoción de ayuno encadenada!" (City of winter... Mordant crusade of a cart that seems to drag along / a feeling of fasting in chains [*Complete Poetry* 111]). The line "ciudad de invierno" is paralleled by the winter (understood figuratively as hardship) that persists through the Chilean spring. In addition, a striking similarity surfaces in the use of the bread symbol. The poetic voice, feeling guilty for the food he has that others do not, states at the end that he would like to "hacerle pedacitos de pan fresco, aquí en el horno de mi corazón" ([*Obras completas* 73] And bake him morsels of fresh bread here, in the oven of my heart [*Complete Poetry* 111]). This description of the "pedacitos de pan fresco" evokes a highly significant episode of the novel. In the first chapter, upon Manuel Sendero's release from prison, he witnesses the murder of a man who is riding a bicycle. Sendero thinks the police are coming for him, when in reality they are calling for the baker on the bike. We are told that the baker is making bread deliveries "con ese barquito cargado de pan fresco recién horneado" (20) (with his little boat laden with bread fresh from the oven [*Last* 14]), a phrase very similar to the verse from the Vallejo poem. The Vallejo poem is about solidarity as well as rebellion. The "padre nuestro" (our father prayer) is converted into "el pan nuestro," a prayer that demands, not requests, the daily bread, which the use of the exclamation point underscores: "El pan nuestro de cada día dánoslo, Señor...!" ([111] Our daily bread, give it to us, Lord!). Similarly, the bread that falls from the bicycle also becomes a symbol of rebellion. According to the myth that grew out of this episode, "el que coma una de estas migas interpretaron ellos en su mejor tono de evangelizadores... jamás olvidará su infancia, como decir... será siempre rebelde" ([*La última* 24] whoever eats one of those crumbs, they expounded in their most evangelizing... tone, will never forget his childhood. That is... he'll always be a rebel, [*Last* 18–19]). Altogether, this episode prefigures Manuel Sendero's own death at the end of the novel.

    Many other passages reinforce the idea that *La última* is a strong allegory, but with a final example, I limit myself to the material in the "Afuera" sections that serves as an embedded allegory. As mentioned, Johnson discusses how an embedded allegory might potentially be a signal that the work as a whole should be interpreted allegorically. First, although the dialogue between Felipe and David is not in itself an allegory, the fact that they openly discuss

Allende, Pinochet, their status as exiles, Felipe's former imprisonment, the boycott of Chilean products, and many other historical details about the situation in Chile is a clue to the fact that the "Adentro" sections should be interpreted allegorically. In addition, the comic strip written by David narrates the adventures of a former Disney cartoonist (Carl Barks) in Chile, where he is invited to create the image of a "superman" from whom the will to fight and rebel (known as the X factor in the novel) has been removed.[3] The reader cannot help but make a connection between these episodes and those in which Manuel Sendero is the protagonist. Finally, the footnotes to David and Felipe's dialogue, as well as the voice of a mother telling a story to her children, relate the legend of David and the dragon Pinchot. The dragon Pinchot is obviously the dictator Pinochet, and thus the reader is cued to associate the events in the "Adentro" section to Chile in the 1970s. I later return to the significance of these other discourses in the construction of melancholia and nostalgia.

On the surface, this discussion of allegory may appear to have led us far afield from my main point, which is that *La última* is ultimately about the expression of a pervasive feeling of nostalgia and melancholia experienced by those who participated in the Chilean socialist project, including the author Dorfman himself. However, many of the examples mentioned above illustrate the principal characteristics that Dorfman uses to create a sense of melancholic feeling throughout the novel. He employs myth (mythic structure and mythic episodes), idealization of the main characters (Sendero and Senderito), a nostalgic tone (created through stylistic choices), and explicit references to nostalgia for Chile, all of which communicate a pervasive feeling of nostalgia and melancholia.

Let us begin by examining the ways in which the technique of idealization is employed. According to Monika Tuszewicka: "Nostalgia is an intense experience and a form of selective memory.... Past events appear in an exaggerated, idealized form that only recall the pleasant things. The past is—to some extent—a myth"(168). Implicit within idealization is the desire to return to this exaggerated state of perfection. This is precisely the situation *La última* creates. As noted, Manuel Sendero's name suggests parallels to God, a form of idealization. Braun notes that this is also true of Manuel Sendero's son who is thirty-three when he returns to Chile, the same age of Christ when crucified. She also states that "Dorfman ... draws implicitly on parallels between the act of belief necessary to accept Christ as the son of God and the faith necessary to accept the existence of the son of Manuel Sendero" (410). Such is the case because the novel presents at least two contradictory versions of almost all events, so that in one version Senderito is aborted as a fetus by the Caballero and is never born, while in another he is born and narrates his father's story to his grandchildren. Readers are left to draw their own conclusions.

Sendero's name is not the only element that idealizes him. His mission is described as a crusade, a word choice that evokes a goal with an aggressive, religious fervor: "Muchas veces, en esta cruzada, Manuel ni siquiera argumentaba: daba besos, tocaba manos, predecía praderas y más que a sus ideas, la gente le creía a él" ([*La última* 64] Often, during this crusade, Manuel didn't even argue: he distributed kisses, shook hands, painted rosy pictures, and the people believed in him, more than in his ideas [Last 73–75]). Sendero is a powerfully charismatic figure, and people believed in him as a religious person believes in God. Such an idealization cannot help but create in future generations a melancholic nostalgia for Sendero after his death.

Another way in which Manuel Sendero is idealized is through his innocence. Eduardo, the pragmatic character who is counterposed to both Sendero and Senderito, describes Manuel Sendero thus:

> Era como un feto . . . que desea que todo en torno suyo sean paredes de leche y afecto. Creía en el Paraíso, en la Tierra de Promisión, en la Edad de Oro. Se ponía a sí mismo . . . como un ejemplo desaforado de la existencia de tales utopías en que no existen conflictos. . . . Era invencible, Manuel. . . . ¿Quién lo paraba? (*La última* 64)⁴

> He was . . . like a fetus that wants everything around him to be walls of milk and of love. Manuel believed in paradise, in the Promised Land, in the Golden Age . . . he presented himself as an outrageous example of the existence of such utopias, where there were no conflicts. . . . He was invincible, Manuel was. . . . Who could stop him? (Last 74)

Even though Eduardo himself is not an idealistic person and immediately states that Manuel Sendero was wrong, his cynicism is undermined by the images of Manuel Sendero that linger from his description. The idea of Manuel's innocence, his goodness, and his desire to create a better world idealize him and so create an effect of nostalgia for the past in the reader and on the part of the implied author.

In that vein, Braun has studied the mythic, fairy tale-like quality of the novel and draws from Dorfman's *Imaginación y violencia en América* in which he connects myth to nostalgia:

> El mito, nostalgia de lo que se ha perdido, falsificación de lo original es también un modo de recuperación, un recobrarse para algo tal vez mejor.... La leyenda se hace no solo en el momento fundador, en la acción humana, sino también en la transmisión, en la elevación o caída de ese instante olvidable e inolvidable." (qtd. in Braun 411)

> Myth, nostalgia for what has been lost, falsification of the original is also a way of recovering, a recovering for something perhaps better.... Legend is made not only in the founding moment, in human action, but also in transmission, in the elevation or falling of that forgettable and unforgettable instance.

Braun points out that the structure of the "Adentro" sections employs this same mythic approach in the oral transmission of Sendero's song from generation to generation. What is of particular interest here is the connection between myth and nostalgia. The second principal way in communicating nostalgic melancholia for Dorfman is through this mythic structure and other related mythic elements.

The symbolic value of bread in the novel and its relationship to Vallejo's poetry is illustrative, as its intertextuality explains how myths are created in the novel. The twins (who are friends of Senderito) pass on the story that those who ate those breadcrumbs that had fallen from the bicycle remained forever young and rebellious. Braun mentions numerous other myths and fairy tales that appear in the novel, including the tale of Sleeping Beauty reenacted through Sendero's wife, Doralisa, who is put to sleep by the Caballero's pills and the mythic tale of Esmeralda. Esmeralda was a cook in a factory cafeteria. When the government closed her kitchen and the workers forced to bring lunch, her breasts became enormous and were used to feed the hungry full-course meals. There is also the myth of the apple that represents solidarity and hearkens back to the mythic apple from the Garden of Eden (426). All of these stories help to create a mythic atmosphere in the novel. However, the myth that is most important in the creation of melancholia and nostalgia in the novel is the central myth surrounding Manuel Sendero's song.

Manuel Sendero's song resonates symbolically throughout the novel. When he loses his voice in prison, some say that has happened because the prison guards took away his wedding ring. The Caballero, instead, insists that his mutism is voluntary, even though Sendero cannot seem to utter a word. At the end of the novel, the Caballero insists he sing for him (that is, he permit the government to use his song for its purposes); if not, then he will abort his son and keep his wife's sexual organs as payment for his outstanding bills. In this version, we are told that Sendero refuses to sing because it signifies a willingness to talk, confess, and possibly betray others; his voice would no longer be his but a tool of evil. Sendero here remains true to himself and his followers; he refuses to collaborate:

> Podría haber cantado. Pero no lo hizo, niños . . . y cuando el mundo, lejos de cambiar, había empeorado, Manuel Sendero había recaído hacia el recurso extremo de la mudez, para no tener que colaborar, se deshizo de lo único valioso que él poseía. (*La última* 320)

> He could have sung. But he didn't, kids . . . and when the world, far from changing, had gotten worse, Manuel Sendero had fallen back on that extreme recourse of muteness, in order not to have to collaborate. He had gotten rid of the only valuable thing he possessed. (*Last* 406)

However, as with the story of Sendero's son, who is simultaneously aborted and born to return to Chile and lead the second fetal rebellion, another contradictory version of events has Manuel Sendero sing. In this version, recounted below by Senderito's lover Pamela, the meaning of singing changes as well. In this case singing is no longer betrayal, but the inspirational words that Sendero (Allende) leaves for future generations:

> Desde que era niña había bebido la fluctuante historia . . . a los pies de su propio padre adoptivo quien . . . había sido uno de los escasos testigos . . . no ya de la última canción sino de la intención proclamada

> de Manuel Sendero de darle cauce.... El pueblo aceptó esa versión....
> Le habían asesinado al hijo... pero nuestro Manuel Sendero que estás
> en los sueños, en vez de echarse a morir, se había puesto a cantar... y
> lo desaparecieron... y seguía cantando y lo seguirá, así dicen hasta que
> nosotros todos seamos capaces de cantarla también. (*La última* 343)

> Ever since she was a little girl, she'd been nourished on the ever-changing story.... She'd drunk it in at the feet of her own adoptive father, who... had been one of the few witnesses... not of the last song itself, but of Manuel Sendero's proclaimed intention to produce it....
> The people accepted that version.... They had murdered his son.... But our Manuel Sendero who art in our dreams, instead of going off to die, had started to sing.... And they disappeared him.... And he kept on singing, and he'll keep on, so they say, until all of us can sing it too. (Last 434–35)

In addition to being the version passed down by the people, this second tale creates a mythic vision of Sendero that expresses a melancholic nostalgia for the figure. And so "nuestro Manuel Sendero que estás en los sueños" parodies "nuestro padre que estás en el Cielo" (our father who art in Heaven), which deifies and idealizes Sendero. He is also portrayed as a martyr who sacrifices his own son (as Christ was sacrificed for mankind) "to serve our cause" (435).

One final myth serves an important function in the novel: that of the legend of David and the dragon Pinchot, which belongs to the "Afuera" sections of the novel, as well as the novel's second epilogue, in which a mother recounts this legend to her children at bedtime. The legend is juxtaposed with the dialogue between Felipe and David in which David finds out that something has happened to his son Lolo in Chile. The reader comprehends from this juxtaposition that the Felipe and David of the legend are the same characters as those in the dialogue/soap opera. In addition to adding to the overall mythic atmosphere of the novel, this particular legend is important for both the interpretation of the character David, as well as that of Manuel Sendero. In the legend, David believes that the dragon Pinchot has taken his son, and so he goes to fight the dragon and bring his son some "future air" to help him survive. Although Felipe also goes to fight the dragon, he does so in this moment only because he does not trust David, fearing that he will fall victim to the dragon and somehow end up on his side, fighting for evil. Obviously, these events parallel those from the dialogue, in which Felipe is angry with David for abandoning the boycott and granting an interview to a conservative newspaper. He feels that David is disloyal to the cause for which they both fought under Allende. However, the legend serves to clear up any doubts the reader might have about David. As the title of the legend shows, David is the hero of the legend, not Felipe. David is pure in his stance against Pinochet and valiant in his attempts to slay the dragon. Although the reader never hears the end of the story, the children want the story to have "un final lindo" (a happy ending), which they clearly anticipate, as does the reader.

The reason that this legend also serves to help in interpreting Manuel Sendero is that, as much of the criticism on *La última* has pointed out, the "Afuera" sections frequently mirror characters and other significant elements of the "Adentro" sections. Felipe, who is the pragmatist, mirrors Eduardo (Senderito's rival for Pamela), while David, the dreamer, parallels Manuel Sendero and his son (McClennen 138). Thus, David's heroic attempts to slay the dragon Pinchot also cast a heroic interpretation on his counterpart Manuel Sendero. That being said, the implied author, rather than suggesting that dreamers are better than pragmatists, posits a fusion or union of the two. Just as Felipe helps David, Eduardo's help is necessary for Senderito (the grandfather) in the "Adentro" sections. When the Caballero is searching for Senderito to kill him, Senderito sends messages through the blind girl to both Pamela and Eduardo. On the last page of the novel, titled as the last epilogue and the first prologue, the blind girl delivers this message in which Senderito asks Eduardo to take care of his children as if they were his own. Although Eduardo claims to promise nothing, the voice of the future generations of children insists: "Pero a nosotros nos pareció a lo lejos como una promesa . . . me atreví a creer que él cuidaría como si fueran suyos a los múltiples nietos de Manuel Sendero" ([*La última* 357] But it seemed like a promise to us, from afar. . . . I dared believe that he'd care for Manuel Sendero's many grandchildren as if they were his own [Last 453]). This ending suggests that the dreamers and the pragmatists must work together in the hope for a better future.

These examples illustrate how important word choice and style are to the creation of myth, melancholy, and nostalgia, as both contribute to creating narrative voice and tone. James Phelan, in this vein, remarks: "voice is a synthesis of style, tone and values in any utterance" and that narrative tone depends on a speaker's attitude toward an utterance, as well as on stylistic and contextual cues, such as "occasion, subject matter, character of the speaker, and prior relationship of speaker and audience" (50). Many other passages from *La última* create feelings of melancholia and nostalgia for the loss of Manuel Sendero and what he has represented via the style of the utterances about him. Note the following passage in which El Flaquísimo, Sendero's best friend, states: "Las cosas que se hacen por amor al prójimo no se realizan para quedar en un libro de historia o para que te levanten una estatua. A mi compadre Manuel le hubiera bastado con tener una paginita en el corazón del pueblo" ([*La última* 15] The things you do out of love for your fellowmen aren't done for a place in a history book or so someone can put up a statue in your honor. The only page my buddy Sendero wanted was a page in the hearts of his people [Last 10]). Obviously, El Flaquísmo's attitude in this utterance is one of affection for his friend Sendero. Through use of the words "amor," "corazón del pueblo," and the affective diminutive "paginita," this utterance suggests a strong sentiment associated with this memory—and thus nostalgia.

Similarly, Senderito's favorite grandson also suggests a melancholic longing for Manuel Sendero and what he represents by referring to Eduardo's vision of his last song as "una de tantas hermosas leyendas que el pueblo ha ido tejiendo en las orillas de su memoria o a modo de indemnización por una eternidad de frustraciones" ([*La última* 15] one among many splendid legends that the people have woven on the shores of their memory, an indemnity for an eternity of frustrations [Last 10]). In this passage, the words such as "hermosas" and "indemnización por una eternidad de frustraciones" also suggest that the grandson is looking back nostalgically on the past represented by Sendero given the subsequent "eternity of frustrations" that the world has had to face. Moreover, it is important to recall here, that nostalgia is solidified by objects that help us to remember and that Manuel Sendero's song serves the purpose of being an object of memory that fulfills this function.[5]

Myth, nostalgia, and melancholia are also elements in the "Afuera" sections of the novel, only more explicit. Just as we observed the recounting of many myths and legends in the "Adentro" sections, the "Afuera" sections contain references in the footnotes to the legend of David and the dragon Pinchot.

Melancholic Allegories

Both Felipe and David are Chilean citizens in exile. Felipe had been imprisoned under the Pinochet government and is now living in Mexico, while David was forced by his own socialist political party to leave Chile after the coup because they felt that his sentimental actions (such as getting his revolutionary group together for a bachelor party) were compromising the resistance movement. David is an autobiographical character who shares many traits with Dorfman (his family fled the Nazis, he is a naturalized Chilean citizen, he is exiled in Amsterdam, and so forth). His love and passion for Chile lead him to perform actions that are not always politically correct, such as abandoning the boycott of Chilean goods or agreeing to an interview with a conservative newspaper, in the hope that such departures may result in his return to Chile from exile in Amsterdam. David's characterization explicitly evokes the melancholia and nostalgia implicitly woven into the "Adentro" sections. Perhaps the best example of David's nostalgia for Chile can be found in his description of how he broke the boycott by eating the last Chilean apple he found in the supermarket:

> Masqué, tragué, pagué.... y aceleré, aceleré, mi mano buena eligió productos autóctonos de los estantes... esperando que... mis tripas me engañaran... que cuando abriera los ojos estaría nuevamente allá, donde estas plantas habían crecido y estas botellas se habían llenado. (*La última* 94–95)

> I nibbled, I swallowed, I paid.... I accelerated, I accelerated, my good hand raked native products from the shelves... hoping that the unique certainty of my guts would deceive me... that when I opened my eyes, I would once again be in Chile, where these plants had grown, and these bottles had been filled.[6]

It is noteworthy that this passage returns to the apple motif present in the "Adentro" sections, which can also be seen here as a symbol for solidarity, which David violates by eating the Chilean apple (Braun 426).

  David also nostalgically remembers the moment of Allende's triumph when his strange melancholia anticipates future events that will destroy Allende's socialist project: "¿Quedaría algo? Me sorprendió la violencia de mi propia *nostalgia anticipada*, la repentina y sucia lluvia triste que me calaba desde el futuro" ([*La última* 122; my emphasis] Would anything remain? The violence of my own *anticipated nostalgia* surprised me, the sudden, sad, dirty rain that was soaking me from the future [Last 151]). Indeed, the entire scene in the Mexican bar, where Felipe and David celebrate the new year with a Mexican man who proposes a toast to Allende, permeates the "Afuera" section with a sense of nostalgic longing for this past, with the "left-wing melancholia" described by Traverso in his book.

One final symbolic element deserves mention before closing the discussion of *La última*. Throughout the novel, hands are repeated as an important motif. Braun claims that hands are a "sinister motif," such as when a passenger tries to strangle Sarah Barks in the comic strip, or the Caballero used gloved hands to abort Senderito. She views David's missing hand, which he purposely slams into the elevator grille as it is moving, as "punishment because he used force, not words, as he planned against the French boy who had been tormenting his son at school" (425). According to Lois Baer Barr,

> Hands as the symbol of the workers' resistance would take on a power significance to the torturers of the disappeared. Of course, the torturers often tried to assure that the corpses would not be identified by removing their fingers and thus the fingerprint.... [B]y smashing Víctor Jara's hands his jailors stripped him of his powers ... Throughout the novel there is a link between helplessness and the loss of use of one's hands. In a moment of frustration, David deliberately injures himself by slamming an iron elevator door on his hand. Carl Barks languishes in a sanatorium ...[where he] first loses any sensation in his hands and later loses control of them altogether. (148)

While these interpretations are plausible, hands are a significant motif in other works by Dorfman in which they serve as an interpretive key. In the novel *Máscara* (1988), hands are the primary symbol employed to develop the importance of memory. The narrator of one of the novel's three sections, Oriana, explains how the lines on one's hands reflect each person's life and memories of who they are and what they have done. When a person died, two men would come and erase their hands. As I explain in another study, Oriana becomes a depository for the memories held through people's hands but then suffers amnesia from trauma caused by the two men (*Masquerade* 135–40). Although *Máscara* appeared several years after *La última*, I see some similarity in the way hands are described in it vis-à-vis *Máscara*. For example, the narrator connects hands to the memories one has prior to birth in the following passage: "la mentira de que el útero es uno en particular en vez de ser una constelación donde todos se encuentran y se sucesivan y se trasponen. Fracturar los dedos de la mano que nos une a ese lugar por donde han pasado todas las mujeres, todos los hombres vivos" ([*La última* 141] the lie that there is a particular uterus not a constellation of uteruses where all meet and succeed each other and change places. Breaking the fingers of the hand that links us to that place through which all living men and women have passed [Last 174]). Here the narrator employs the metaphor "breaking the fingers of the hand" to refer to memory of womb, which is envisioned not as an individual uterus, but a collective womb of the unconscious that unites all humankind.

In another instance, the subterranean prisoners have had their hands thrown into the sea by the guards, which are likened to bottles without messages. The narrator indicates that the hands will be the first thing rescued (*La última* 233). The hands separated from the individual are like the empty bottles that contain no message because a person's identity, life, and memories are written on their hands. This is the same reason that in David's comic strip, the people, like Marras, who have been rejuvenated need to wear gloves because their hands still look old. The hands contain the past, their memories, and therefore cannot be erased. In this same vein, it is possible that when David severs his hand in the elevator, it is an attempt to sever his memories. At that moment, he is frustrated because his wife Cecilia is returning to Chile with their children and threatens to have her father, a military man, impede David's return from exile. This is the moment in which David smashes his hand into the elevator grille. However, still with one hand, David cannot forget his family or Chile. Just as in *Máscara*, hands are connected to the past, and the act of remembering is an explicit theme in both novels.

I have chosen, in light of this evidence, to conclude my discussion of *La última* with an analysis of hands as a representation of memory that is, at once, melancholic and nostalgic of the Chilean socialist movement. Nostalgic memory is not only the novel's overarching theme but also the primary connecting factor between Dorfman's novel and Eltit's *Jamás*.

While *La última* constitutes a strong allegory, *Jamás* is a weak one. Weak allegories, as discussed, remain allegories for the reader, but their transformation or equivalency of novelistic elements is often indeterminate. Eltit's novel includes many repetitions (Todorov's syntagmatic elements of excess) as well as many contradictions (syntagmatic elements of lack), which encourage the reader to find symbolic meanings for these elements. All the critics who have written on Eltit's novel agree that it is allegorical, but each attributes a different allegorical meaning to the textual elements, which supports the notion of weak allegory.[7] Consequently, there is little consensus about what the novel means (the themes to which the allegory contained in *Jamás* points). For example, Rubí Carreño has interpreted the novel as fundamentally a love story between the female narrator and the man who shares the bed with her (191), while Carolina Díaz insists that the novel is about gender roles and how women are "capaz de subvertir totalitarismos" ([182] capable of subverting totalitarianisms). While I agree that gender roles and a love story figure in *Jamás*, the fundamental allegory that the work establishes is that of memory versus forgetting, which critics such as María Rosa Olivera-Williams have indicated without full explanations. Olivera-Williams focuses on the bed, undoubtedly an important element of the allegory, as a ruin "de donde surjan los retazos, los despojos del pasado" ([49] from which the pieces, the spoils of the past appear). The bed, the space of memory, allows the narrator to "mirar de frente el fracaso para poder dirigir una mirada al futuro" ([53] to look failure in the face in order to be able to look toward the future). Olivera-Williams and Carolina Díaz share a positive take on the novel, suggesting that the novel includes some hope for the future. Díaz states: "La paranoia . . . se presentaría como una práctica alternativa al testimonio latinoamericano o al trabajo melancólico de la memoria. . . . Mas allá de lamentar aquello que ha desaparecido, el objeto de la dramatización paranoide de la narradora es, por lo tanto, un "reparative knowing" ([191] Paranoia . . . would be presented as an alternative practice to Latin American testimony or the melancholic work of memory. . . . Beyond lamenting that which has disappeared, the objective of the paranoid dramatization of the narrator is, thus, a "reparative knowing").

Unlike Dorfman who went into exile, Eltit (1949–) lived and wrote under the Pinochet dictatorship. She was, as Michael J. Lazzara details, cofounder of the avant-garde group CADA (Art Actions Collective) that sought to fuse art, life, and politics (Corral ed. 320). She has written numerous novels, most of which are to some degree allegorical and the first of which was *Lumpérica* (*E. Luminata*) published in 1983. According to Lazzara, her novels "offer a searing reflection on the ways in which individual bodies and the social body have suffered and resisted the pressures of dictatorship, colonialism, imperialism, and the imposition of neoliberal economic policy that has been the hallmark of Chile's transition to democracy" (320).

In contrast to *La última*, which includes specific elements that point toward a better future,[8] Eltit's novel concretely points to the opposite: a future that is clearly as bad as the past. It is important to note that, despite confusion on the matter, both protagonists are dead, and the female protagonist/narrator is narrating from an indefinite point far into the future: "Hace más de cien años que murió Franco ... No, no, me dices, no un siglo, mucho más, más" ([18] It was more than a hundred years ago that Franco died. ... No, no, you tell me, not a century, it's more than that, much more [7]).[9] The narrator repeats this idea of a thousand years having passed throughout the novel (*Jamás* 21, 110–11, 154, 158; *Never* 9, 75, 110, 112).

Given the imprecision of "when," Franco's death in 1975 would mean that the earliest the narrator speaks would be 2075. On this matter, Carolina Díaz proposes three related possibilities: that the narrator is dead and her companion alive, that they are both alive, or that both are dead ("Allegorical Spectors" 253–54). Nonetheless, the narrator explicitly states that both are dead: "Ya no estamos exactamente vivos (muertos, sí, muertos) después de los cien, de los mil años que hubimos de sobrellevar" ([*Jamás* 177] We are no longer exactly alive (dead, yes, dead) after the hundred, the thousand years we had to endure [*Never* 129]).

What is more is that the future from which the dead narrator speaks is always cast in forbidding terms. "Están asaltando prácticamente todos los bancos ... están apedreando cientos o miles de autos ... mientras en las casas lujosas se desencadena un terror no exento de culpa" ([*Jamás* 185] They're robbing almost all the banks ... they are stoning hundreds or thousands of cars ... while in the luxury houses a terror is unleashed that is not altogether blameless [*Never* 135]). Although memory of the past and the present alternate constantly throughout the narration, this citation appears to refer to the city in the narrator's present, which is to say, one overrun with murders and bank robberies. That the rich are terrified points to their complicity in an unequal system that privileges them at the expense of and on the backs of the poor.

Finally, the novel's full title, *Jamás el fuego nunca*, as I have mentioned, comes from Vallejo's bleak poem "Los nueve monstruos." The poem repeats the word "dolor" (pain) fourteen times. The line "never did the fire ever play better its role of dead cold" from Vallejo's poem suggests the motifs of death and coldness that Eltit develops throughout her novel. From the title and then subsequently Eltit fills her novel with an atmosphere of mourning, melancholia and nostalgia for the lost socialist revolution—and especially its failure in delivering justice to the poor. Eltit, like Dorfman, employs allegory to construct these emotions.

I would like to begin with a discussion of those allegorical elements that are most obvious and then move on to some of the more indeterminate elements of the novel, the allegorical value of which is difficult to establish. The novel begins with the two protagonists lying in bed as one of them, the female narrator, is trying to recall when the Spanish dictator Francisco Franco died. This sets up an important dynamic, lasting the entire novel, that pits the woman, who remembers events and attempts to engage her companion in remembering and clarifying details of those events, against the man who prefers to forget the past. In post-dictatorial Chile, fraught with conflict over what Stern terms Chile's "memory box," this tableau can only mean that the woman symbolizes remembering, while the man symbolizes forgetting (which is one of the memory narratives discussed in the introduction). Despite the fact that they are both former left-wing revolutionaries, the novel posits their relationship as a metaphor for the Concertación governments in Chile. As I explain in chapter 1, the Concertación was a coalition of center-left political parties established in 1988. Their governing pact included a policy of forgiveness toward the right wing at a time when Chileans advocated forgetting the past as a way to return to democracy and to a more inclusive future. This pact between center/right and left is allegorized by the couple as seen in the following citations:

> Mi empeño se centra en controlar cualquier indicio de rencor para formar parte de esta paz que nos hemos concedido. (*Jamás* 18)
> ...
> Más adelante ... tomamos el acuerdo de no rememorar. Decidimos suspender todo juicio sobre el pasado. Quien lo decidió, como se

formuló nuestro pacto, fue acaso implícito, me pregunto ahora. (*Jamás* 55)[10]

My own determination is focused on controlling any glimmer of bitterness in order to be a part of this peace we have granted ourselves. (7)

...

Later ... we reached an agreement not to remember. We decided to suspend all judgment of the past. Who made that decision, how was our pact formed, could it perhaps have been implicit, I wonder now. (Never 34)

The novel repeats similar ideas, notably regarding the couple's agreement to share their room and their bed (Never 25, 179). For someone familiar with Chilean history from 1988 to the present, the emphasis on "peace" and the constant repetition of the word "pact" can only evoke the agreement made between the political parties to forget the past for the sake of democracy and neoliberal economic prosperity. Stern remarks of this arrangement:

> The fundamental objective of Patricio Aylwin's administration was to build a new *convivencia*—a living together in peace—after a period of immense violence, fear, and polarization and thereby [to] achieve an irreversible recovery of democracy.... In this vision, strong and sustained growth would reduce poverty and provide political and economic underwriting to sustain equity-oriented reforms.... In the minds of Aylwin and his most important advisors, such goals required broad social backing.... The memory question, understood as "truth," was inherently paradoxical—both indispensable and dangerous. Political adversity in a more general sense constituted a second major challenge to building *convivencia*, let alone a vibrant democracy. (*Reckoning* 17–22).

Jamás allegorizes the Concertación government and its politics of forgetting through the relationship established between the man and the woman. Some of the above citations refer to this pact specifically occurring after the death of the woman's son, at once allegorically significant and confounding, as three separate versions of the son's death are told, each contradicting the other. This contradiction (Todorov's syntagmatic element of lack) paints the reader into the corner of having to read the son allegorically.

The first and most pervasive version of the son's death figures when he is two and spikes a high fever. The man and the woman cannot bring him to the hospital because they are part of a revolutionary cell, presumably during the dictatorship. Under the circumstance, it would be dangerous for them to abandon their clandestine quarters and identities, an act the would jeopardize both their safety and the fate of their political movement. The son perishes from the fever, and ever after the woman questions their actions. And so, in the wake, she asks her partner why they did not take him to the hospital.

The second version of the son's death appears toward the end of the novel. Both the man and the woman are each separately captured and tortured—and both eventually released. When the woman returns to their apartment, she is pregnant—the victim, we think, of multiple rapes while she was incarcerated. Since it would be too risky to give birth in a hospital (for the same reasons as before), the man assumes the role of delivering the baby. But during childbirth, he gives the woman too much ether (acquired from an intermediary), either accidentally or on purpose. As a result, she and her son die.

The third version of the son's death also appears at the very end of the novel. When the woman returns pregnant from her imprisonment, the man is enraged and asks her why she didn't get rid of the baby. In a fit of passion, he beats her and the unborn child to death with a stick.

What is important in these three different versions is not the question of which is correct, but rather what the total effect of the different versions has on the reader. From that confusion, the reader is left not knowing what happened to the son. This indeterminacy is one of the two major factors that transform the dead son into an allegory of the disappeared in Chile whose families often never had closure on the fate of their offspring. Thus, the reader's inability to find out what happened to the son allegorizes the disappeared under the Pinochet dictatorship.

The second factor that reinforces the idea that the dead son represents the disappeared is the way in which the woman expresses her feelings over the son's death. An overwhelming feeling of melancholia and nostalgia surrounds every mention of the son throughout the novel. This feeling, which any mother would have under the circumstances, undoubtedly distills the feelings of the loved ones who lost family members to systematic atrocity:

Su carita de dos años y sus angustioso rictus de muerte. De pronto la imagen fue interceptada por una impresión insólita. No avanzaba. La realidad física de esa calle en la ciudad se había detenido. Solo yo me movía en un escenario único que no dejaba de suceder. . . .
　　　　Prácticamente no respira . . . y recuerdo como llorábamos juntos. . . . Una cara que estaba de salida y que ahora lucho por reconstruir.
. . .
Hasta llevar a su fin los latidos imprescindibles de su pequeño amado corazón. (*Jamás* 41, 85, 138)

That little two-year-old face and his anguished grimace of death. Suddenly, the image was intercepted by an unusual impression. I wasn't moving forward at all. The physical reality of this street in the city had stopped. I alone was moving in a unique setting that didn't stop happening.
. . .
He's hardly breathing, not breathing at all, and I remember how we cried together. . . . A face that was on its way out and which I now struggle to reconstruct.
. . .
Until it [the paraffin gas] put an end to the indispensable beatings of his small, beloved, heart. (Never 24, 57, 96)

Words such as "carita," and "su pequeño amado corazón" suggest an affectionate nostalgia for the lost child. In addition, the narrator emphasizes the issue of melancholic memory by asking the man if he remembers the child's face. As already noted in this chapter, concrete objects aid in the construction of a nostalgic vision of the past. This is borne out in the woman's reflection on the single photograph she possesses of the child:

Ahora miro la fotografía que guardo entre las hojas del cuaderno. . . . Pequeño, bello, una sutil criatura. . . . Fue el único viaje al mar que hicimos con el niño. . . . Ah, si nos hubiésemos ahogado en esas aguas (*Comentan que nos hundimos entre las aguas, que no dejamos huella alguna*). . . . Una foto, la única, que lo confirma, al niño . . . quiero mostrarte la foto, a la que acudimos en los momentos más intensos de nostalgia. (*Jamás* 111; my emphasis)

> But now I look at the photograph I keep between the pages of the notebook.... Small, beautiful, a delicate thing.... It was the only trip to the sea we took with the boy.... Oh, if we'd drowned in those waters. (*They say that we drowned in the waters, that we left no trace*).... A photo, the only one, confirming him, the boy. I get up with the photo in my hand, I want to show you the photo . . . the picture we go to . . . [in] the most intense moments of nostalgia. (Never 76)

Note that the italics in the passage above evoke the disappeared when the narrator states that they drowned in the water and left no trace at all, since frequently disappeared bodies were dumped into the ocean. This nostalgia for the dead child extends to a general feeling of melancholia regarding the past and the couple's participation in revolutionary cells during and after the Allende government. The description of the various revolutionary cells to which the pair belonged, her role as a copyist and his as secretary in charge of one of the cells, are important for establishing not only the traditional gender roles but also the allegorical connection to Chile. Although Chile is never directly mentioned in the novel, the divisions between members of the cells suggest parallels to their corresponding historical counterparts. Several passages (*Jamás* 31, 50; Never 16–17, 31) articulate these factional differences through references to reformist versus more militant ideals within revolutionary cells, as well as the narrator's partner's alignment with the reformist wing. This divide parallels a similar split that occurred between Chilean revolutionary cell members. According to Liborio Justo, the *Unidad Popular* became polarized between "un ala reformista . . . y un ala radicalizada" ([217] a reformist wing and a radical wing). Although initially the Communist Party in Chile (affiliated with the Soviet Union) had the majority of proletariat members and seemed to be the primary revolutionary force that would lead to the establishment of socialism in Chile, eventually, with what Justo calls "la degeneración del proceso de la Unión Soviética" (the degeneration of the process of the Soviet Union), the mission of the Communist Party would change from extremist to reformist, peacefully leading to socialism. Justo adds:

> No obstante, su alarde [el del partido comunista] de contar con un 75% de la clase obrera, distribuidas en 10,000 células, su preocupación eran los intereses de la pequeña burguesía mientras que al proletariado

se le exigían más sacrificios... el partido socialista se transformó en el organismo político mayoritario... presentándose en general como "más revolucionario." (222)

Despite the display [of the Communist Party] of counting 75% of the working class as members, distributed in 10,000 cells, their concern was the interests of the petit bourgeoisie while they demanded more sacrifices form the proletariat... the Socialist Party transformed into the main political organism... presenting itself in general as "more revolutionary."

The narrator's discussion of the cell divisions is a cue to interpret the text allegorically as a reference to historical events in Chile from the 1970s and beyond. Moreover, the man's tendency to distance himself from the radical left suggests a gravitational pull toward the political center, which at least obliquely decodes the opening scene of the novel, the man and woman abed, as an allegory of the Concertación government era in Chile.

Another allegorical element that seems relatively identifiable in the text is the relationship between the narrator and her clients when she leaves the house to go to work as an aide to the elderly who cannot bathe themselves. During the course of the novel, she travels to several homes to take care of these clients. Since the narrator appears to be dead, these episodes seem like flashbacks to when she was alive and working outside her home. In two of the three episodes, the clients served by the narrator, who are wealthy and can afford such service, meet her efforts with scorn and hostility. For example,

Está enojada y leo en sus ojos una mezcla de terror y de desprecio... Voy rápido con el aceite y sé que se aproxima el momento más difícil entre nosotras.... Me esquiva abiertamente torciendo la cabeza.... Abre los ojos y me mira con un rencor penetrante. (*Jamás* 61–66)

She's angry and I can read a mixture of terror and contempt in her look.... I go quickly with the oil and I know we're approaching the moment that's the trickiest between us.... She openly tries to dodge me, twisting her head. She opens her eyes and looks at me with a spitefulness that is piercing. (Never 41–42)

Similarly, a second client kicks the narrator in the face while she is attempting to bathe him in the shower (*Jamás* 124–29: *Never* 85–86). These two episodes share a hostile attitude on the part of the wealthy clients toward the narrator, whom they regard a servant. This repetition suggests how these episodes allegorize the social hierarchy in Chile at the time of the Pinochet coup. The female client is verbally abusive to the narrator, while the male client physically attacks her. Eltit uses these episodes to re-create Chilean class conflict.

Another episode critics have paid attention to involves a dress that the narrator spies in a shop window. As Olivera-Williams states (51), the dress betokens neoliberalism. For that reason, the narrator battles between her desire to own the dress and her knowledge of the capitalist exploitation it symbolizes:

> De pronto experimenté el impacto ante ese vestido, que . . . ocupó enteramente mi deseo y se apoderó de mi mente . . . detrás de cada una de las vitrinas yacía el fantasma expansivo de una dominación . . . como pude olvidar la frase: "Mediante la explotación del mercado mundial, la burguesía ha dado un carácter cosmopolita a la producción y el consumo de todos los países." (*Jamás* 144)

> And suddenly I experienced the impact of that dress, which . . . occupied my dreams and took control of my mind . . . behind each one of the shop windows lay the expansive ghost of a domination . . . how could I have forgotten the line, the motto . . . "the bourgeoisie has through its exploitation of the world market given a cosmopolitan character to production and consumption in every country." (*Never* 100–02)

The novel includes other neoliberal symbols, such as the calculator and television set, both rejected by the protagonists (*Jamás* 11).

The last relatively clear symbolic element that adds to the allegory of Chilean history is the constant insistence on the cold. Once again, this element, as for Manuel Sendero, hearkens back to the Vallejo poem that speaks of "el frío muerto" and concentrates on human pain and suffering. The constant reference to the cold underscores the pain and suffering of Chileans under the dictatorship and in the postdictatorial era. "El frío" is referred to in *Jamás* on pages 38, 43, 59, 68, 116, 137, 188, 195, and 204; and in *Never* 22, 25, 37, 43, 79, 96, 137, 142, and 151. The contexts, in most cases, deal with cold weather; one deals with exposing the dying son to the cold by shutting the paraffin gas; and another to the "cold process," which refers to the eventual murder of the protagonist in childbirth in one version of her death. The repetition of the cold helps to create an atmosphere of hardship and feelings of sadness.

Finally, the novel presents a series of allegorical elements that are highly indeterminate. These elements have led me to categorize *Jamás* as a weak allegory. The most prominent indeterminate elements are the bed, the wall, the ceiling, and the room. As already noted, the two protagonists share a bed in a room populated by the dead members of their former revolutionary cells. These members are in the room, at the foot of the bed, but not on the bed itself, with the exception of Ximena. The protagonist makes numerous comments about how she and the man prefer to face the wall that "marca un límite" ([95] marks a limit) than face the ceiling. However, there are no textual cues in the novel to explain the meaning or allegorical role of the ceiling and the wall.

The significance of the bed has been extensively commented upon in the literary criticism on the novel. Olivera-Williams analyzes the bed as a ruin that contains fragments of past memories. According to Olivera-Williams: "La cama eltiana impulsa a "La nostalgia reflexiva." . . . La nostalgia reflexiva no intenta restaurar un tiempo pasado, sino que vuelve al mismo desde una perspectiva crítica y con la conciencia de que ese pasado es irrevocable" ([49] The Eltian bed propels toward a "reflexive nostalgia." . . . Reflexive nostalgia does not attempt to restore a past time, but rather to return to it from a critical perspective and with the cognizance that this past is irrevocable). The bed is also the site of death and birth, which Díaz, among others, reads as a tomb that holds the phantoms from the past ("Allegorical Specters" 253). However, if the bed is a site of memory and reflexive nostalgia, or even a tomb that contains the haunting dead, what does the room in which we find the bed symbolize? "La pieza"[the room] is a distinct entity that is referred to repeatedly within the novel. Perhaps the bed is the conscious memory, and the room represents the unconscious? This division is potentially suggested when the narrator states that she only tolerates Ximena's presence on the bed, while her partner would allow all the former cell members to take over their bed (*Jamás 208*; *Never* 153). Perhaps the unconscious elements (the cell members) are trying to enter conscious memory (the bed)? On the other hand, the narrator appears to consciously remember and speak about the dead cell members, which would undermine such a reading. In short, few textual cues guide the reader, other than the presence of the former cell members who attempt to climb on the bed.

In addition to the "reflexive nostalgia" identified by Olivera-Williams, and the melancholia and nostalgia associated with the death of the protagonist's son, several nonallegorical passages add to the feeling of melancholic nostalgia for the lost revolutionary past. The narrator repeatedly speaks of their participation in the revolutionary cells as an attempt to change or form a part of history, suggesting the "reflexive nostalgia" that Olivera discusses or melancholy for a failed cause (*Jamás* 44–45, 80, 135, 139–40; *Never* 26, 53, 94, 97).

Narrative tone (as Phelan explains) depends on the reader's perception of textual cues such as style and the speaker's attitude toward his utterance. The repetition of the word "history" in the utterances mentioned above suggests the narrator's feeling of the importance of her participation in the revolutionary movement and a melancholic nostalgia over its disappearance. The sadness for this lost moment is expressed in words such as "ineludible" and "imperioso compromiso," among others, referring to the importance of their historical role. Just as with the death of her son, the melancholia expressed is not an explicit theme, but must be extracted from the style and word choices of each utterance.

In summary, allegory is employed as the frame that contains and expresses the overall tone of both *La última canción de Manuel Sendero* and *Jamás el fuego nunca*. Both novels focus on a lost utopian dream, but from very different perspectives. In Dorfman's 1982 novel, hope still exists for a socialist or, at least, an egalitarian future. In contrast, Eltit's 2007 novel registers the persistence of the Chilean neoliberal state, rife with inequalities, in which any real reform of the state seems far more remote under a new neoliberal reign. As Enzo Traverso puts it:

> Does the concept of Sattelzeit [saddle time] help us to understand the transformations of the contemporary world? We may suggest that . . . the years from the end of the 1970s to September 11, 2001 witnessed a transition whose result was a radical change of our general landmarks

of our political and intellectual landscape. During this quarter of a century, market and competition—the cornerstones of the neoliberal lexicon—became the "natural" foundations of post-totalitarian societies. . . . The extremities of such Sattelzeit are utopia and memory. . . . On the other hand, the concrete utopias of collective emancipation turned into individualized drives for the inexhaustible consumption of commodities. Dismissing the "warm stream" of collective emancipation, neoliberalism introduced the "cold stream" of economic reason. Thus, utopias are destroyed by their privatization into a reified world. (3–7)

The neoliberal present leads to a nostalgic and melancholic view of the past in *Jamás*. Although neoliberalism exists under the dictatorship, Dorfman is still able to maintain the dream of its disappearance in a postdictatorial future. Eltit, twenty-five years later, cannot do the same, which is why she ends the novel with the following line: Debemos llevarlo [al hijo al hospital], después de todo, ya no tenemos nada que perder" ([*Jamás* 212] We should take him [the son to the hospital], because, after all, we have nothing left to lose [Never 156]). The novel ends on a melancholic note, indicating that nothing can be lost when nothing is left to lose.

Despite the pessimism expressed at the end of Eltit's novel, it is important to emphasize here both Dorfman's notion of myth and nostalgia as a form of recovery to improve in the future: "un recobrarse para algo tal vez major," recovery for something perhaps better, a point he makes in *Imaginación y violencia* (218), and Olivera-Williams's idea of "reflexive nostalgia," which implies the possibility of learning from the past and moving forward, despite feelings of melancholia and nostalgia. Both novels suggest this possibility of learning from the past. Otherwise, simply wallowing in nostalgia and melancholia would represent a contradiction with the Marxist ideology of both novels.

CHAPTER 5

Betrayal and Abjection in Luce Arce's *El infierno*, Arturo Fontaine's *La vida doble*, and Carlos Franz's *El desierto* and *Almuerzo de vampiros*

IN 1993, LUZ ARCE PUBLISHED her controversial memoir titled *El infierno* (Inferno). Arce, who confessed under torture of being an Allende supporter, though later became a DINA functionary,[1] has, in some quarters, been heralded as a victim of the Pinochet regime. In other quarters, however, she has been reviled as a self-serving betrayer of her leftist colleagues for having secured protection from prosecution by testifying before the Truth Commission in Chile.[2] Michael J. Lazzara has studied Arce in two works, his single-authored *Chile in Transition* (2006) and an edited collection, *Luz Arce and Pinochet's Chile* (2011). In the introduction to *Luz*, he refers to the notion of abjection, which Arce employs in her testimony:

> [S]crutinizing Luz Arce's discourse . . . can be illuminating insofar as it confronts us directly with the terrible *abjection* to which certain bodies were subjugated under dictatorship. . . . [I]t raises questions about how the dictatorship unmade revolutionary longings by literally unmaking bodies, turning them into *abject*, depoliticized shells devoid of any sense of futurity. . . . Sometimes she [Arce] appears as a corrupt, hardened criminal of DINA/CNI; at other times she appears as a poor, pathetic, *abject* collaborator. (2–4; my emphases)

Within a few pages, Lazzara employs the terms "abject" or "abjection" to refer both to the tortured victims of the Pinochet government and to Arce herself. According to Rina Arya, "abject" has two similar meanings: "Extremely unpleasant and degrading" and "completely without pride and dignity" (3). Similarly, *Merriam-Webster Online Dictionary* states that abject means: "1) sunk to or existing in a low state or condition; 2) cast down in spirit; showing hopelessness or resignation; 3) expressing or offered in a humble and often ingratiating spirit"; abjection is the substantive. Whether adjective or noun, it has thematic significance in *El infierno*.

Three novels written after Arce's testimony, Carlos Franz's *El desierto* (2005) and *Almuerzo de vampiros* (2007) and Arturo Fontaine's *La vida doble* (2010) also use abjection in comparable ways. I argue here that Fontaine's novel answers Arce's testimony through contradiction. He does that by using Julia Kristeva's psychoanalytic concept of abjection to depict Arce (through the protagonist Lorena) as an abject being for her betrayal. *El desierto* also employs Kristeva's abjection, though in a different manner and sans Arce or her testimony; likewise, *Almuerzo* explores abjection in a novel way through the theme of the double and techniques of the grotesque.

In *Powers of Horror* (1980), Kristeva defines the concept of abjection as a threat from the outside that encroaches upon a person's identity:

> There looms, within abjection, one of those violent, dark, revolts of being, directed against a threat that seems to emanate from an exorbitant outside or inside, ejected beyond the scope of the possible, the tolerable, the thinkable. It lies there, quite close, but it cannot be assimilated. It beseeches, worries, and fascinates desire. . . . Unflaggingly, like an inescapable boomerang, a vortex of summons and repulsion places the one haunted by it literally beside himself. (1)

The self is simultaneously attracted and repelled by the abject, which constitutes an assault on identity.

Kristeva's theory of the abject is quite complex and has been the subject of various analyses. According to Rina Arya in *Abjection and Representation* (2014),

> [a]bjection describes an experience between a subject and a source of abjection. The encounter, the abject source, threatens the subject's sense of self, but it cannot be objectified. . . . [I]t is not a subject or an object but displays features of both. . . . [T]he non-object impresses on the subject's stability, causing the subject to become (so that it is

part of ourselves) that which we have to reject and expel to protect our boundaries. We are unable to rid ourselves of it completely and it continues to haunt our being. (Arya 4)

In addition to Kristeva's citation of bodily fluids and corpses as examples of sources of abjection (*Powers* 3), Arya cites anything that reminds us of our animal origins as a source of abjection (Arya 2).

Two important aspects of Kristeva's theory that make it relevant to the novels at hand are 1.) the relationship between the abject and the mother's body; and 2.) the relationship between the abject and morals. In the first instance, Kristeva states that the original manifestation of the abject is the mother's body, which the infant experiences as abject. Arya indicates that,

> The process of feeding is simultaneously a process of moving towards the breast and suckling and rejecting and withdrawing when satiated. This movement of identification and rejection . . . constitutes the ambivalence that the mother's breast signifies. . . . Abjection is the process by which the infant separates from the mother. The feelings of revulsion and horror and the action of expelling the mother shatter narcissism and result in feelings of insurmountable horror. . . . Making the infant abject is a necessary step for the infant to be able to establish its own subjectivity. (Arya 17)

In the second instance, Kristeva signals that abjection can also be moral: "It is thus not the lack of cleanliness or health that causes abjection but what disturbs identity, system, order. . . . The in-between, the ambiguous, the composite. The traitor, the liar, the criminal with a good conscience, the shameless rapist, the killer who claims he is a savior" (4).

Both *La vida* and *El desierto* illustrate Kristeva's abject through the feelings of their protagonists. *La vida* is, in addition, directly connected to Arce's *El infierno*, as it contains many intertextual references to her testimony. These echoes help to construct a dialogue between the two texts on the figure of the traitor who confesses under torture and is epitomized by Arce. According to Mikhail Bakhtin in *Problems of Dostoevsky's Poetics*, "Two discourses equally and directly oriented toward a referential object within the limits of a single context cannot exist side by side without intersecting dialogically, regardless of whether they confirm, mutually supplement or (conversely) contradict one another" (188–89). If we view texts on the Chilean dictatorshsip as a "single context," the relationship between *La vida* and *El infierno* becomes clear. Yet to comprehend how Fontaine constructs his protagonist as an abject figure suffering feelings of horror, we must first examine how the novelist structures his novel as a response to Arce's testimony.

In *El infierno*, Arce emphasizes three aspects of her story: 1.) its truth value; 2.) her conversion from traitor to a repentant Christian; and 3.) her ability to reclaim her name as a result of her confession. The prologue to the novel, written by her priest, José Luis de Miguel, emphasizes the truth value of Arce's testimony: "¿Cuál es el precio de la verdad? . . . En las páginas que siguen, su autora, Luz Arce, vierte la que ha sido su verdad, la verdad de su experiencia en el infierno durante . . . el periodo dictatorial del general Augusto Pinochet" ([*El infierno* 11]. What is the Price of truth? . . . In the following pages, their author, Luz Arce, pours out what has been her truth, the truth of her infernal experience . . . with the dictatorship of General Augusto Pinochet [Inferno xv]). Fontaine's novel also begins with a reference to the truth in the form of a question that, surely, is no coincidence: "¿Podría yo decirte la verdad? Esa es una pregunta para ti. ¿Me vas a creer o no? A eso solo respondes tú" ([*La vida* 11] Can I tell you the truth? That's a question for you. Are you going to believe me? That's a question only you can answer [La vida 3]). By beginning the novel with a reference to truth, Fontaine establishes an immediate connection to Arce's testimony and the truth of *El infierno*. *La vida* goes on to emphasize that the protagonist is telling her story, not to a journalist who plans to write a factual article, but to a novelist who plans to write a fictional story. In like manner, Alfonso de Toro examines how the novel specifically emphasizes the incommunicability of the feelings and experiences of its protagonist, stating that: "Un tercer gran tema es la 'representabilidad' o 'irrepresentabilidad,' lo decible o indecible en relación a la tortura física y psíquica" ([36] A third great theme is the "representability" or "irrepresentability," the tellable or untellable, in relation to physical and psychological torture). De Toro also notes that intertextuality (including that in Arce's book) helps to transmit and articulate all the central themes of the novel.

A second organizing principle of both *La vida* and *El infierno* is the question of religious belief and conversion. Arce testifies to her redemption through religious conversion: "Conocer a Dios cambió mi vida.... Me hizo reflexionar acerca de quien fui, quien soy y naturalmente eso implicaba asumirlo no solo en la dimensión personal, sino también en la colectiva. La tantas veces infiel, la Luz que se sentía miserable comenzó a poder decir sí al Señor" ([*El infierno* 417] Knowing God changed my life ... made me think about who I was and who I am; it also meant coming to terms not only with myself, but also with my relationships with those around me. The Luz who had been unfaithful so many times, who felt so miserable, started wanting to be able to say yes to the Lord [Inferno 322]). Fontaine sets up his novel in direct contrast, emphasizing that his protagonist does not believe in God or religion. Lorena tells her interviewer that a priest left her a statue of the Virgen of Guadalupe to inspire her to pray and asks: "¿Crees tú que ayude rezar si uno no cree?" ([*La vida* 52–53] Do you think it helps to pray if you're not a believer? [La vida 45]). The protagonist's failure to believe in God is set in direct contrast to Arce's religious conversion by which she seeks forgiveness and justification.

A third key element that structures *La vida* as a response to *El infierno* is the question of identity and name. Luz Arce begins and ends her book by emphasizing her loss and eventual recovery of her name: "Me llamo Luz Arce. Me ha costado mucho recuperar este nombre. Existe sobre mí una suerte de leyenda negra ... elaborada al tenor de una realidad de horror, humillación y violencia" ([*El infierno* 15] My name is Luz Arce. It has been very difficult for me to recover that name. There is kind of a black legend about me ... created out of a horrific, humiliating, and violent reality [Inferno xix]). Similarly, *El infierno* ends with the words "Ahora puedo decir otra vez mi nombre: es Luz, Luz Arce" ([*El infierno* 479] It was important, indispensable to tell myself once more: my name is Luz, Luz Arce [Inferno 372]), suggesting an initial loss of identity through her torture and collaboration with the Pinochet government and its recovery through religion and repentance. In contrast, *La vida* never reveals the real name of its protagonist. She is referred to by various names that reflect her various identities: Lorena (her name when she escapes to Stockholm); Irene (her communist sympathizer name); and la Cubanita (her torturer name). The protagonist tells the novelist who is listening to her story that she lives under a new name with false documentation: "Llámame Lorena. No Irene. Yo quiero ser tu Lorena. Nunca sabrás mi nombre real ([*La vida* 37] Call me Lorena. Not Irene. I want to be Lorena to you. You'll never know my real name [La vida 30]).

Lorena's inability to recover her name and identity are linked to the fact that after betraying her comrades, she is transformed into a Kristevean abject being. Lorena's eventual descent into abjection is, interestingly, prefigured by her rejection of her mother, which recalls Kristeva on the infant's rejection of the mother as abject. When Lorena is a child, her parents divorce. This leads to what she herself describes as a split in her personality (similar to the split caused by the threat of abjection in Kristeva's theory) and to a rejection of her mother because she was unable to stay married to her father:

> Mi imposibilidad de coincidir conmigo misma, ¿cuándo habrá comenzado? La distancia de mí misma que sentí siempre.... Vuelvo entonces forzosamente al desgarro por el divorcio de mis padres, mi brusco desdén por mi madre cuando mi padre se fue. (*La vida* 58)

> My inability to coincide with myself, when did that begin? The distance from myself that I seem to have always felt.... I go back then, inevitably, to the rupture that came from my parents' divorce, my harsh disdain for my mother after my father left. (La vida 49)

Lorena blames her mother for her parents' divorce even though the father is the one who is unfaithful. Her mother is abject, the object of disdain, because she was unable to keep her father happy. This causes a rift between Lorena and her mother, if not a crack in Lorena's identity, which anticipates her eventual abjection later on in the novel.

In contrast to Arce's testimony in which she portrays herself as a victim forced to collaborate, Fontaine portrays Lorena as a woman who goes far beyond mere collaboration. In fact, she vehemently comes to hate her former comrades and even takes an active role in torturing them. On several occasions, moreover, she freely and willingly offers information that compromises her former colleagues just to gain the affection and approbation of the military men with whom she is having affairs. In direct opposition to Arce's assertions that "Manuel Contreras ordenó que yo pasara a la categoría de empleado civil femenino a la de civil con categoría de oficial... en esos días... las tres sentíamos que la alternativa era ser funcionaria o morir" ([*El infierno* 197] When Manuel Contreras promoted me... from the category of female civilian employee to a civilian employee with the status of officer... [i]n those days I think... our only alternative was to be employees or die [Inferno 144]), Lorena is portrayed as having *chosen* to give information and to have reveled in the torture of others. The two most conspicuous cases are, first, when Lorena is anxious to please her lover, Flaco Artaza, a top agent at DINA. She betrays to him that El Hueso, one of head communist organizers, was secretly a smoker. This detail will allow the military to track him down more easily. In the second case, Lorena turns against her friend Rafa, who was initially the person who befriended her and brought her into Allende's camp. Although once on the mission to trap Rafa, she has second thoughts, but it is too late; her former friend is captured.

In contrast, and in answer to Luce Arce's portrayal of herself as a repentant victim, Lorena is portrayed as an individual who allows the abject to take control of her identity. She is the traitor Kristeva speaks of, the individual who gives herself over to complete moral turpitude. Her portrayal as abject also relies on a variety of techniques. The first is the description of her character as transformed into an animal when tortured:

> El amo logrará ir doblegándome como si llegase a ser un animalito suyo.
> Eres una cucaracha a la que cualquiera tiene derecho a reventar de un pistón.
> Te han vaciado. Y sin embargo, sobrevives con la tenacidad inútil del insecto aplastado que sigue moviendo sus patitas.
> La mordaza que se roba mis quejidos de animal, de chancho.
> Soy un animal que declina aceleradamente reducido a deseos mínimos.
> (*La vida* 15, 16, 17, 27, 43)

> The master would slowly bend me to his will as though I were an animal that belonged to him.
> You become a cockroach that everyone has the right to trample and crush. They have emptied you. And still you survive, with the useless tenacity of a crushed insect still waving its legs.
> The gag that steals my animal cries, my piglike squeals.
> I'm an animal reduced to basic desires. (La vida 7, 8, 19, 36)

Lorena describes what Lazzara referred to as the "unmaking of bodies," (and the unmaking of revolutionary identity), which is the first step in Lorena's process of abjection.

The second step signaling her path to total degradation are her sexual proclivities once she becomes a traitor, which are frequently described as base and animalistic. There are several highly detailed sexual encounters that emphasize Lorena's participation on a purely animalistic level: when she attempts to goad a prisoner into having sex with her; when she has sex mandated by Flaco Artaza with him and two of his colleagues, and when she has sex with two other women.

In the first episode, Lorena describes the sex she imagines with the prisoner as cannibalistic, that she would eat his flesh as animals do in preying on other animals:

> Me imaginé la carne bajo la piel y pensé que debía ser rico comérsela. En otros tiempos, cuando éramos antropófagos, me habría comido esa carne a mordiscos.... Escúpeme, por favor, méame la cara. Y él no me hizo nada. Fóllame, le dije.... Tienes miedo a que yo te guste y se te vaya a la mierda tu celo revolucionario, le dije. (*La vida* 170–73).

> I imagined the meat under the skin and I thought it must be delicious to eat. Other times, when we were cannibals, I would have devoured that meat by the mouthful.... "Spit on me, please, piss on my face." And he did nothing to me.... "Fuck me," I told him.... "You're afraid you'll like it and your revolutionary zeal will all go to shit," I told him. (La vida 166–68)

Similarly, Lorena has a sexual encounter with Flaco Artaza and two of his colleagues with whom he orders her to have sex. The foursome is described in animalistic terms. Indeed, one of the three men is named Conejo (Rabbit) who, we are told, approaches Lorena with:

> Dientes de *conejo* detrás de una sonrisa que tiembla. Rozo sus pechos con mis pezones ... y lenta, muy lentamente le voy bajando el cierre.... Miro al Flaco, a Jerónimo, sus ojos afiebrados, su boca entreabierta, Los tengo me dijo.... Saco la lengua, la estiro, la siento vibrar en el aire como *víbora*.... Y entonces, obedeciendo al Flaco, que me lo ordena ... me tiendo, lánguida , en el sofá de felpa negra.... Y él me lo ordena y me someto, que sí. que lo haga ... y yo quiero ... complacerlo hasta

> que no quede nada de mi salvo *un borrón*. . . . Me sometí y me encontré haciéndolo y, te lo juro, me gustó. (*La vida* 164; my emphases)

> Rabbit teeth behind a trembling smile. I brush his chest with my nipples . . . and slowly, very slowly, I lower his zipper. . . . I look at Flaco, at Jerónimo, his feverish eyes, his half-open mouth. "I have them," I think to myself. I put out my tongue, stretch it out, I feel it vibrate in the air like a viper's. . . . And then, obeying Flaco, who orders me . . . I lie down, languid, on the black velvet sofa. . . . And he gives me orders and I submit; "Yes, let him do it," Flaco murmurs . . . and I want to obey him and please him and them all until there's nothing left of me, just a stain. . . . I cross an invisible barrier and I do it. . . . [I]n the end its wonderful. (La vida 159)

Lorena emphasizes her submissive, degraded position throughout the encounter. She repeats several times that she "obeys" or "submits" to Flaco's orders, but that she enjoys it. One participant is described as a rabbit and Lorena's tongue as a snake, the whole an exercise in abject degradation. Despite her insistence of titillating pleasure, we are told that the experience destroys her identity; left behind is "un borrón" (a stain).

Finally, under the influence of amphetamines, Lorena has sex with two other women, an encounter that she also describes as bestial:

> *Las tres abrazándonos . . . un amor lento. . . . Yo podía . . . aceptarlo todo, desearlo todo y la piel de mi alma de bestia omnívora que suprimimos se fascinaba, se arrojaba al vértigo. . . . somos animales carnívoros mal disfrazados y sin inocencia. . . . El infierno es un espejo del que no puedes apartar la vista.* (*La vida* 206)

> The three of us . . . intertwined. . . . Until the kisses returned and a slow loving . . . [e]nergized by amphetamines. . . . I could endure all, embrace all, accept all, desire all, and the skin of my soul, of the omnivorous beast that we usually suppress, was captivated and threw itself headlong into the frenzy. . . . Because we are disguised barbarians. . . . Hell is a mirror that we can't look away from. (La vida 202)

In describing her ecstasy, Lorena alludes to the abject when she speaks of the "omnivorous beast that we usually suppress." At another level of exegesis, her reference to hell also uncovers the title of Arce's book (*infierno*) and part of its contents, namely, her morally abject role in torturing others.

Another way in which *La vida* represents Lorena as morally abject is through her illness, as she is dying of cancer. Susan Sontag (*Illness as Metaphor* [1990]) says that cancer has a long history of being an abject illness:

> Punitive notions of disease have a long history.... Ostensibly, the illness is the culprit. But it is also the cancer patient who is made culpable... and conventions of treating cancer as no mere disease but a demonic envoy make cancer not just a lethal disease but a shameful one.... In the last two centuries, the diseases most often used as metaphors for evil were syphilis, TB, and cancer.... Cancer was never viewed other than a scourge; it was, metaphorically, the barbarian within.... In cancer, non-intelligent ("primitive," "embryonic," "atavistic") cells are multiplying, and you are being replaced by the non-you. Immunologists class the body's cancer cells as "nonself." (57–67)

Sontag's characterization of cancer bears upon how Lorena's illness can be seen as a manifestation of abjection and moral culpability. That is, her cancer cells invade the individual and make the self a "nonself," which recalls Kristeva's description of how the abject attempts to invade and impinge upon the self and one's identity.

A final sign of Lorena's abject status is in her relationship with Roberto. Once in Stockholm, she finds love with him yet she never seems comfortable in her own skin because in constantly testing his love, she silently discloses how she feels so unworthy and abject that she cannot fathom being loved. For example, one night she deliberately spills water on Roberto's side of the bed so that he must sleep on the sofa. She does this because she considers herself an abject traitor who is undeserving of affection. After repeated episodes like this, she succeeds in alienating Roberto so completely that he finally leaves her (*La vida* 254; La vida 251–52). Lorena thus drives Roberto away because she recognizes her own abjection as an unloveable being. She reflects that others went through the same torture she suffered but did not become traitors.

Unlike them, however, she drinks "el cáliz de mi propia abyección" (from the chalice of my own abjection) and has survived at the cost of becoming a worm, "un gusano" (*La vida* 257–58; La vida 253–55).

Fontaine's emphasis on Lorena's abjection and horror over what she has done constitutes a direct answer to Arce's attempts at self-justification in *El infierno*. Lorena indicates that she is not able to ask for forgiveness and is, in that respect, unlike Arce, whose Christian repentance invites forgiveness. Lorena states: "Me pregunto por qué estoy aquí.... ¿Estoy tratando de ser perdonada? ¿Y quién podría perdonarme?... lo que hice no tiene justificación.... ¿Se pide perdón, entonces por lo injustificable?... Estaría pidiendo un regalo. Porque el perdón es eso, un regalo" ([*La vida* 296] I wonder why I am there ... am I hoping for forgiveness? And who could forgive me?.... [T]here's no justification for what I did. Can one ask for forgiveness, then, for the unjustifiable?... It would be asking for a gift. Because that's what forgiveness is: a gift [La vida 294]). Various critics have noted this connection between *La vida* and *El infierno*. For example, Viviana Plotnik emphasizes how Lorena stands in direct contrast to Arce because she never repents for what she did, which "podría interpretarse como una critica autorial a Arce," given that Arce "enuncia su discurso como una confesión cristiana" (could be interpreted as an authorial criticism of Arce [since] she enunciates her discourse like a Christian confession [89]). Similarly, Ksenija Bilbija points out the parallels between testimony in the novel and Arce's testimony: "Mientras que las historias de Arce y Lorena coinciden en muchos puntos, el personaje de Fontaine también contiene algunos de los caracteres que Arce ... siempre negó pero que sus críticos no han dejado de resaltar ... el interrogatorio y la tortura de excompañeras" (While the stories of Arce and Lorena coincide on many points, Fontaine's character contains some of the characteristics that Arce always denied but that her critics have not stopped underscoring ... the interrogation and torture of former comrades [302]). However, none of the previous work on *La vida* illustrates how abjection is important in connecting the novel to Arce's text.

Many subtle connections between *La vida* and *El infierno* reinforce how Fontaine constructs his novel by contradicting Arce's work. These connections include a reference to Príncipe de Gales (the code name of the communist leader El Hueso in *La vida*; in Arce's testimony, it is the street on which Manuel Contreras lived). Similarly, the parallels between el Flaco Artaza in V*ida* and

Arce's lover Rolf Wenderoth are too many not to register, particularly how each participated in the work of Chile's Truth Commission. Nor are the allusions to Dante's *Inferno* by happenstance, as they target Arce's *El infierno*. The more important point is that such intertextuality creates a dialogue between both novels.

Abjection is also the central theme of another important novel based on the Pinochet dictatorship, Carlo Franz's *El desierto* (2005). The condemnation of the political prisoners in Pampa Hundida in this novel is part of the famous Caravan of Death, the army death squad that flew to different locations to condemn prisoners between September–October 1973, thus constituting another important Chilean memory knot. The protagonist Laura Larco is the judge in the town of Pampa Hundida during Allende's government. She becomes a victim of the Pinochet dictatorship when she challenges the local military authorities who have set up a concentration camp for political prisoners in the town. Laura agrees to hide an escaped prisoner but reveals his whereabouts under duress when Major Cáceres tortures and rapes her. Laura then enters into a "pact" with Cáceres whereby he promises to free a prisoner each time she submits to him sexually. Her relationship with Cáceres, one of submission and humiliation, makes her feel abject, even though she rationalizes it as a way of achieving justice for the prisoners. Only later does she learn that Cáceres has lied to her—he has freed no one. Laura, pregnant and suffering from Stockholm syndrome, returns repeatedly before eventually running away and beginning a new life in Germany with her daughter. The novel alternates chapters of third-person narration[3] with the first-person narration of Laura in a letter to her daughter, the crux of which answers the question of where she was and what she did during the dictatorship.

El desierto develops the concept of abjection in various ways: (1) through Laura's rejection of her mother as abject; (2) through parallels established between Laura and Cáceres's horse; (3) through Laura's explicit comments that show her view of herself as a traitor to justice; and (4) through the philosophical and legalistic dichotomy that the novel establishes between Apollonian and Dionysian principles.

In an interesting parallel with the character Lorena in *La vida*, *El desierto*'s Laura also rejects her mother in Kristevean fashion. We are told that her mother left when she was a baby and that her father never spoke about the mother. One day, when Laura is fourteen, she finds her mother's papers and belongings and manages to reconstruct her mother's story as that of a passionate actress trapped in an unhappy marriage with her father. From that day on, Laura becomes unhappy and rejects her mother, stressing how she hates her for having abandoned her and choosing to study law because it was the furthest thing from "esa escuela de pasiones que es el teatro" ([*El desierto* 106–08] that school of passions which is the theater [*Absent* 83–85]). Laura rejects her mother's passion and emotion associated with the theater as something undesirable, something abject. Laura will, perforce, spend a good part of her life valuing the rational and objective over of emotions and feelings, which she views as abject. Moreover, she sees the divorce of her parents and early rejection of her mother as the ultimate source of her later state of abjection: "*¿Qué era eso que coceaba y bufaba en mi interior, Claudia? De donde me venía eso que... he llamado, por ahora, una 'culpabilidad abyecta'... La respuesta... debería ir a buscarla muy lejos en mi memoria, a mi infancia*" ([*El desierto* 102] *What was that something kicking and snorting inside me, Claudia? Where had it come from, this thing that,... I have until now called an "abject guilt"*[?]... [*F*]*or that part of my reply... I would have to look somewhere deep in my memory, in my childhood* [*Absent* 80]).

The second way in which Franz establishes a connection between Laura and abjection is through the parallels developed between Laura and Cáceres's horse. We have already seen how association with animals and animal behavior constitutes a form of abjection in Kristeva's theory. Thus, the parallels between Laura and the horse emphasize the abjection in which she is submersed. When Laura first sees Cáceres's horse, it is inside a small metal trailer, kicking and spitting to get out. Laura emphasizes how Cáceres simultaneously threatens and comforts his horse, which is thirsty and mired in feces because of his confinement:

> Costaba imaginar al animal... que venía en esa caja de metal plateado, no le hubieran dado agua ni le habían limpiado el habitáculo—que hedía a diez metros a la redonda.... El mayor consolaba a su caballo... con el chasquido de la lengua y al mismo tiempo... lo amenaza con el restallido de la fusta. (*El desierto* 50–51)

Betrayal and Abjection

> It was also difficult to imagine that the animal ... so recently arrived inside that silvered metal box had not been given water nor had its quarters cleaned—for the stench was felt for ten yards around. ... The Major comforted his horse ... with the click of his tongue and at the same time ... he threatened it with the crack of the riding crop. (Absent 39)

Laura first compares herself to the horse when she is angry over the government's abuse of the free press and wishes to take up the issue with Cáceres. She states "(algo bufaba y pateaba en mí como el caballo queriendo ir tras su amo)" ([Franz, *El desierto* 53] (something was snorting and kicking inside me, like the horse wanting to follow after its master) [Absent 41]). This connection is repeated several times: "empecé a saberlo desde el amanecer del golpe militar, cuando presentí que, desde ese momento, algo inexpresado y abyecto me acusaría ... presentí al animal encerrado en el remolque plateado, la bestia que pateaba y bufaba ... como mi memoria u otra cosa dentro de mí misma" ([*El desierto* 109] I started to become aware of it on the morning of the military coup when I had the feeling that from that moment on, something unexpressed and abject would call me to account .... I had a presentiment of the animal locked inside the silver-plated trailer, that beast which was kicking and snorting and whinnying ... like my memory—to get out [Absent 86]). However, Laura's connection to the horse goes far beyond these initial comments. Her relationship with Cáceres, replete with torture and the "reward" of sex, parallels the actions of punishing with the whip and then calming the horse with comforting noises:

> *Y yo, desesperada. ¿Por qué? ... Para que me lo agradezcas cuando me detenga. Y luego volvió a azotarme ... habíamos creado entre los dos algo vivo ... mi abyecto agradecimiento de que el dolor se hubiera interrumpido y la esperanza animal de que esa magnanimidad durara ... yo creí oír el caballo que relinchaba desde su establo (o tal vez había sido yo). ... En algún momento abrí los ojos y me encontré montada sobre él. ... Y creí que cabalgaba de noche a golpe tendida en la oscuridad ... y me pareció oír que el purasangre relinchaba desde su establo. (El desierto 264–67)*

> *I was desperate. "But why?"...*
> *"So you'll thank me for it when I stop."*
> *And then he hit me some more... we had created something...*
> *In my abject "gratitude" for the interruption of the pain together with the animal hope that such magnanimity would last...*
> *I thought I could hear the horse neighing from the stable...*
> *At a certain point I opened my eyes and found myself mounted on top of him.... and I thought I was riding through the night at full gallop ... and it seemed to me I was hearing the thoroughbred from its stable.* (Absent 211–13)

This likening of Laura to the horse underscores the animalistic and abject nature of her relationship with Cáceres.

The third way Laura portrays abjection is in her failure as a judge to enact justice in Pampa Hundida. She suffers from the guilt she feels for her inadequacy in standing up to the regime as a form of horrifying abjection, which she describes as *"una corazonada abyecta, un presentimiento de abyección (abyección, que viene de humildad)* ([*El desierto* 30] I was sanctioning an abject impulse, a premonition of the abjectness (abjectness, which comes from being put to shame [Absent 22]).

During the military trials that condemn numerous prisoners to death, Laura is present and attempts to devise an argument to contest the unfair proceedings on legal grounds. Just when she thinks she has found the right words, the trials end, and she has failed to speak. This inability to stand up for what is right renders Laura so abject that she compares herself to a rat:

> *Cuando por fin creo haber hallado los argumentos... el mazo cae... Las sentencias de muerte son dictadas... y entonces... cometo el acto... me siento... sentarse cuando había de mantenerse de pie... puro miedo... un miedo que corría a esconderse como una rata en el agujero de mi razón, en el escondite de mis argumentos legales.* (*El desierto* 151)

When I believe I've finally found the arguments for intervening... the gavel falls.... The sentences of death are read.... At that point... I do it. . . . I sit back down. . . . Pure fear. . . . A fear that ran to hide like a rat in a hole, the hiding place of my legal arguments. (Absent 120–21)

The military represents what is abject and threatening to the identity of the self; for Laura, the military men evoke "un cortejo, un desfile de suplicantes coronados de vides . . . una corte de bacanal y de los desaforados ministros de su culto danzando y devorando carne cruda" ([*El desierto* 240] a procession, a parade of suppliants crowned with vines, writhing in a Bacchanalian orgy, and the terrifying ministers of his cult dancing and gnawing on raw meat [*Absent* 191]). The representation of the military men as abject derives from their association with the animal behavior of eating raw meat. This description also introduces the fourth and final motif of abjection: that of acting according to Apollonian or Dionysian principles.

According to *Oxford Online Dictionary*, Dionysian refers to "the sensual, spontaneous, and emotional aspects of human nature," while Apollonian is defined as "the rational, ordered, self-disciplined aspects of human nature." When Laura was in law school, her professor and mentor, Professor Velasco, taught the students to act according to Apollonian principles, which Laura did during the early years of her career. Once she moved to Germany, she left the law profession and became a philosophy professor. In this capacity, she wrote a celebrated book titled *Moira*, in which she argues that "Ante el poder sin fondo de Dionisio . . . solo quedaba reconocer y practicar una justicia de lo posible . . . era terrible pactar y era necesario pactar con lo terrible" ([*El desierto* 281–82] "Faced with the boundless power of Dionysus . . . the only thing left is to recognize and practice a justice of the possible. . . it was terrible to make a pact and it was necessary to make a pact with that which was terrible" [*Absent* 224]).[4] In other words, the fate of justice (Moira, from moirai, the three fates), rests not simply on rational principles but must take into account the factor of human desire and emotion, which frequently controvert justice: "No es posible hacer justicia sin tener poder y una vez que se tiene poder, éste tiende naturalmente a la injusticia" ([*El desierto* 378] it is not possible to have justice without having power, and once this power is exercised it tends naturally toward the unjust [*Absent* 303]). Laura's theory moves from an idealistic foundation in Apollonian justice to a more practical Dionysian-influenced concept of justice.

The constant tension of the Apollonian and Dionysian suffuses the novel and, especially, its theme of abjection. During Velasco's course, he refers to the Dionysian students as "instintivos como animales, eran un grupo dionisíaco, una manada trágica olfateando en busca de fiestas" ([*El desierto* 229] you were as instinctive as animals, a Dionysian group, a tragic herd sniffing out every party [Absent 181]). Those same students, once they become Apollonian and use reason as their guide, are welcomed into "la edad adulta" (*El desierto* 229; adulthood). Military personnel, by contrast, align themselves with Dionysus, as they only follow their pleasure and their passion.

The idea of compromise between of Dionysus and Apollo, which is enacted by the Concertación governments (the center/left coalition that negotiated the return to democracy through pacts with members of the right) is not, however, seen as something positive in the novel. Velasco, a Concertación government minister, is a symbol of the flaws underlying the pacts negotiated between the new government and former members of the military dictatorship. Once a proponent of Apollonian reason, Velasco tries to obscure justice and maintain the status quo as both serve his own self-interest, principally his grip on official power and station. He bribes the young lawyer Martínez Roth with a promotion to dissuade him from pursuing a court case that would subject the town of Pampa Hundida to prosecution for using a fake image of the town's patron saint, who had been burned in a fire. Martínez Roth planned to use this case as leverage to get the townspeople to testify to the existence of prisoners who had been disappeared by the military. The novel's somewhat ambiguous ending, however, suggests the possibility that perhaps the Dionysian principle can be employed to enact justice. The pieces fall in place at the end of the novel when Laura has her ex-husband announce on his radio program a new sighting of the patron saint at the very site of the former concentration camp, the one where Major Cáceres now resides. This occurs during the annual pilgrimage to Pampa Hundida. The pilgrims all rush to the site as Major Cáceres disappears in the crowd. However, it is unclear whether he is trampled by the group (a form of Dionysian justice, since he is finally punished for his crimes through an impassioned act by the crowd) or whether he just disappears during the hubbub, lost among the celebrating crowd: "El Dr. Ordóñez habla de un cuerpo atropellado y luego medio devorado por animales . . . el cuerpo no puede ser identificado con seguridad. . . . Hay por supuesto otra versión . . . se confundió con el pueblo festejante" (*El desierto* 464–68] Dr. Ordóñez describes a body outraged and then abused and partially eaten by animals. . . . [T]he body cannot even be identified with certainty. . . . There is of course another version . . . he disappeared into the celebrating mob of people [Absent 371–72]). The idea of the masses trampling Cáceres like a herd of wild animals clearly aligns with the idea of the animalistic nature of the abject. Yet here Laura has instigated this act as a potential punishment for the horrific acts committed by Cáceres. Thus, Dionysian principles serve Apollonian justice.

Although abjection is a central theme in *La vida* and *El desierto*, the abjection of each protagonist and their ultimate portrayal differs greatly. While Lorena represents an unrepentant traitor who chooses and wallows in abject behaviors, from torture to orgiastic sex, Laura is a highly intellectual and civilized individual who has been swept up in a wave of abjection caused by the military dictatorship. Laura eventually breaks free from her abject relationship with Cáceres and works on behalf of societal justice, despite her recognition of the Dionysian principle as operative in society.

Carlos Franz's second novel on abjection, *Almuerzo de vampiros*, also presents an ambiguous character through the figure of the narrator's teacher. When the narrator was fifteen, during the Allende government, he had a language and humanities teacher who seemingly represented an uplifting figure who taught his students correct language, classic literature, and high-minded ideals. The narrator was even chosen to participate in a special group organized by the teacher that would meet on Tuesdays to read and discuss literature, politics, and philosophy. The narrator, an orphan, loved and admired the teacher, but after the coup, the teacher disappeared, rumored to have been tortured and murdered by the government. But when, toward the end of the novel, the narrator professes to hate that teacher, readers learn that under torture he had betrayed his students by revealing the names of those in the special group. All, with the exception of the narrator (whose uncle may have had connections that saved him), were expelled from the school. Some even met worse fates, such as exile and disappearance.

The narration in *Almuerzo* occurs thirty years after the military coup. The narrator left Chile a few years after the dictatorship began and, as he tells his story, lives outside the country, even though democracy has returned at home. He comes to visit Chile once a year and, as the novel opens, is having lunch with his friend, who has remained in Chile. They eat at Le Flaubert, an elegant restaurant, and he narrates his tale from "la dichosa terraza del presente" ([47] the fortunate terrace of the present).[5] He does not refer to his friend by name, calling him, instead, Zósima, a character from *The Brothers Karamazov*. During the luncheon, Zósima claims that he saw a figure wandering around Santiago, who looked a lot like their teacher from the past. Zósima says to the narrator: "Si yo fuera escritor ... inventaría una historia a partir de ahí" ([25] If I were a writer ... I would invent a story with that as my departure point). This comment is immediately followed by the beginning of the narrator's account of his experience as a night-shift taxi driver during the dictatorship at a point when he met the "double" of their high-school teacher. The positioning of his narration about the teacher's double suggests the possibility that the entire episode is the narrator's invention, and he is just writing a story. However, whether a real or invented story, the tale of his teacher's double is the central axis of the novel.

Søren Landkildehus has contended that the one character is not the double of the other, but rather that a pair of doubles are two parts of the same whole. Within this framework, he distinguishes between an outward and inward (what he terms experiential) double.

> In the case of the former [outward double], features of similarity are largely related to physical appearances. In the case of the latter [inward double], features are more subtly relational.... When we speak of the inward double, what we need to look for is a shared interiority, as for example in moral/spiritual values and belief systems.... On a lesser scale, however, the outward double can also be detected on the level of "semblance' as in the case of family resemblance. This variety of similitude is what I term "symmetrical exteriority" ... [which] is a weaker outer resemblance that provides multiple means of distinguishing one from the other. Such symmetrical exteriority is sometimes used to great effect by writers to contemplate on the intertwined destinies of different characters, as well as the choices made in life that *will inevitably fuse individuals into an organic whole or expose their divergent paths*. (67–68; my emphasis)

Betrayal and Abjection 147

In other words, doubles can share both outward and inward characteristics, or they can be similar on the outside but different on the inside (or vice versa). I underscored Landkildehus's emphasis on the use of the double to signal organic wholes or divergent paths in life, since this is one of the essential features regarding the pair of doubles, to whom I will refer as "el profesor" (Víctor Polli) and "el maestrito" (Víctor Jiménez-Polli) in *Almuerzo*.

When the unnamed narrator sees el maestrito (the double of the teacher Víctor Polli) for the first time at the Oliver bar, he describes him thus:

> Este maestrito . . . imita . . . a aquel profesor de lengua y literatura que tuvimos (si el profesor hubiera sido un Cantinflas afectado por una severa coprolalia). . . . Pero se parece a él, a Polli, oído por el revés, en reversa. . . . "Si me fuera permitido expresar todo lo que siento, tendría que reconocer que me duele. Que experimento una inesperada lástima, una piedad, que no puedo conciliar con mi ira hacia el profesor original. Ni con mi desprecio hacia este doble de pacotilla. ¿Es piedad por este monigote que lo imita? ¿O es lástima indirecta por el profesor imitado? Y en ese caso, ¿para quién es la ira? ¿para esta caricatura grotesca o para el original, como lo creí siempre? (66–67)

> This teacher . . . imitates . . . that professor of language and literature whom we had (if the professor had been a Cantinflas affected by severe coprolalia). . . . But he looks like him, Polli, heard backwards, in reverse. . . . "If I were allowed to express everything I felt, I would have to recognize that it hurts me. That I experience an unexpected pity, a compassion that I cannot reconcile with my anger toward the original teacher. Nor with my scorn for this trashy double. Is it compassion for this puppet that imitates him? Or is it indirect pity for the imitated teacher? And in this case, for whom is the anger? For this grotesque caricature or for the original, as I always thought?

Although the narrator states that he laughed at the "maestrito's" dirty language and crude jokes, he indicates his scorn for this "trashy double" and "grotesque caricature" of his intellectual teacher. As I show below, the "maestrito" is an abject version of "el profesor," who inspires disgust and repulsion in the narrator. Both el maestrito and Víctor Polli build their worlds around words, but their paths diverge in opposite directions: el maestrito employs dirty language for cheap comic effects, while Polli teaches high-level vocabulary and literature to his students.

After the narrator meets el maestrito in the Oliver bar, he becomes involved with a group of individuals who inhabit the Santiago "underworld" of bars and whorehouses during the curfew imposed by the dictatorship, which prohibited anyone from being outside after hours. The leader of the group is a lawyer named Lucio, who invites the narrator to help him write the screenplay for a film titled "La gran talla de Chile" (Chile's Big Joke). The narrator's assignment is to write down the "maestrito's" jokes, but he helps Lucio in other endeavors as well. The job of the maestrito (Victor Jiménez-Polli), then, as authorized by the dictatorship, is to repossess goods from the houses of poor people during curfew hours. The narrator, it turns out, aids Victor-Jiménez-Polli in this unscrupulous task, which contributes to maestrito's picture as the degraded version of the "profesor." That he is referred to as "el maestrito" is in itself debasing, as Spanish-speakers use the diminutive to belittle and diminish someone. However, the diminutive is also a sign of affection, thus rendering the narrator's attitude toward el maestrito ambiguous.

The narrator's own description of el maestrito applies the term "grotesque" to this figure. According to the *Oxford Advanced American Dictionary*, grotesque means: "strange in a way that is unpleasant or offensive" or "extremely ugly in a strange way that is often frightening or amusing." Many critics have studied the grotesque as an art form (both in literature and the plastic arts), the most famous of whom is Mikhail Bakhtin in his landmark study *Rabelais and His World* (1968). He observes,

> [e]xaggeration, hyperbolism, excessiveness are generally considered fundamental attributes of the grotesque style.... The exaggeration of the inappropriate to incredible and monstrous dimensions is ... the basic nature of the grotesque. Therefore, the grotesque is always satire. (302–06)
>
> ...
>
> Finally, debasement is the fundamental artistic principle of grotesque realism; all that is sacred and exalted is rethought on the level of

> material bodily stratum or else combined and mixed with these images. We spoke of the grotesque swing, which brings together heaven and earth. But the accent is placed not on the upward movement but on the descent. (370)

Bakhtin emphasizes that the grotesque is an ambivalent art form that writers use to create rebirth and regeneration. Geoffrey Harpham's definition of the grotesque confirms Bakhtin's grotesque as an ambivalent art form: "The grotesque is always a civil war of attraction/repulsion.... Most grotesques are marked by such an affinity/antagonism, by the co-presence of the normative ... "high" or "ideal" and the abnormal, unformed, degenerate, low or material" (11). Harpham likens the grotesque to a paradox: "like the grotesque, paradox is a sphinx who dies once its riddle is solved" (23).

Finally, Bakhtin's analysis also coincides with Frances Connelly's categorization of the subversive grotesque, which is carnivalesque. Connelly defines three different types of grotesque in Western plastic arts:

> Accordingly, this history of the grotesque is organized into chapters on improvisation, subversion, trauma, and revelation, and considers significant historical developments within these. This approach emphasizes that the grotesque is an action.... It also demonstrates that, although the grotesque courts ambiguity and flux, it is remarkably consistent in its operations, especially in its intermixture of high and low. The improvisational, witty grotesque interrogates the forms and conventions of visual and literary representation, testing the limits of art. The subversive grotesque puts social roles and hierarchies, as well as cultural conventions into play, challenging the limits of propriety. And most unsettling by far, the traumatic grotesque threatens the limits of our identity, rupturing the boundaries between self and oblivion through the monstrous, the uncanny, or the abject. (14)

Connelly's second category, the subversive grotesque, corresponds to Bakhtin's notion of the carnivalesque. She also shares Bakhtin's emphasis on the positive aspects of the grotesque, indicating that grotesque art often has "revelatory powers." The revelatory grotesque "does not comprise a strand in itself, but the extreme limits of existing ones, pushed to the breaking point in an effort to express a profound truth" (149). This "noble grotesque" is from John Ruskin's classification, which Connelly applies exclusively to plastic arts. However, as I argue below, in *Almuerzo*, Franz uses the grotesque "maestrito" and his underworld not only to criticize the dictatorship that makes people abject but also to illustrate a process of regeneration through Victor Polli's process of abjection.

Throughout the novel and his encounters with el maestrito, the narrator describes this character in abject terms and reacts to him with disgust:

> Unos zapatos que sugieren irresistiblemente la herencia de un difunto más grande. Y que jamás habría usado el pretencioso maestro de lengua que me hizo clases. Quien tampoco se habría dejado ese bigotillo irregular, caído mostacho con un ala más larga que . . . parece destinada a cubrir una cicatriz o hendidura en la mejilla izquierda. . . . Honestamente, profesor, si es que ese fuera Ud., daría la impresión de haber caído muy abajo. . . . Sin embargo . . . Cuando le cierro el paso creo reconocer . . . la corbata de pajarita amarilla. (32–33)

> Shoes that overwhelmingly suggest an inheritance from a larger dead person. And which the pretentious language teacher who taught me classes would never have used. Who also would not have grown that uneven moustache, a fallen moustache with one side longer than the other . . . it seems designed to hide a scar or fissure on the left cheek. . . . Honestly, teacher, if this were you, you would give the impression of having fallen very low. . . . However, . . . [w]hen I block his way, I think I recognize his canary yellow tie.

El maestrito is made further abject by his use of colloquial language for the genitals. The narrator tells us that el maestrito "suelta las groserías más gruesas, los garabatos malolientes, las palabrotas más sucias" ([55] Lets fly the thickest curse words, the smelliest scrawls, the dirtiest swear words). He also tells us the following joke is typical of the sort that el maestrito would tell: "Sabís por qué a los hombres inteligentes nos gusta casarnos con enanas de cabeza plana . . . Porque así tenemos donde apoyar el vaso de whisky mientras nos están chupando el pico. Y estalla en una carcajada" ([91] Do you know why intelligent men like to marry dwarves with flat heads . . . Because that way we have a place to rest a glass of whiskey while they are sucking our cocks. And he explodes in laughter).

Bakhtin emphasizes that the grotesque focuses on bodily fluids and functions, genitals, and orifices, among which he particularly singles out the gaping mouth. It leads, he remarks, "to the lower stratum . . . the bodily underworld," where

> [t]he gaping mouth is related to the image of swallowing, this most ancient symbol of death and destruction. . . . The exaggeration of the mouth is the fundamental traditional method of rendering external comic features, as pictured by comic masks. (325)

It is interesting that el maestrito also corresponds to this physical feature. The scar on his cheek lifts his mouth into what the narrator describes as an "eternal smile," which for mindful readers recalls Bakhtin's gaping mouth:

> La brocha larga del bigote disparejo y teñido ha quedado un poco alzada, mostrando una cicatriz de unos cuatro o cinco centímetros que sube desde la comisura izquierda de la boca. . . . Podría deberse, espéculo . . . a una mala cirugía dental, lo que explicaría la depresión que agrava el resto de la mejilla. O podría ser, y esto ya es pura y legítima fascinación, lo que el hampa llama "la sonrisa eterna." Esa venganza practicada en las cárceles y los callejones, especialmente contra los delatores, que consiste en agrandarles la boca abriéndoles las mejillas desde las comisuras con una navaja. (92)

The long brush of the dyed and uneven moustache has remained a little raised, showing a four- or five-centimeter scar that extends from the left corner of his mouth. . . . [I]t could be due, I speculate, to a badly done dental surgery, which would explain the hollowing that aggravates the rest of his cheek. Or it could be, and this is pure and legitimate fascination, what the underworld calls "the eternal smile." That revenge practiced in jails and alleyways, especially against snitches, which consists of widening their mouths, opening the cheeks in the corners with a knife.

Finally, in the last episode in which we see el maestrito, he is about to be shot by Lucio, who then tells him he was joking and never intended to kill him. El maestrito then defecates in his pants and chases his friends who are trying to escape from the foul smell. All of these examples involve bodily functions and fluids associated with the grotesque and the abject. There are many more examples, but these suffice to show how "el maestrito" is an abject version of "el profesor," who, in contrast, is described only in the most elegant terms, as seen in the following: "Nos inspiraba un respeto instintivo, que en algunos de nosotros llegaba a la veneración, o incluso al amor" ([36] He inspired in us an instinctive respect, which in some of us reached veneration, or even love [see also *Almuerzo* 38, 61).

It is clear that "maestrito" is a symmetrical double of Víctor Polli who shares some of his outward physical characteristics. The lofty "profesor" reflects the Allende years in Chile, while the degraded "maestrito" reflects the debasement of the dictatorship. In this sense, "el maestrito" is Polli forced down a divergent path—to live as a crude, uneducated individual under the dictatorship. However, Franz's use of the double in his novel goes deeper than that. Whether the narrator actually met el maestrito or simply invented him, this double of Victor Polli serves the function of helping the narrator come to terms with his feelings about his high-school teacher, which passes from love to hate. This process has two main threads in the novel. First, the text develops inward similarities between el maestrito and el profesor, despite el maestrito's abject condition; and second, through his adventures in the underworld, the narrator discovers his own abject side—or his potential for abjection.

The inward similarity between el maestrito and el profesor stems mainly from the desire of each character to mentor and look out for the narrator. Although el maestrito is crude and uneducated, in his own way he is protective of the narrator. This primarily comes into focus in el maestrito's attempts to dissuade the narrator from pursuing a relationship with Lucio's girlfriend, the prostitute Vanesa, to avoid revenge by Lucio. Lucio orchestrates a feigned retaliation against the narrator in a scene where he orders el maestrito to cut off the narrator's balls. El maestrito refuses, once again illustrating his desire to help and protect the narrator, even though this means adverse consequences for el maestrito who does not know it is all a joke. These episodes strangely parallel Victor Polli's solicitous behavior toward the narrator, whom he invites into his special group of students. He also helps the narrator in coming to terms with his mother's death by telling him it was okay to cry. Interestingly, both men are described as resembling comics. El maestrito "parece un cómico natural" ([55] seems like a natural comic), while Polli is described as having "maneras exageradas, de comediante" ([36] exaggerated mannerisms, like those of a comedian). Similarly, el maestrito was "un académico de la lengua" (academic of language), which is a shibboleth for comics "de mala muerte" (seedy comics), while Polli is "profesor de lengua y humanidades" ([116] professor of language and humanities).

The inward similarities between the two characters are important because they signal that perhaps el maestrito is not totally abject—that underneath that persona something remains of the beloved teacher. More significant, el maestrito allows the narrator to work through the feelings of hate he harbors over his teacher's betrayal of his students. Helping el maestrito in his adventures in the underworld, the narrator discovers his own potential for abjection. In one episode, he is so angry with el maestrito he almost punches him in the face; in another, he sits in his car masturbating while waiting for Vanesa to appear. Like others, he employs street language; he even laughs at el maestrito's dirty jokes. However, above all, the narrator discovers his own potential for betrayal. When Lucio discovers the narrator's betrayal, the narrator, in turn, betrays el maestrito (with whom Lucio is also angry for not finishing the screenplay) by revealing his whereabouts. He later confesses his betrayal of el maestrito in the following dialogue:

> Lo entregué, maestrito—le confieso. . . . No hay condena ni reproche en él; solo una apenada resignación ante lo previsible, en sus ojitos verdes. Parecen más que nunca los de mi auténtico profesor.—Me entregaste y ni siquiera te salvaste tú. No aprendiste ni eso, pendejo. No. No aprendí ni a sobrevivir. Traicioné la nobleza de vivir que me enseñaba el profesor original. Y ni siquiera aprendí a sobrevivir traicionando cualquier nobleza, como me quería enseñar Ud. (244)

> I turned you in, teacher—I confess to him. . . . There is no condemnation or reproach on his part; only a pained resignation faced with the predicable, in his little green eyes. They look like those of my authentic

> teacher more than ever.—You turned me in and you didn't even save yourself. You didn't even learn that, idiot. No. I didn't learn to survive. I betrayed the nobility of life that my original teacher taught me. And I didn't even learn to survive by betraying nobility, as you wanted to teach me.

The narrator, like Víctor Polli, is guilty of betrayal. His adventures with el maestrito help him to learn that under the right circumstances, anyone is capable of betrayal and that this does not necessarily make someone into a terrible person. It is through this underworld episode, that the narrator comes to realize that Víctor Polli was just trying to survive, and the ability to survive is also the lesson el maestrito attempts to teach to the narrator. Thus, his love for Polli is regenerated, which leads him to ask el maestrito to tell Polli that if he ever sees him, that he, too, would have tried to survive at any cost. Yet despite everything, he still admires and loves him (249). The grotesque and abject maestrito has resulted in the rebirth of the narrator's admiration for his teacher. Víctor Polli is able to become a positive figure again, despite the abjection he underwent because of the dictatorship.

The theme of survival is also important in the novel's title. It could be argued that the vampire is the perfect figure to symbolize survival, because by drinking blood, he remains immortal. According to Nina Auerbach in *Our Vampires, Ourselves,*

> Vampires are easy to stereotype, but it is their variety that makes them survivors. . . . As parasites, they stretch back through folklore to the beginnings of recorded history, but they begin their significant literary life in 1816, with the self-creations of Byron. The Byronic Lord Ruthven has something in common with his American cousin today, Anne Rice's Lestat who preys on 1980s and 90s America. Both are enchanting media companions, both are media stars, but each feeds on his age distinctively because he embodies that age. (1)

As embodiments of their age, postdictatorship Chilean vampires clearly represent survivors. Although the teacher who is allegedly roaming around Santiago as a vampire probably did not survive the dictatorship and would be long dead anyway, the spirit of intellect, inquiry, and high ideals that he represented, potentially lives on. His figure contrasts with the postdictatorship era of "peace without honor" (qtd. in Bram Stoker's *Dracula*) but has not been totally eradicated. Moreover, Zósima, the narrator, and many other Chileans are also survivors or vampires:

> Todos nosotros ... seríamos unos expertos en sobrevivir a toda costa. Y, en cierto sentido, sobrevivir no es vivir. La supervivencia consiste en seguir estando aquí "sobre o luego de la vida" ... Un superviviente no está vivo ni muerto. ¡Como los vampiros! Como ese hombrecito idéntico a nuestro profesor de castellano que Zṕsima vio en el centro el otro día, todavía vivo e igual a sí mismo, cuando debería llevar muerto tantos años. (211)

> All of us ... were probably experts at surviving at all costs. Survival consists of continuing to be here over or after life. A survivor isn't alive or dead. Like vampires! Like this little man identical to our Spanish professor whom Zósima saw downtown the other day, still alive and the same as always, when he should have been dead for so many years.

Eric Rojas sees the vampire more as a figure that symbolizes the suppressed memories of the dictatorship during the Concertación government in the immediate postdictatorship period: "el vampiro ... sirve también para referirse metafóricamente a memorias suprimidas, las que en cierto sentido afloran a la consciencia después de haber sido enterradas" ([253] the vampire ... also serves the function of metaphorically referring to suppressed memories, those that in a certain sense come into consciousness after having been buried). The endurance of suppressed memories can also be seen as a form of survival embodied in the figure of the vampire and, as Rojas indicates, the critique of the politics of forgetting is clearly another central theme of *Almuerzo*.

A final important point is the ultimate destiny of the two survivors who share the "vampire lunch." Both Zósima and the narrator are highly intellectual and linguistically talented individuals. They constantly cite literary texts and engage in wordplay. Zósima is expert in palindromes and speaks various languages. The narrator offers erudite definitions of many words, though often they are part of the dirty language of the underworld. One must recall, however, that the narrator worked on an unfinished dissertation titled "Grosería y Humor en el Dialecto Chileno" (Coarseness and Humor in Chilean Dialect) and thus combines low Chilean slang with high-level intellectual analysis. In other words, both the narrator and Zósima have followed in the footsteps of their original teacher, even if the narrator retains some of el maestrito's predelictions for language. At the novel's end, "el maestrito" and "el profesor" in fact fuse into one, as Landkildehus has indicated. The narrator cannot decide whether the "vampire" he sees wandering around Santiago has the frightened eyes of the teacher or the astute eyes of the maestrito; whether he should call him profesor or maestrito (259). In the end it does not matter because they are one and the same.

  The abject double is a somewhat different manifestation of feelings of abjection than those seen in *La vida*, *El desierto*, and *El infierno*. The construction of el maestrito as an abject figure is a projection of Víctor Polli's abjection derived from torture and betrayal, as well as the narrator's own fears of becoming abject. However, just as in Bakhtin's notion of the grotesque or Connelly's "revelatory grotesque," the abject figure of the maestrito serves a purpose of regeneration by revealing a profound truth about love and survival, ultimately making him an ambiguous rather than a negative figure.

CHAPTER 6

Affect and Empathy in Nona Fernández *La dimensión desconocida*, Alia Trabucco Zerán's *La resta*, and Fátima Sime's *Carne de perra*

IN CONTRAST TO THE OTHER chapters in this book, each of which focuses on a specific emotion as expressed in Chilean novels about the dictatorship, this one explores the concept of affect. One of the founding fathers of affect theory is the psychologist Silvan Tomkins, who defines it as a "density of neural firing" to refer to physiological shifts that individuals experience as a reaction to different stimuli. Depending upon the intensity of neural firing, a person may react by being startled, or with fear, interest, or anger. Affects in themselves are not emotions, though emotions may be attributed to the affects experienced by an individual. In other words, affects are physiological responses to a phenomenon, while emotions are labels attributed to different affects. For example, a feeling of distress might be the emotional response attributed to a person who experiences a rapid heartbeat. However, the heartbeat itself is an affect or physiological reaction to a situation.

Affect obviously bears a close relationship to emotions, which is one of the reasons these two words tend to be conflated. Indeed, all of the terms that Tomkins employs to define affects are also words used to designate emotions. One might think of affect as part of the overall process of creating these emotions. Tomkins defines both a set of positive/neutral affects and a set of negative affects. For an analysis of novels of dictatorship, negative affects are clearly more pertinent. Yet the "surprise-startle" affect, which is considered neutral, is so strikingly important that I focus most on it in this chapter. The negative affects include distress-anguish, fear-terror, anger-rage, shame-humiliation, contempt, and disgust/dissmell. In addition to surprise-startle, this chapter will also concentrate on the affect of disgust/dissmell, which bears a close relationship to the condition of abjection studied in chapter 5.

While the other chapters in this book elucidate character emotions as a reflection of what Chilean citizens felt and experienced because of the Pinochet dictatorship, this chapter emphasizes the emotions an audience experiences in reading novelistic representations of dictatorship. I am particularly interested in how reader identification and empathy are created in these novels by using affect and emotions. I posit that by startling the reader with unusual or unexpected actions, the reader is made to identify and empathize with the characters more strongly than in other types of novels.

According to Adam J. Frank and Elizabeth A Wilson, Tomkins's surprise-startle affect is characterized by such physical reactions as eye blinks, mouths open, and eyebrows up. Experiencing this affect has a "resetting effect." In other words, for Tomkins "the salient characteristic of the startle mechanism—its 'capacity for interruption of any ongoing activity' gives it the role of 'a circuit breaker.' . . . Surprise-startle has the function of clearing the central assembly to prepare for a subsequent central assembly that takes into account the information that activated the surprise response in the first place" (ch. 5). Tomkins emphasizes that the surprise-startle affect is often part of a process by which interest is enhanced:

> Despite some interference between startle and interest their more general relationship is one of mutual facilitation in which growing interest may activate startle, which then activates interest. This may be seen most clearly in the way in which startle and interest interact to expedite a revisit of a particular message to the central assembly, in the "double take." In the "double take," information reaches consciousness and leaves, but a moment later further information retrieved from memory may enlist further interest or fear to amplify the bare bones of memory information, and this ensemble produces a sufficiently steep gradient of high neural density of firing to activate the startle, which in turn gives way to the double take, which is essentially a more rapid orientation reflex, ordinarily accompanied by rapidly increasing intensity of interest or any other affect. (*Positive Affects* 507)

All three of the novels discussed in this chapter—*La dimensión desconocida* (2016) by Nona Fernández; *La resta* (2014) by Alia Trabucco

Zerán; and *Carne de perra* (2009) by Fátima Sime—strategically re-create the affect of surprise-startle in the reader. Its use helps to process the information that stimulated this physiological reaction. That is, since this narrative material is likely to be foreign to many readers or difficult to adjust to and make sense of, the surprise-startle reflex can help by triggering the "resetting effect" that, in turn, heightens interest and attention. Often this contributes to the reader's identification with and empathy for the characters of each novel. However, as I show below, empathy can be a complicated and variable concept, depending on numerous factors, not least the morality of the characters.

According to Walter Kintsch, readers construct what he terms "situational models" to aid in their comprehension of literary texts. In other words, when we read, what we read reminds us of past situations—the sorts of things that we experienced, whether directly or vicariously. Readers relate what they read to their existing knowledge structures (Gernsbacher 141–42). Gernsbacher has theorized, based on experiments he conducted on readers, that, in addition to activating temporal and spatial knowledge, these situational models also trigger knowledge about human emotions that help readers to "build mental representations of fictional characters' emotional states" (143). Readers were given two sets of paragraphs to read: one in which the last sentence contained the emotion word evoked by the content of the passage and another in which the emotion word did not match the emotion stimulated by the content of the passage. Gernsbacher reports his findings as follows:

> Subjects read the target sentences considerably more rapidly when they contained an emotion word that matched the emotional state implied in the story as opposed to when they contained an emotion word that mismatched the emotional state implied in the story. . . . Gernsbacher et al. suggested that these data illustrate the roles that activation of previously acquired knowledge plays in how readers understand fictional character's emotional states. The hypothesis that the ability to understand fictional characters' emotional responses is based on exposure to actual or vicarious emotional experiences predicts that the more emotional situations a person encounters, the more memory traces are stored, and therefore the more emotional knowledge is available during comprehension. (145–54)

In other words, previously acquired knowledge about emotions helps readers to comprehend and identify with characters' emotions. Fernández's *La dimensión* relies on the situational models provided by the once-popular television series *The Twilight Zone* (1959–1964), as one of the ways to help readers process the horrific events of the Pinochet dictatorship.

La dimensión narrates the disappearance, torture, and murder of several individuals who appear in a torturer's confession published in the journal *Cauce*, another memory knot of the dictatorship. *Cauce* (Channel) first appeared in 1983 during a period of political openness in the dictatorship. The Minister of the Interior, Sergio Onofre Jarpa, thought that it would be a good idea to allow the publication as a vehicle for public thought, especially the views of the Social Democrats, as a way of reducing the tense political climate of the era. The journal's eventual goal was to lead to the restoration of democracy in Chile ("Periodismo de oposición: 1979–1989"), but after it published a torturer's confession, it was shut down. The challenge that Fernández faces is in how to make readers comprehend and identify with torture, an experience most have never had and to many an atrocity that would be both unimaginable and unbelievable in a country such as Chile. According to Van Alphen, one of the principal ways in which affect is created in readers is through visualization:

> Reading for meaning [allegorical reading] has to leave out a lot to be efficient.... But texts and images are full of details in excess of any allegorical reading. Another textual aspect that is usually neglected in the pursuit of allegorical meaning is powerful physical depictions. Elaborate descriptions enable the reader to visualize a text.... These visualizations can have an especially strong affective impact on the reader. (26–27)

Van Alphen emphasizes the connection between visualization and affect. In *La dimensión* , Fernández employs two visualization techniques. The first is her highly visual descriptions of torture; the second puts those descriptions to use through the re-creation of and parallels with episodes from the television series *Twilight Zone*. That adaptation stimulates the surprise-startle affect by reproducing the strange and often supernatural events that occurred on the show. In turn, this startle affect helps to create the emotion of surprise/shock in the reader, as well as identification with the characters' feelings of fear, distress, and anguish. In other words, through movies and television programs, visual media enable people to participate vicariously in situations that they have never personally had or experienced. These media serve as bridges that help readers to formulate the situational models of characters' emotions that Kintsch and Gernsbacher speak of, given that most readers, mercifully, will never have to endure the sorts of occurrences Fernández narrates. Specifically, Fernández employs the affects and feelings that *Twilight Zone* episodes prompt, such as surprise, fear, disquiet, and unsettlement to create a form of identification between the feelings of the characters who are subjected to abduction and torture and those of the reader who have not had these experiences. If Fernández had simply chosen to include excerpts from the *Cauce* article or other historical documents (which do appear in other historical novels such as *Yo el Supremo*), the reader would not necessarily experience the same connection to the events and consequently would not forge such a strong identification with characters. The familiar television series serves as a "situational model" or bridge between readers and shocking occurrences to help readers process actions that might seem very foreign to them, even though the television series itself had no explicit connection to politics.

One of the first episodes that the narrator recalls is that of Carlos Contreras Maluaje, who threw himself under a moving bus to escape capture and anticipated further torture by government officials. The narrator prefaces this episode by mentioning *Twilight Zone* and the specific episode featuring Captain Cook (the episode titled "Probe Seven"):

> En los años 70 . . . veía los capítulos de la *Twilight Zone* . . . *tengo grabada esta sensación de inquietud que me seducía*. . . . El coronel Cook, viajero en el océano del espacio, con su nave destruida e incendiada, no volverá a volar jamás. Adolorido y asustado, envía mensajes a su hogar para que alguien vaya a su rescate, sin embargo, eso parece imposible . . . un pequeño planeta en el espacio, pero para el coronel Cook es la dimensión desconocida. (*La dimensión* 47–48; my emphasis)

> In the seventies . . . I watched episode after episode of *The Twilight Zone*. . . . I'm forever marked by the seductive feeling of disquiet. . . .

> Colonel Cook, voyager across the ocean of space, will never fly the smoldering wreck of his ship again.... Hurting and afraid, he sends messages home pleading for someone to rescue him, though that appears to be impossible... on a small planet in space, his very own twilight zone. (Twilight Zone 39–40)

The reason that Captain Cook's compatriots cannot act to save him is that his country is engaged in a war between good and evil that is on course to lead to its total destruction, a battle that the narrator sees as similar to the one fought in Chile during the dictatorship. The memory of this *Twilight Zone* episode is immediately followed by the story of Contreras Maluaje. One day over lunch, the narrator's mother relates the following:

> Un hombre se había lanzado a las ruedas de un micro.... Dice que de pronto apareció un grupo de personas que lo venían a buscar.... El hombre, cuando vio a estas personas, comenzó a gritar *como si hubiera visto al demonio o un grupo de gnomos* que lo acosaban. Decía que eran agentes de la inteligencia; que se lo querían llevar para seguir torturándolo, que por favor lo dejaran morir en paz.... Un auto apareció y... subieron al hombre que se fue a desaparecer definitivamente de los límites de la realidad. (*La dimensión* 49; my emphasis)

> A man had thrown himself under the wheels of a bus.... [A] group of people moved decisively toward the injured man.... As soon as he saw them, he yelled *as if he'd seen the devil or a pack of gremlins hounding him.* He said they were intelligence agents, and they were going to take him away to torture him again, and could he please be left to die in peace.... A car drove up and... they maneuvered the man into it, who then vanished forever outside the bounds of reality. (Twilight Zone 40–41)

In addition to the parallel between Captain Cook and Contreras Maluaje suggested by the juxtaposition of these two episodes, the narrator makes specific reference to *Twilight Zone* with "as if he had seen the devil or a group of gnomes who were pursuing him." This reference for anyone familiar with *Twilight Zone* conjures forth the episode "Nightmare at 20,000 Feet" in which a gremlin appears on the wing of a plane to dismantle it, while a horrified passenger watches his actions.

Another episode with parallels to a *Twilight Zone* episode works on reader empathy and identification through the character Carol Flores. Flores, another historical figure, is arrested and tortured along with his two brothers. The narrator informs the reader that Flores turned government informer and became a torturer to save his brothers, who were then released.[1] Ultimately, Flores is murdered by the military for an alleged betrayal.

Fernández casts Flores into another *Twilight Zone* episode titled "The Four of Us Are Dying." In it, the main character, Arch Hammer, who can make his face change into anything he wants, uses his gift to obtain money. However, at the end of the program, he is killed by a man who mistakes him for his own son, an occurrence that surprises and shocks the viewer. The reader of Fernández's novel experiences similar affects of surprise-startle upon reading about Carol Flores's torture and subsequent betrayal. After the narrator describes what happened to Flores, she states:

> Recuerdo otro capítulo de la dimensión desconocida. En él un hombre cambiaba de rostro cada vez lo necesitaba. Era el hombre de las mil caras, así le decían. . . . Si hubiera estado en Chile en los 70 hubiese sido un feliz trabajador de la municipalidad . . . y luego un agente feroz, capaz de torturar y delatar a los suyos.
>
> ¿Cuántos rostros puede contener un ser humano? . . . ¿Cuántos yo? (*La dimensión* 92)

> I remember another episode from *The Twilight Zone*. In it a man could choose a new face whenever he needed to. He was the so-called man of a thousand faces. . . . If he had been in Chile in the seventies he would have been a happy municipal employee . . . and then a savage agent, willing to torture or turn in his loved ones.
>
> How many faces can a human being contain? . . . What about me? (Twilight Zone 84)

Fernández's narrator incorporates *Twilight Zone* as a means of creating identification with the character Carol Flores, despite Flores's being a traitor who aligns himself with the torturers. By questioning how many different "faces" any of us has, including the narrator herself, she emphasizes that under similar circumstances any of us might have done the same as Flores.[2] Meir Sternberg discusses what he terms primacy and recency effects in characterization. Primacy effects refer to the initial impressions created about a character, which can be either confirmed or negated by subsequent character development (see Sklar 461). Primacy effects establish the first idea that a reader has about a character, so if the primacy effects are strong enough, they may, as in the case of Carol Flores, have greater influence on the reader's assessment than any subsequent information does. In other words, the reader's initial positive impression of Flores is not overshadowed by the later negative impression (when he betrays his cause and sides with the enemy), not only because the reader understands his motive (saving his brothers) but also because the initial positive impression was strong enough to counteract the ensuing information.

This technique of creating identification is central to *La dimensión*. In addition to incorporating *Twilight Zone* episodes, the novel's narrator draws constant parallels between ordinary Chilean citizens and the fewer numbers who were abducted, tortured, and murdered; this technique also firms up the connections readers make with the victims they read about. For example, one of the first atrocities that the narrator describes involves the fate of José Weibel Barahona, who disappears from a bus one morning as he sets out to take his children to school. The narrator emphasizes the similarity between that morning in 1976 and a typical morning in her own home, or any home with children, before relating Weibel's disappearance and the ultimate difference between the past and present:

> Desconozco como habrá sido la rutina mañanera en la casa de los Weibel Barahona en 1976 ... pero con un poco de imaginación puedo ver esa casa ahí en La Florida y a esa familia comenzando la jornada. No creo que su rutina se haya diferenciado mucho de la que día a día yo misma ejecuto con mi familia, o de la que día a día todas las familias con niños de este país desarrollan desde hace años.
>
> El 29 de marzo de 1976 a las 7:30 horas, la misma hora en la que mi hijo y su padre se van a diario de nuestra casa, José y María Teresa salieron con sus niños para llevarlos al colegio. (*La dimensión* 30)

> I don't know what the morning routine must have been like at the Weibel Barahona household in 1976 ... but with a little imagination I can see that house in La Florida and the family beginning their day. I doubt their routine was much different from the one I follow daily with my family, or the one that all families with children in this country have been following daily for years.
> On March 29, 1976, at 7:30 a.m., the same time my son and his father leave the house each day, José and María Teresa left to take their children to school. (Twilight Zone 21–22)

The strategy of drawing parallels between the normality of the narrator's life and that of the tortured victims before their disappearance is repeated numerous times by Fernández's narrator. She employs this same technique with respect to ambiguous or "gray zone" characters, such as the torturer turned informant who is the axis of the novel. At the beginning of the book the narrator asks regarding Antonio Valenzuela Morales:

> ¿Qué habría hecho yo si a los dieciocho años, igual que Ud., hubiera ingresado al servicio militar obligatorio y mi superior me hubiera llevado a hacer guardia a un grupo de prisioneros políticos? ... ¿Qué haría mi hijo en este lugar? (*La dimensión* 26–27)

> What would I have done if, like you [Morales Valenzuela], I had reported for military service at eighteen, and my superior had sent me to guard a group of political prisoners? ... What would my son do in the same place? (Twilight Zone 17–18)

By asking this series of difficult questions, the narrator imagines herself in the place of Andrés Antonio Valenzuela Morales, "the man who tortured," which also makes readers put themselves in Morales's place and wonder what they might do in a similar circumstance. According to Van Alphen, this type of "idiopathic identification" has great affective power:

> Identification makes reading concrete, in the sense that reading is no longer a matter of signifying transactions but of an event that one

> experiences directly and even bodily.... Some forms of identification are more affectively powerful than others. One form involves taking the other into the self on the basis of (projected) likeness... idiopathic identification.... Here, the self doing the identification takes the risk of... becoming like the other. This is both exciting and risky... but at any rate, affectively powerful.... When we identify with the inner states or ethical dilemmas of a narrator or character, we are no longer reading signs to which we have to attribute meaning, but we are living or experiencing them. (28)

In other words, strategies that cause the reader to identify with a character are another way in which the reader is made to experience the same affects (physiological responses) and emotions (feelings of fear, anguish, shock) as the character in question.

It is important to note that just as in the other chapters that focused on melancholy, despair, loss, and abjection, Fernández's emphasis on emotion is not employed as a method to distance the reader from historical occurrences, but rather to preserve the memory of history through the memory of affects and feelings engendered by historical events. To a large degree, the novel achieves and maintains this connection to history through the creation of empathy and sympathy in the reader. The "idiopathic identification" discussed by Van Alphen leads the reader to experience both empathy and sympathy. The process of identification, and not the emotions themselves, is risky because it causes readers to feel as if they are undergoing the same dangerous or difficult experiences as those of the characters. Empathy has been variably defined, as summarized by Howard Sklar:

> Social psychologist Lisa Myyry... suggests that empathy "could be defined as an affective response more appropriate to another's situation than one's own." Similarly, Suzanne Keen... suggests "we feel what we believe to be the emotions of others."... Educational philosopher Nel Noddings proposes... "I do not project; I receive the other onto myself and I see and feel with the other, I become a duality."... Empathy operates as a "chameleon emotion" in the sense that, when we experience it, we take on the emotional experience of the other as our own. (453)

Sklar goes on to distinguish empathy from sympathy. In his opinion, the two entail different processes. While empathy, as we have seen, involves idiopathic identification or a type of fusion with the character, sympathy:

> involves greater distance between the individual who feels it and the person toward whom it is ... directed. ... [T]he following elements [are] essential to the definition of sympathy: 1) awareness of suffering as "something to be alleviated"; 2) the judgment that the suffering is unfair; 3) negative, uncomfortable feelings on behalf of the sufferer; 4) desire to help. (453)

Although Sklar sees empathy and sympathy as two distinct processes, they are often concurrent and not mutually exclusive in the development of readers' emotional responses to characters. Jaén's definition of empathy, in fact, seems to have much in common with Sklar's definition of sympathy, suggesting that the creation of empathy and sympathy are intertwined processes. Jaén relies on Jean Decoty's definition of empathy:

> The natural capacity to share, understand, and respond with care to the affective states of others. This definition includes ... the three fundamental steps involved in the affective function of historical memory narratives—feeling with (sharing); feeling for (understanding), and reacting (responding with care) to the affective states of others—embracing a notion of empathy as a complex experience that encompasses feeling (both felt and witnessed) and behavior. (807)

"Feeling with" is clearly what Sklar defines as empathy, while "feeling for" and, consequently, "ethically responding to" coincide with Sklar's notion of sympathy. In Decoty's definition, the empathy one feels for a character (the sharing of feelings) ultimately leads the reader to sympathize with that character (understanding the character), which in turn stimulates an ethical response (responding with care) in the reader. This ethical response is the result of the emotive reactions (both empathy and sympathy) that the reader experiences.

Eliciting empathy and sympathy from the reader in no way detracts from the memory of historical events but is a technique employed that ultimately keeps ever present the atrocities of the Pinochet dictatorship. Fernández fuses history and feeling in the novel as a form of political activism that encourages future generations to remember past events, to act ethically in the future, and to fight fascism, dictatorship, and authoritarianism in general. According to Sergio Alzate, who interviewed Fernández about *La dimension* and *Space Invaders*:

> Recuerda e imagina porque sabe que tiene que escribir. Que si nadie más lo hace, ella lo tiene que hacer. Porque hay un boquete oscuro por el que pasa la memoria de su país y ella quiere saber qué fue lo que sucedió, iluminar las esquinas, confrontar a sus compatriotas con el recuerdo del horror para no olvidar y evitar que algo así se repita: "Ha sido en la escritura donde realmente he tomado completa conciencia de lo pasado." (n.p.)

> She remembers and imagines because she knows that she has to write. That if no one else does it, she must do it. Because there is a dark hole through which the memory of her country passes, and she wants to know what happened, to illuminate the corners, to confront her compatriots with the memory of the horror so as not to forget, and to avoid that something like this repeat itself: "It has been through writing where I have really become aware of the past."

In another interview with Ivana Romero, Fernández states:

> La democracia pactada con los militares el año 90, pactó a la vez con la justicia y pactó también el olvido. Entonces el proceso ha sido lento y voluntarioso. Tenemos la construcción de un relato oficial que cuenta las verdades a medias y que busca tranquilizar conciencias. Y tenemos también la construcción inacabada de un relato que no termina nunca de contarse, y donde todos van aportando fragmentos. La memoria política chilena es un ejercicio en construcción que, probablemente, no tendrá nunca un fin y dejará muchos vacíos, muchos hoyos negros. *La dimensión desconocida*, este libro, es también un intento por aportar y despertar esa memoria colectiva. (n.p.)

The democracy agreed upon with the military men in 1990 also concluded a deal with justice and also forgetting. Thus, the process has been slow and changeable. We have the construction of an official story that tells only half the truth and that soothes consciences. And we also have the unfinished construction of a story that never finishes being told and to which everyone has contributed fragments. The Chilean political memory is an exercise in construction that, probably, will never have an end and will leave many empty spaces, many dark holes. *The Twilight Zone*, this book, is also an attempt to contribute and awaken that collective memory.

Fernández points out the need to "awaken collective memory" and "gain consciousness of the past" so that it will not be repeated. These comments imply that a segment of the Chilean population wants to forget what happened or is resistant to the antiauthoritarian message of her texts. According to Guillermo García-Corales, many writers from this second generation, including Fernández, "revisan las prácticas político-culturales que . . . intentan dominar el imaginario colectivo y blanquear u olvidar los episodios más oscuros y traumáticos de la reciente historia nacional. Además, erigen estrategias de sospecha con respecto a la ideología neoliberal postdictatorial que propone la panacea de la estabilidad y el progreso" ([3] revise the political and cultural practices that attempt to dominate the collective imaginary and whitewash or forget the darkest and most traumatic episodes of recent national history. Moreover, they build strategies of suspicion with respect to postdictatorial neoliberal ideology, which proposes the panacea of stability and progress).

Isabel Jaén studies this phenomenon of implied political activism in Spanish Civil War (1936–1939) narratives, with a focus on Dulce Chacón's novel *La voz dormida* (The Sleeping Voice). These novels are comparable in many ways to novels of the Chilean dictatorship. Jaén, employing Jo Labanyi's term "haunting," explains the historical past as "something that chases us, obsesses us. . . . What matters about the past is its unfinished business, which requires critical reflection and action in the present" (806). That explains why Fernández criticizes post-Pinochet neoliberal governments and the continued influence of Pinochet in Chilean politics well after the restoration of democracy. The author achieves this criticism through the following principal techniques:

(1) use of the different zones from the Museo de la Memoria Chilena; (2) a parody of Nicanor Parra's poem "Noticiero 1957" (Newscast 1957); and (3) the constant juxtaposition of imagination and memory.

El Museo de la Memoria Chilena opened on January 11, 2010, in Santiago. The museum focuses on the abuses of the Pinochet dictatorship and the subsequent transition to democracy. Miguel Caballero Vázquez argues that the museum was built as a way for the Concertación government to control memory of the dictatorship. The Allende government is barely mentioned in the museum, while the Concertación Government (the neoliberal Coalition government of left and centrist parties established upon the transition to democracy) is institutionalized by the museum as the best form of government to ensure future democracy, morality, and the destruction of evil (514–15).

A compelling example of how Fernández employs the zones of the museum to criticize Chilean politics is found when the narrator and her son arrive at the "Zona Fin de la Dictadura" (End of the Dictatorship Zone). The narrator explains to her son that Pinochet, who caused all the destruction documented in the museum, was also the man who created the new laws for the country after the dictatorship. When her son reacts by laughing in a disconcerting fashion, the narrator states that: "A los 10 años mi hijo se daba cuenta ya de las malas bromas de la historia chilena" ([*La dimensión* 37] At ten my son was already wise to the bad jokes of Chilean history [Twilight Zone 29]). The narrator satirizes here the continuance of Pinochet and the right's influence in the Chilean transition to democracy. Similarly, the narrator criticizes the fact that the end of this museum section displays a huge photograph of President Patricio Aylwin (1990–1994), the first president after the Pinochet years, who is represented as Chile's savior, even though he initially supported the coup that brought Pinochet to power. Alywin, then a member of the Christian Democratic party, was "instrumental in the breakdown of the 'Dialogue' between the Unidad Popular government and the Christian Democrats. In August 1973, Patricio Aylwin provided a Green Light to the Chilean Armed Forces led by Augusto Pinochet on behalf of the CD" (Chossudovsky n.p.).

Toward the end of the novel, Fernández's narrator further emphasizes the absurdity of Pinochet's continued influence as Senator for life through her parody of the poem "Noticiero 1957." Parra, its author, is known for writing irreverent, nihilistic poetry that questioned and criticized traditional institutions.

"Noticiero 1957" evokes the notion of absurdity through its juxtaposition of important national and international events with insignificant occurrences during a newscast. Each stanza ends with something trivial that contrasts with serious news, such as "el autor se retrata con su perro" (the author sits for a portrait with his dog)[3] or "Jorge Elliot [a Chilean writer] publica una antología" (Jorge Elliot publishes an anthology). The fact that these items are mixed in with events like "Terremoto en Irán: 600 víctimas" or "nuevos abusos de los pobres indios/quieren desalojarlos de sus tierras," ([Parra 164–67] Earthquake in Iran: 600 victims or new abuses of the poor Indians/they want to evict them from their lands) creates a sense of the absurdity of history. Fernández's narrator achieves this same effect in her parody in which she blends major events from Chilean history since the beginning of the dictatorship with commonplace daily activities. The poem begins with "Golpe Militar en Chile" (Coup in Chile) and contains lines about the creation of the National Intelligence Directorate and the assassination of General Carlos Prats mixed with others about the narrator's wearing a school uniform and carrying a tin lunch box or going to the National Stadium to see El Chapulín Colorado with her squeaky plastic hammer (*La dimensión* 212–25; Twilight Zone 198–213).

Finally, although the narrator repeatedly invites the reader to imagine the feelings and experiences of the tortured victims, she engages in a constant counterposing of imagination to history, the effect of which underscores that despite the need to fill in certain details with imagination, what we are reading is a retelling of actual historical events. A typical example occurs when the narrator discusses the disappearance of Alonso Gahona: "No imagino, sé que don Alonso Gahona fue trasladado a este lugar. No imagino, sé que cruzó la Puerta del número 037 de la calle Santa Teresa y desde ese mismo momento ingresó a una dimensión de la cual nunca regresaría" ([*La dimensión* 99] I know—I'm not imagining—that Don Alonso Gahona was transferred to this place. I know—I'm not imagining—that he crossed the threshold of 037 Calle Teresa and at that very moment he entered a dimension from which he would never return [Twilight Zone 91]). Despite being immersed in imagining the characters' feelings, the reader is never left to doubt or forget the connection between the novel and history.

Lazzara astutely notes in his study on memory of the dictatorship that "Chilean artists have confronted disappearance by employing two primary strategies that coexist in a profound dialectical relation: marking the presence and marking the absence" (102). Throughout the novel, Fernández records the absence of the disappeared who are swept up in the "Twilight Zone"— the parallel universe of disappearance, torture, and death that coexisted with "normal" everyday living in Chile during the 70s and 80s. However, Fernández also registers the presence of these individuals in her narratives by describing their photographs, which give a physical concreteness to their existence despite the passage of years since their death. She indicates that by clicking on these images, one can obtain information about each individual (*La dimensión* 45; Twilight Zone 36–37). In another instance in the novel, when a lawyer is showing photographs of the disappeared to the former torturer so that he can identify them and provide information, the narrator states: "Cada una de estas fotos es una postal enviada desde otro tiempo. Una señal de auxilio que pide a gritos ser reconocida ... recuerda quien soy, dicen. . . . recuerda lo que me hicieron." ([*La dimensión* 79–80] Each of these photographs is a postcard sent from some other time. A cry for help begging to be heard. . . . . Remember who I am, they say. Remember where I was, remember what was done to me [Twilight Zone 71–72]). Thus, remembering the victims and their suffering and giving presence to their existence are fundamental to *La dimensión*.

Trabucco Zerán's novel, *La resta*, though in many ways very different in approach from Fernández's, is also centered on the question of affect and feelings. While Fernández emphasizes history, Trabucco Zerán's novel is both symbolic and allegorical.[4] Moreover, while Fernández elicits mostly positive empathy in her novel,[5] Trabucco Zerán whips up the surprise-startle affect to produce feelings of shock, leading to what Stefano Ercolino calls "negative empathy." Ercolino combines Theodor Lipps's concept of "negative empathy" for an object with Adam Morton's ideas about how aesthetic objects are different from other types of objects. He states that Lipps views empathy as a form of "self-activation" in relation to an object, which can be either positive or negative:

> For Lipps, the feeling of accord is a feeling of pleasure (Lust) towards the object, whereas the feeling of conflict is a feeling of unpleasure (Unlust). The self-activation is experienced in both cases as a demand originating from the object. In positive empathy, the subject freely and

willingly consents to such demand—which is why Lipps also refers to "positive empathy" as "sympathetic empathy"—whereas in negative empathy, the subject experiences a sort of resistance against what is perceived as an "enemy request" by the object; a resistance against the introduction of something unpleasurable inside of her/himself, which generates interior detachment.... Lipps's conception of negative empathy as a partial form of empathy, generating interior detachment and the consciousness of the separability—of a distance—between the empathizing subject and the other individuals, is perhaps his most significant contribution to a definition of negative empathy. (244)[6]

Ercolino goes on to cite Morton's ideas about how the aesthetic object allows for more empathy than one would feel in similar real-life situations:

Morton's reasoning has an important implication for our thinking on negative empathy. Unlike life, works of fiction can provide the reader with a lot of information about characters, the motives of their actions, the different situations they live in, and which require them to act. In fictional worlds, complex historical and social contexts can be easily reconstructed with a very high level of precision, offering a rich background to the actions of negative characters with whom we can establish an empathic relationship: an empathic relationship that would be nearly impossible in a real situation because, among other things, the information we would have on flesh and blood monsters would probably be much more limited. (250)

Thus "negative empathy" refers to a limited or reduced empathy because of how a reader can interpret characters negatively based on their actions. Although such actions can be abject, they are not always that, as they may also be perceived as negative character traits for other reasons. Ercolino illustrates negative empathy with Jonathan Littell's novel *The Kindly Ones*. In it, the fictional protagonist Maximillien Aue, a former Nazi SS officer and key actor in the Holocaust, serves as narrator. For Ercolino, this work evinces an example of negative empathy and "permanent shock": "the negative affect of permanent shock is strictly functional to stir negative empathy which cannot be assimilated with the ugly feelings theorized by Ngai.... The aesthetic dimension of negative empathy is at the exact opposite of that of an ugly feeling; it is mostly a tragic one, ceaselessly pondering and questioning the boundaries of human agency" (254).

Ercolino's theory is in keeping with studies done to measure affect (frowning reflex) in readers who read narratives about both morally good and morally bad characters. Bjorn t. Hart and his fellow researchers have found that "Bad things happening to bad people resulted in neither an increase nor a decrease in corrugator EMG [electromyography], while description of bad characters experiencing a positive event elicited a decrease in [frowning] activity (indicative of positive affect)" (11). These findings line up with those literary characters who, despite their failings or repugnance, can still elicit empathy thanks to mitigating circumstances. Such is the case in Alia Trabucco Zerán's *La resta*, in which some of the characters, though not morally corrupt, exhibit undesirable characteristics.

La resta's two principal narrators are Felipe and Iquela. Both are children of Marxist supporters during the Pinochet years. Throughout the novel, both recall events from their childhood. Among them is that after Rodolfo/Víctor, Iquela's father, was captured by the military, he betrayed Felipe's father who was subsequently murdered by the government. Another character, Paloma, who is the daughter of Iquela's mother's best friend Ingrid, also recalls childhood events. When Pinochet came to power, her parents, Ingrid and Hans, fled the country. Now that her mother has died Paloma is attempting to grant her last wish of returning her body to Chile for burial.

Nelly Richard, in that vein, has in *Cultural Residues* described the important role of art in literature as converting what she terms the "remains" and "residues" of memories that cannot be represented within the "disciplinary framework of philosophy and sociology" into a "poetics of memory" (50). Perhaps no coincidence, Richard speaks at length of "remainders wrapped in an overabundance of artifice destined to repair the contents of lessness (... enduring violence) with the luxury of a form of more... with a proliferating and mobile diversity of creative signifiers" (50). Thus the title of Trabucco Zerán's "the remainder" (la resta) purposefully recalls Richard's notion of the use of creative signifiers to express the violence experienced during the dictatorship. Among these "creative signifiers," Richard highlights the use of the "allegorization of ruins" or allegorical mode, which she examines at length in *El padre mío*, Diamela Eltit's novel. As I similarly argue below, Trabucco Zerán's novel relies on this same allegorical mode (Felipe's cadaver counting and the violent childhood games) to represent the atrocities of the dictatorship and the postdictatorship struggle to come to terms with them.[7]

Although *La resta* does not employ every characteristic of allegory, it does exhibit at least three of the five major traits of allegorical fiction Angus Fletcher indicates.[8] The first, according to him, is "daemonic" agency, which he describes as a character identified with a single, obsessive idea: "If we were to meet an allegorical character in real life, we would say of him that he was obsessed with only one idea, or that he had an absolutely one track mind . . . I shall therefore use the word 'daemon' for any person . . . acting as if possessed by a daemon" (40–41). Fletcher's description fits the character Felipe Arrabal. Felipe is portrayed as an odd, troubled, and even pathological individual. For example, he kills his pet parrot because he wants to look inside it to understand more about the origin of the parrot's voice. In another instance, he beats Iquela up when she refuses to beat up another student. He does this because he claims that the only way Iquela can recover from her father's death is through inflicting pain on someone else. At one point, Paloma asks Iquela "¿por qué Felipe era así?" ([*La resta* 173] "why Felipe was like that?" [Remainder 123]), confirming the impression that the reader already has of Felipe, that he is very strange. Two elements make him "abnormal."[9] The first is his obsessive habit of counting cadavers. This fixation started sometime in Felipe's past, probably due to the atrocities of the dictatorship. Despite the end of the dictatorship, it continues into the present:

> Así empezaron mis muertos . . . sorprendiéndome sin falta en los lugares más extraños . . . flotando rapidito Mapocho abajo . . . entiendo que debo apurarme de una vez por todos, aplicarme para llegar a cero . . . ¿Cómo saber cuántos nacemos y cuántos quedamos? ¿Cómo ajustar las matemáticas mortales y los listados ¿sustrayendo . . . usando la aritmética del fin de los tiempos para así de manera rotunda y terminal, amanecer el último día, apretar los dientes y restar. (*La resta* 11)

> That's how my dead began ... catching me unawares in the strangest of places ... floating down the Mapocho. ... I have to shake a leg, really knuckle down if I'm going to get to zero. ... How will I work out how many are born and how many remain? How can I reconcile the death toll with the actual sum of the dead? by deducting ... using this apocalyptic math to finally, once and for all, wake up on that last day, grit my teeth, and subtract them. (Remainder 2)

Throughout the novel, Felipe obsessively continues to contemplate how to arrive at a zero sum of dead bodies, considering such issues as how to account for disinterred people (a reference to when the body of Chilean poet Pablo Neruda was disinterred in 2013 to see if he had been murdered by the Pinochet government [101]). He does this as a way of coping with the atrocities of the Pinochet dictatorship. The chapter titles reflect this theme; they appear in descending order, from 11 to 0. In contrast, the chapters narrated by Iquela are indicated by () with no number. Felipe's obsession makes him a "daemonic agent," pointing to the allegorical functioning of the episodes, in the sense Fletcher attributes to allegory.

During his cadaver counting, Felipe constantly points to the failure of arithmetic to solve his problem. He questions how to count the "living-dead," whether or not he should include Paloma's mother, who died of natural causes, and what to do if he finally gets to zero, repeatedly acknowledging that math is imperfect (*La resta* 75, 126; Remainder 49, 85–86).

Felipe's insistence on the failure of arithmetic is important to the way the novel rejects logic, as well as all the factual or historical approaches to what happened under the Pinochet dictatorship. The failure of arithmetic or logic coincides with an emphasis on affect, feeling, and emotion in the novel. Arithmetic is normally considered rational and precise; whereas, emotions are often associated with the irrational and imprecise. By rejecting arithmetic as a solution to how to make sense of so many murders and disappearances, the novel, as it were, suggests an affective and allegorical pathway to comprehending the past.

It is also worth noting that Felipe's cadaver counting gives rise to the novel's title, *La resta*. "La resta," or "the remainder" not only is a mathematical term, as in Felipe's calculations but also refers here to what is left, namely, the aftermath of the Pinochet dictatorship. Thus, the novel's title, like its techniques, is also symbolic in nature.

Felipe's odd behavior, particularly his cadaver counting, is one of the many ways in which *La resta* startles the reader, since most would not think of it as a normal activity. The presence of cadavers scattered throughout Santiago is, as well, likely to cause the startle affect in the reader. In turn, the affective physiological responses Trabucco Zerán induces are likely to leave the reader surprised, indignant, or emotionally disturbed and disoriented.

Another central way that *La resta* creates affective allegory is through the aggressive childhood games that Felipe and Iquela once played. Other than the game in which they pretended to be their parents, Felipe and Iquela's play was violent. In one instance, Iquela recalls how they played a "hanging" game in the backseat of the car:

> Hagamos algo nuevo, Ique, juguemos al colgado ... saca de su mochila uno de sus lápices y un largo pedazo de hilo negro, me toma la mano. ... Mi mano inmóvil sobre sus rodillas, palma arriba, mientras Felipe dibuja concentradísimo, puntos negros como ojos, un círculo a modo de nariz y una línea recta para indicar la boca en cada una de las yemas de mis dedos ... Felipe, el elegido, pasa al frente. Saliste tú ... mi mano, mis cinco obedientes *soldados* sostienen el hilo, el largo cordel que mi *ejército* ata con determinación, Ique, más fuerte, apriétalo, dice esa voz. ... Hasta ver estancada su sangre, sudando estrangulado, los ojos salidos, el hilo hundido en el primero de los nudillos, una cabeza a punto de estallar y nuestras risas ahogadas. (*La resta* 143; my emphases)

> "Let's try something, Ique, let's play hangman." ... [H]e would pull out a pencil and a long piece of black thread from his rucksack. ...
> With my hand resting steadily on his knees, palm facing upward, on each of my fingertips Felipe would painstakingly draw two black dots for eyes, a circle for a nose, and a straight line for a mouth. ... One of Felipe's fingers (the selected one) would come to the front ... while my hand (my five obedient soldiers) took hold of the thread, the long rope, and tied it firmly.
> "Tighter, Ique, tie it tighter," he would say. ...

And I would watch as the blood built up at the tip of his strangled finger, those drawn-on eyes bulging as the thread cut deep into the top joint, a head on the brink of bursting, and our stifled laughter. (Remainder 99–100)

If we recall Tomkins's definition of rapid neural firing as triggering the startle response (495–96), we might think it the expected reaction readers would have to hangman—or any of the other games the narrators describe linking play and actual physical pain that they consciously inflicted on each other—and even appeared to enjoy. On a symbolic level, this episode evokes the sadistic pleasure of the torturers during the Pinochet era and fits into Fletcher's allegorical category of symmetrical plots/double meanings (282-300). Iquela unconsciously highlights this connection in referring to her fingers as "soldiers" and her "army."

A second violent game involved Iquela trying to blind Felipe (167), while in a third, Felipe scattered rocks and shards of glass on the ground and goaded Iquela to walk on them, until she could no longer bear the pain of their cutting into the skin on her feet (*La resta* 260–61; Remainder 188). These painful games also involved other children. Iquela recounts a scratching game she played with a fellow classmate named Camila, which, yet again, allegorizes the violence of the Pinochet era:

Dejar que la otra se rascara el anverso de la mano el mayor tiempo posible. . . . Su uña se movía a un ritmo constante. Raspaba, abría . . . hasta que bajo su uña ya no quedaba más espacio porque lo invadía mi piel descascarada. Porque mi sangre se amontonaba. . . . Mi mano tardaba semanas en sanar. (*La resta* 166)

Her finger would move to a constant beat. She scratched. My skin came apart. . . . My hand would take weeks to heal. (Remainder 117–18)

The representation of children's aggressive play during the Pinochet era is an illustration of affects in children stimulated by the threatening and violent atmosphere of the dictatorship. In *Aggression in Play Therapy* (2018), Lisa Dion demonstrates that aggressive play is a neurobiological reaction (as is affect; cf. Tomkins) that results from memories enacted in play. She states that

> [w]hen we look at aggression from this perspective [neurobiology], we begin to understand that children's biology is attempting to integrate their sympathetic (hyper-aroused) and dorsal parasympathetic (hypo-aroused) states as they work through their traumatic memories and sensations.... Aggression ... is a normal biological response that arises when our sense of safety or our ideas about who we think we are, who others are supposed to be, and how we think the world is supposed to operate are compromised.... The playroom is the children's safe and contained place for exploring whatever they need to explore to help them feel better. (9–22)

Dion's ideas stem from earlier studies on this aspect of play. For example, Jaqueline Jukes and Jeffrey Goldstein define aggressive play to include "mock fighting, rough and tumble play, and/or fantasy aggression" (127). They also explain reasons for aggressive play, one particularly relevant: that it "affords the child an opportunity to come to terms with war, violence, and death," the stuff of "adult behavior and values" (131). At the same time, as they contend, aggressive play allows for exploring various environments from within a context of safety: "In play, children explore not only their physical environment but their emotional, social, and cultural environments also. According to Dolf Zillmann, play is a means for achieving emotional and physiological self-regulation" (137–39). Finally, Eleanor Palmer Bonte and Mary Musgrove, who conducted a study of children's play in Hawaii during World War II, found that war-play occurred extensively among kindergarten children whom they observed.

Thus the violent play of Felipe and Iquela's childhood, as the research on play confirms, has them work through the trauma of the violence they experienced as children in the only way they could. On a larger scale, this is what the novel does as a whole: it comes to terms and moves past the trauma caused by the Pinochet dictatorship. Later in the novel, we learn that Felipe and Iquela had a tacit agreement never to speak of certain things they had overheard as children, especially not that Iquela's father had betrayed Felipe's father to the government, which led to his death. That prohibition against speaking did not keep either from acting out through the accommodating indirections of play, including its muted forms of violence. However, their participation in these activities does not necessarily imply that they themselves subscribe to violent values, but rather that they were trying to deal with the stories of the dictatorship through play. Indeed, the novel suggests that the two are attempting to break free from this violent past identified with their parents. This can be observed at the end of the novel when both reject their parental past.

A series of episodes revolving around same-sex relationships is still another way readers may get physiologically startled. On one occasion, while Felipe is counting cadavers, another man tells him that he has a "lindo pecho" ([*La resta* 105] nice chest [Remainder 72]). After a brief discussion, Felipe asks him whether he has seen the cadavers and, following that, the two have a sexual encounter that is graphically described (*La resta* 108–09). *La resta* also includes a sexual relationship between Iquela and Paloma (174).

In an interview in 2019, Trabucco Zerán commented on the importance of these same-sex relationships in her novel:

> The three characters have sexual encounters with same[-]sex partners. When I ask about this she replies: "I'm glad you mention the queerness of the characters because that is something that is not very commented on in Chile, especially because it's something that is still taboo. The three characters have a queer relationship with their bodies and with the others because it gave them the desire to transgress and for me that made them a lot more complex and different than their parents' generation." (Rothlisberger n.p.)

For many readers, seeing graphic sexual acts depicted in a novel could potentially trigger a startle response, particularly when those acts are "queer." However, the larger point is that Trabucco Zerán intends transgressive representation, which lies at the core of those children of the dictatorship who act up and rebel against their figures of authority and the burden of the past in anticipation of a different kind of future. This tendency also affects Felipe and Iquela beyond their sexual practices.

Iquela, as readers know, has a somewhat problematic relationship with her mother throughout the novel. At the beginning, she declares that the 1988 plebiscite in Chile was not her own memory, but one that her mother foisted on her (15). Later on, when Paloma convinces Iquela not to tell her mother about their trip to Mendoza to recover Ingrid's corpse (which was diverted there when a volcanic ash storm[10] hit Santiago), Iquela imagines a mother-daughter conversation in which her mother criticizes her for wasting her time, including the impending trip to Mendoza (*La resta* 140; Remainder 96). Iquela refuses to return to Santiago with Paloma and to her mother; she remains, instead, in Mendoza, while Felipe drives the hearse back to Santiago. The point is this: Iquela is trying to free herself from the past through acts of defying and rebelling against her mother. The birds in the following passage capture that:

> Vi ... a decenas de pájaros preparando su vuelo ... y la [a Paloma] vi partir sin más, dejando frente a mí ... la perfecta sincronía de los pájaros en vuelo, desprendiéndose de la tierra en medio de un arrullo desconocido, un rumor que estalló de pronto en una algarabía incontenible. (*La resta* 278–79)

> I noticed, in the near distance, dozens of birds preparing for flight ... and I watched her [Paloma] as she drove away, leaving only those wings beating in steady unison before me, the perfect harmony of birds in flight, taking off to the sound of a strange lullaby, a murmur that burst suddenly into an uncontainable din. (Remainder 195)

In a similar manner, Felipe asserts his distance from his father. The first time occurs when his grandmother Elsa used to tell him that his eyes were just like his father's. He would say "no, eso es mentira ... No tengo los ojos de ningún papá, mis ojos son míos ... Eso soy, hijo de mí mismo" ([*La resta* 257] no, that's a lie. ... I don't have the eyes of any father, my eyes are mine, mine, mine. ... That's what I am, my own son [Remainder 186]). The second time happens at the novel's end when Felipe imagines that he is like a bird that can fly away and be reborn: "Corro por el centro como corren las aves grandes ... arde Santiago completo y son sus llamas que alumbran ... mientras me nazco a mí mismo, mientras me engendran las llamas, debo quemar el aire con mi voz ... con mi cifra, menos uno, menos uno, menos uno" ([*La resta* 276–79] I run through the center like long-legged birds run. ... [T]he whole of Santiago is on fire and I shine in the light of those flames. ... [A]s I give birth to myself, as the flames give life to me I have to scorch the air with my voice . . . with . . . my final sum, minus one, minus one, minus one [Remainder 199–202]). In Felipe's imagination, he is reborn, while the old Santiago, site of the destruction caused by the dictatorship, burns up. Moreover, his new number "menos uno" (minus one, no longer zero), suggests that he is one less person held under the influence of the past. This is the "remainder" alluded to in the novel's title.

In addition to the double meanings, Angus Fletcher identifies a third allegorical element, the symbolic battle or questing journey: "There is usually a paradoxical suggestion that by leaving home the hero can return to another better 'home.' Self-knowledge is apparently the goal" (151). In *La resta*, the questing journey takes the form of a road trip in search of Ingrid's body. Paloma, Iquela, and Felipe travel in a hearse across the border to Mendoza and eventually locate the body in an airport hangar. The following passage narrated by Felipe suggests a symbolic association between the corpses found in the hangar and those disappeared and murdered during the dictatorship: "Eran decenas. No, muchísimos más. Cientos de ataúdes . . . Cientos de muertos queriendo volver, retornar, repatriarse" ([*La resta* 246] There were dozens of them. No. Many more than that. Hundreds of coffins . . . Hundreds of dead men and women wanting to go back, to move back, to be repatriated [Remainder 177]). In this context, Ingrid's missing body symbolizes the disappeared. The journey of recovering her body and returning it to Chile has much resonance, as that act symbolizes putting the past to rest, which the protagonists Felipe and Iquela have wanted all along. Also, as we have already seen, both Iquela and Felipe appear to find themselves, their own identity, and freedom at the end of the novel because of the journey to Mendoza.

Felipe's cadaver counting, Felipe's and Iquela's aggressive play as children, and the discovery of multiple bodies in the airport hangar are all symbolic elements designed to cause a physiological reaction that startles the reader. These episodes stimulate affects in the reader, which in turn lead to surprise, shock, indignation, and other like responses. Despite the negative quality of the children playing violent games, Felipe killing his pet parrot, or the same-sex relationships that some readers may disapprove of, the readers are able to identify and feel empathy for these characters because they are made to understand the circumstances under which Felipe, Iquela, and Paloma were raised. However, rather than the positive empathy the reader feels in Fernández's novel toward innocent torture victims, the empathy in *La resta* qualifies as somewhat "negative" because the reader feels a more distant empathy due to the violent actions and, for some, because of the same-sex relationships.

A third novel that relies heavily on the creation of affect and emotion is Fátima Sime's *Carne de perra*, which stands out among novels about torture for its vivid descriptions of sexual torture that the protagonist María Rosa, a sufferer of Stockholm syndrome, undergoes. The novel relies heavily on two affects: surprise-startle and disgust/dissmell. The descriptions of violence and sexual torture often elicit in the reader a physiological reaction of startle with the accompanying emotions of shock and disgust. While the character María Rosa experiences the physical affect of disgust/dissmell throughout the novel, the provocation of moral disgust in the reader creates a parallel between the character and the reader and thus serves as a means of identification between the two. The novel's emphasis on María Rosa's sensory perceptions of disgust suggests a close connection to the condition of abjection detailed in chapter 5. However, I have chosen to include *Carne de perra* in this chapter because its textual strategies are very similar to those employed in *La dimensión* and *La resta*.

Carne begins with the physical torture of María Rosa who has been detained because her boyfriend is a leftist leader. She is "rescued" from this torture by a lieutenant named Emilio Krank who refers to himself as *El Príncipe* throughout the novel. According to Cristián Montes Capó, Krank is based on Edwin Dimter Bianchi, whose real-life nickname was "The Prince" and who has been unofficially credited with murdering the famous singer Víctor Jara in Estadio Chile (69). The book provides vivid descriptions of Krank's sexual torture of María Rosa. It also describes how María Rosa, a nurse, is drafted by Krank to help revive tortured prisoners so that they can continue to be tortured, as well as how she is enlisted to help with an important political assassination. Montes Capó points out that the patient murdered in the hospital with María Rosa's help is based on the death of former president Eduardo Frei Montalva, who, it is believed, was murdered during his stay at the Santa María Clinic for a minor procedure on January 22, 1982 (69). After this important episode, which can be considered another memory knot in Chilean history, María Rosa is abruptly freed and flown to Stockholm. Her exile there is not coincidental but rather an indicator of her suffering Stockholm syndrome. After twenty years, she returned to Chile, but the scars from her experience were evident, particularly in her inability to sustain normal relationships with men, as well as her inability to eat food (she mostly drank beer for sustenance). The reasons for her social and food disorders relate to the sexual torture she experienced, which I discuss below.

Emilio Krank does not rape María Rosa by sexual penetration. Rather, Krank's sexual preferences border on sexual fetishism, since he is only capable of sustaining an erection outside of a woman through the use of other stimuli. According to Krueger and his research team, sexual fetishism is the "Reliance on some non-living object as a stimulus for sexual arousal and sexual gratification. . . . Fetishism should be diagnosed only if the fetish is the most important source of sexual stimulation or essential for satisfactory response" (1533). In addition, fetishism as a "paraphilic disorder" should only diagnosed when it involves "sexual arousal patterns that focus on non-consenting others or are associated with substantial distress or direct risk of injury or death" (1544). These conditions describe Krank's sexual encounters with María Rosa, who has no choice but to participate because of her status as political prisoner. The stimulus upon which Krank generally relies to orgasm is food, which he pours over María Rosa's body, particularly her vagina. He eats the food off of her body as a way to reach orgasm, as is evident in the following passage:

> Rellenando de aserrín una muñeca de trapo. Así lo imagina cuando el hombre empieza a embutir, frenético, los higos. Los aplasta entre sus dientes y luego los empuja. Como si su vagina fuera la tripa de un animal. ¡Animal! ¡Mil veces animal! Parece un cerdo con el hocico chorreando harinilla. Estaba errada. ¡Odia esos labios que rezuman pulpa de higo! . . . Siente sus entrañas ahítas, a punto de reventar. Aúlla de dolor. . . . Los pelos del bigote hieren los labios de la vulva. . . . El hombre continúa chupando, alimentándose hasta el orgasmo, hasta explotar ahí, con la cara entre sus piernas. (ch. 6)

> Filling a ragdoll with sawdust. That's how I imagine it when the man begins to frenetically cram in the figs. He crushes them in his teeth and then he pushes them. As if her vagina were an animal's intestine. Animal! A thousand times an animal! He looks like a hog with his

snout dripping flour. She was mistaken. She hates those lips that ooze fig pulp.... She feels her entrails full, on the point of exploding. She howls in pain.... The hairs of his moustache bruise the lips of her vulva.... The man continues sucking, feeding himself until he orgasms, until he explodes there, with his face between her legs.[11]

In this passage, Krank satisfies the definition of "paraphilic disorder" as the Krueger research team has defined it. Moreover, most readers will find this passage highly disturbing. Krank is likened to a hog, while the discomfort Maria Rosa feels is highlighted by her "howling in pain." Her vagina is described as being "wounded" by Krank's beard. All the details of this description create a surprise-startle reaction in the reader who most likely was not expecting to encounter such a description. The second phase of this affect-development relates to the creation of the disgust/dissmell affect, which subsequent passages in the novel provoke. After this sexual torture with the figs, María Rosa takes a shower to attempt to rid herself of the fruit shoved into her vagina:

> Está bajo la ducha.... Se concentra en el jabón. La espuma... se enreda en los vellos del sexo, se dispersa bajando por las piernas. No soporta la idea de acarrear la fetidez si los restos de fruta se descomponen en su interior. Presiente que aún hay más, que no todo cayó en el retrete.... Entonces, con el índice y el anular lubricados de jabón hurga en su interior hasta encontrar el bulto blando de fruta mascada. Desesperada, raspa con las uñas... Siempre quedan restos entre las rugosidades de la vagina. (ch. 7)

> She is under the shower.... She concentrates on the soap. The lather ... becomes entangled in the hairs of her vagina, it disperses as it goes down her legs.... She cannot stand the idea of carrying the fetidness of the remains of the fruit decomposing inside of her. She has the feeling that there is still more, that not all of it fell into the toilet.... Then, with her index and ring fingers lubricated with soap, she rummages around inside herself until she finds the soft lump of chewed fruit. Desperate, she scratches with her nails.... There are always remainders among the ridges of the vagina.

In another passage, María Rosa describes how she likes to air out her vagina on the balcony because the cream that Krank stuffs in it is difficult to expel from its folds and crinkles (ch. 22).

In *Anatomy of Disgust* (1997), William Ian Miller has examined those elements constituting the affect (physiological response) of disgust and how they provoke disgust as an emotion. Disgust itself

> indicate[s] a complex sentiment that can be lexically marked in English by expressions declaring things or actions to be repulsive, revolting, or giving rise to reactions described as revulsion and abhorrence as well as disgust. Disgust names a syndrome in which all these terms have their proper role. They all convey a strong sense of aversion to something perceived as dangerous because of its powers to contaminate, infect, or pollute by proximity, contact, or ingestion.... Disgust ... is not so much [a feeling of] nausea as of the uneasiness, the panic, of varying intensity, that attends the awareness of being defiled. (109)

Miller cites Paul Rozin's work on disgust, noting that Rozin focuses on "oral incorporation and food ejection" as the central axis of disgust. Rozin's later work on disgust adds "bodily products, and animals and their wastes and then five additional domains: sex, hygiene, death, violations of the body envelope (gore, amputations) . . . and sociomoral violations. All of these are gathered under one new generalizing theory of disgust: a psychic need to avoid reminders of our animal origins" (160). Finally, Miller indicates that disgust "deals with harms that sicken us in the telling things for which there could be no plausible claim of right: rape, child abuse, torture, genocide, predatory murder and maiming. Sadism and masochism belong here too" (ch. 2).

If we now return to the previously cited descriptions, we can see how disgust occurs in both María Rosa and the reader. The description of Emilio Krank's actions unites several of the elements normally associated with disgust: defilement, sex, and oral incorporation of food, torture, and sadism. The interesting point is that the novel simultaneously produces disgust in the character María Rosa, who feels defiled by both the food and the sexual torture and then in the reader who, upon reading descriptions of sexual torture, feels shock initially and, after that, moral disgust. According to Miller, shock and disgust are intimately related: "Disgust shocks, entertains by shocking and sears itself to memory" (17). The ability to make the reader experience the same sensations that the protagonist experiences results in a strong reader identification with the character. The "resetting effect" of the surprise-startle affect allows the reader to better process the scene and then to experience the full impact of Krank's actions. As María Rosa experiences physical disgust and defilement, the reader experiences moral disgust. Mentally visualizing María Rosa's suffering causes readers to experience a "mirror neuron" effect (see ch.1), that is, the same affects and emotions as those of the character—and hence to experience empathy.

In at least one instance as well, María Rosa experiences moral disgust. When she is enlisted to prepare poisoned compresses for application on a patient deemed an "enemy" of the government, María feels nauseated and wants to vomit. Nausea and vomiting are physiological responses associated with the disgust/dissmell affect, and are usually associated with unpleasant smells or foods. Nonetheless, in the following passage, they are keenly linked to María Rosa's moral disgust with her own actions: "Ayer, cuando el contacto confirmó que la intervención sería hoy, le pareció que alguien le tensaba una cuerda entre las sienes. Se siente mareada. Antes de entrar a la clínica tiene que apoyarse en un poste. Tiene una vaga sensación de nausea. Trata de vomitar. Pero no puede" ([ch. 27] Yesterday, when the contact confirmed that the intervention would be today, it seemed like someone was tightening a rope between her temples. She feels dizzy. Before entering the clinic she has to lean on a post. She has a vague sensation of nausea. She tries to vomit. But she can't).

The degree to which the reader identifies with and feels empathy for María Rosa depends on how readers choose to interpret the character. If they view her as a morally ambiguous and willfully collaborative, then they will be less empathetic than those who view her as suffering from Stockholm syndrome, which gives her no choice but to collaborate. The former interpretation might find some support in her euphoria after the murder and her desire to celebrate with Krank. Either way, the reader feels "negative empathy" for María Rosa because of her participation in the murder. The torture and trauma she has endured, by contrast, serve as mitigating circumstances that allow the reader to feel empathy despite her morally abhorrent acts.

Returning to the affect of disgust/dissmell, it is highly significant that the novel *Carne* dwells on María Rosa's olfactory and gustatory reactions, not just during torture, but after her experience as a prisoner in her subsequent "normal" life. The fact that she is very sensitive to smells can be interpreted as a long-lasting result of her experiences with sexual torture and the smells emanating from her vagina after being stuffed with food. On more than a dozen occasions, both during and after her time as a prisoner, those sensory perceptions are described. In the flashbacks to her past as a prisoner, for example, readers learn repeatedly that Krank smells "a alquitrán, a ferrocarril" ([ch. 25] of tar, of the railroad); when Krank brings her a bag of figs that he will later stuff into her vagina, he tells her first to smell what is in the bag: "¡Huele, mierda! Con el cambucho pegado a la boca y la nariz, la sensación de asfixia aumenta. El papel se infla y desinfla. . . . ¡Son higos, son higos!, grita con el último aliento" ([ch. 6] Smell, shit! With the paper bag stuck to her mouth and nose, the feeling of asphyxia increases. The paper inflates and uninflates. . . . They are figs! They are figs! She shouts with her last breath); or when she recalls her days in Krank's thrall: "Recuerdo cuando me rescató. Pensé que me estaba salvando. Luego, ¿cuántos días me tuvo aislada en ese baño? Me rodeaba la humedad y había un olor pútrido, mohoso como el de una tumba. La mía" ([ch. 12] I remember when he rescued me. I thought that he was saving me. Later, how many days did he keep me isolated in that bathroom? I was surrounded by humidity, and there was a putrid smell, moldy like that of a tomb. Mine); or when the torture area is described as having "un olor a mierda" ([ch. 16] a smell of shit). Krank's car, we learn, smells of plastic (ch. 18), as do the pieces of furniture in María Rosa's new apartment (ch. 21). Similarly, in the following passage, Krank makes her eat peanuts even though she finds them revolting and is allergic to them:

> Luego se acerca, la toma, la sienta sobre sus rodillas. ¡No quiero! Dice ella cuando le mete maní en la boca, sabes que me salen ronchas. No quiere. La atrae hacia sí. Ella siente la cacha de la pistola hundirse en su nalga derecha . . . sin mascar se traga los granos de maní. (ch. 15)

> Then he approaches, takes her, and sits her on his knees. I don't want to! She says when he puts peanuts in her mouth, you know that my skin breaks out. She doesn't want to. He pulls her toward him. She feels the handle of the pistol sink into her right buttock. . . . [W]ithout chewing, she swallows the peanuts.

Still in another scene, Krank force-feeds María Rosa oysters, even though they taste acidic and metallic to her (ch. 15). María Rosa is, in sum, repelled by the odors and tastes forced upon her. Just as many examples surface in the present—the smell of the slaughterhouse, the hospital, the guitarist who approaches her in the restaurant and smells like Krank); only pleasant odors, such as the scent of roses, can counteract negative smells. All of these seemingly incidental details contribute, in other words, to the development of her affects and the feelings of physical disgust, which register as moral disgust in readers who are the "witnesses" of her torture and trauma.

The toll of trauma María Rosa has suffered catches up with her once she returns to Chile at the end of the dictatorship. Although she remembers her family fondly, she has resisted contacting any of its members during her many years of exile in Stockholm. She is unable to sustain normal relationships with men. Her relationships are reduced to a series of brief sexual encounters with different taxi drivers. She is also incapable of eating as the consequence of her years of sexual food torture. She limits herself to a snack from time to time and only buys cans of beer at the supermarket (ch. 5). Put simply, María cannot sustain normal loving relationships with men or eat normal meals because of what Krank did to her. Her life after Krank bears the scars of life with Krank, a fact that mitigates the moral disgust readers might still harbor over her participation in the hospital patient's murder and that opens the door to negative empathy.

Elaine Scarry has traced how torture and confession destroy the worlds of their victims in *The Body in Pain* (1985). In the throes of that unmoored state, confession is meaningless to the tortured. The interrogation techniques that victims endure amount to a fiction manufactured to justify the action of torture and to assert the power of the regime. According to Scarry, torture has a structure that "entails the simultaneous and inseparable occurrence of three events ... First, the infliction of physical pain; second, the objectification of the central attributes of pain; and third, the translation of those attributes into the insignia of the regime" (18). To this she adds,

> This translation is made possible by and occurs across the phenomena common to both power and pain agency. The electric generator, the whips and canes ... the prisoner's sexuality ... the telephone, the chair ... the prisoner's ear drums—all these and many more ... ha[ve]

become part of the glutted realm of weaponry, weaponry that can refer equally to pain or power.... As an actual physical fact, a weapon is an object that goes into the body and produces pain. As a perceptual fact, it lifts the pain out of the body and makes... it act like a bridge or mechanism across which some of pain's attributes... its incontestable reality... its power of... world dissolution can be lifted away from the source, can be separated from the sufferer and referred to power; broken off from the body and attached instead to the regime. (56)

Scarry emphasizes that sexual torture is a way in which one's own body is made into a weapon against one's own self. She also emphasizes how the victim's world is obliterated through torture. We see this in María Rosa when she claims that Krank has become her world: "Él era el amo, mi amo. Me producía terror. También me excitaba. Una mezcla que no lograba entender. Estaba presa. ¿De él? No. Más que de él, de mi apego a la vida. Me dejé llevar" ([ch.12] He was the master, my master. He produced terror in me. He also excited me. A mixture that I didn't manage to understand. I was a prisoner. Of him? No. More than of him, of my attachment to life. I let myself get carried away). When she claims that more than Krank's prisoner she was a prisoner of her attachment to life, the reader can grasp how life/Krank became synonymous. To survive at all, she had to align herself with Krank because her old world had disappeared. The only other option was to die.

María Rosa's relationship with Krank leads to the novel's somewhat ambiguous ending. Krank, a patient in the hospital where María Rosa works, is dying of laryngeal cancer. He asks her to kill him. At first, María tortures him by taking away his oxygen and pain medication. However, in the end, she decides to assist him in his requested euthanasia, telling him that she is doing it not for him, but for herself, because she has feelings (ch. 30). Most critics have interpreted her act as necessary to her ultimate freedom from Krank, and thus her motivation here. Brintrup and Montes Capó both offer this interpretation (Brintrup 142–43; Montes Capó 75–76). However, I would argue that there is some ambiguity in her decision, since it is prefaced by the following dialogue with the bartender:

¿Usted cree que llevando una vida miserable, ... peor que en una cárcel, uno paga sus culpas? Depende, dijo él ... De la gravedad de lo que le

> hizo a la otra persona. Las heridas de amor son cosa seria. Digamos que la persona cometió algo espantoso, algo horrendo, inimaginable. ¿Quiere que le diga algo?, dijo él, ... Nada es tan terrible cuando ha habido amor.... Yo sentía ese algo sin nombre aflorando dentro de mí.... No sé cuánto tiempo pasó o cuántos vasos me tomé. Pero ya no podía seguir engañándome. (ch. 29)

> Do you think that having a miserable life, ... worse than in a jail, one pays for his offenses? It depends, he said ... [o]n the gravity of what you did to the other person. The wounds of love are a serious thing. Let's say that the person did something frightful, something horrendous, unimaginable. You want me to tell you something, he said, ... Nothing is so terrible when there has been love.... I felt that something without name flowering inside me.... I don't know how much time passed or how many shots I drank. But I could no longer go on deceiving myself.

This passage suggests to the reader that María Rosa admits to herself that the reason she assisted Krank in the murder was because she loved him. The fact that the next day she goes to the hospital and helps him die implies a relationship between the conversation with the bartender and her actions. Thus, when she tells Krank that she is not doing it for him, but because of her own feelings, this statement would be consistent with the protagonist's recognition that on some level, she did love Krank despite the horrible things he did. These feelings constitute Stockholm syndrome and incline the reader toward empathy for María Rosa.

La dimensión, *La resta*, and *Carne* rely on affects, particularly Tomkins's surprise-startle and disgust/dissmell, to help readers to comprehend the shocking torture and atrocities suffered under the Pinochet dictatorship. This technique also aids in the creation of both "positive" and "negative" empathy for the characters in each novel. Readers are made to feel both the shock and disgust of the protagonists, which leads to the ability to empathize with characters even when they are morally ambiguous or exhibit other undesirable characteristics.

CHAPTER 7

Conclusion

The Chilean Dictatorship Novel in Context

THE CHILEAN NOVELS WRITTEN ABOUT the Pinochet dictatorship are a subgroup of a larger corpus known variably as the Latin American dictatorship novel or dictator novel. Carlos Pacheco has suggested the term "narrativa de la dictadura" (narrative of dictatorship) to refer to those works whose "tema principal sea la figura del dictador (aunque él no sea necesariamente el personaje protagónico) o el régimen dictatorial" ([38] main theme is the figure of the dictator [though he is not necessarily the protagonist] or the dictatorial regime), noting that many works are set during dictatorships; however, the dictatorship itself does not constitute a main theme of the novel and therefore these works do not belong to this body of fiction. Pacheco traces the history of the development of dictatorship narrative from Romanticism (Jorge Mármol's *Amalia* (1851) is considered the first novelistic example of it) through the early 1980s, largely adopting an aesthetic criterion that moves from the dictatorship novel as pamphlet or political tool to the progressively more aesthetic concerns of the now-classic dictator novels of the 1970s (Augusto Roa Bastos's *Yo el Supremo* (I The Supreme), Alejo Carpentier's *El recurso del metodo* (Reasons of State), and Gabriel García Márquez's *El otoño del patriarca* (The Autumn of the Patriarch).

Karl Kohut, who specifically studies the Argentine dictatorship novel, categorizes these novels into three groups: "En la llamada literatura de la dictadura, podemos distinguir tres momentos: el primero precede inmediatamente a la dictadura del *Proceso*, el segundo la acompaña, y el tercero es posterior a ella" ([171] In the so-called literature of dictatorship, we can distinguish three moments: the first immediately precedes the *Proceso* dictatorship, the second takes place during the dictatorship, and the third is posterior to the dictatorship). The first of these categories is specific to Argentine history. It refers to the period in which Isabel Perón was president and during which her minister José López Rega essentially governed as dictator and prepared the path for the right-wing military takeover. The second and third are equally applicable to many other countries in which dictatorship novels are generally divided into those written during the dictatorship and those written after as postdictatorship/postmemory novels. Both Kohut and Pacheco emphasize the relationship between this subgenre of Latin American fiction, which belongs to the larger body of historical fiction, and Latin American historical reality. Pacheco notes,

> Podemos observar intervenciones militares que dan paso a tales regímenes en Argentina (1962, 1966, 1976) Perú (1962 y desde 1975), Guatemala, Honduras, República Dominicana y Ecuador (1963), Brasil (1964), Bolivia (1971, 1974, y 1989), Uruguay y Chile (1973). Mientras tanto, Paraguay, Haití y Nicaragua (hasta 1979 esta última) permanecían bajo el yugo de dictaduras que personal o dinásticamente, habían sobrevivido en el poder por largos años. (34–35)

> We can observe military interventions that give rise to such regimes in Argentina (1962, 1966, 1976), Peru (1962 and since 1975), Guatemala, Honduras, The Dominican Republic, Ecuador (1963), Brazil (1964) Bolivia (1971, 1974, and 1989), Uruguay and Chile (1973). Meanwhile, Paraguay, Haiti, and Nicaragua (the last of these until 1979) remained under the yoke of dictatorships that personally or dynastically had survived in power for many years.

The body of works considered "dictatorship narrative" has been expanded by a number of critics who work on US Latino/a literature. Both Daynali Flores-Rodríguez and Jennifer Harford Vargas (*Forms of Dictatorship* [2018]) have explored the lingering presence of Latin American dictatorships in the works of writers such as Julia Álvarez and Junot Díaz, among many others. Both Flores-Rodríguez and Vargas underscore how Latino/a novels focus on ordinary citizens affected by dictatorship, rather than on the dictators themselves. While Flores-Rodríguez studies the role that families play in these works, Harford Vargas examines how narrative structure intertwines "the critical concerns of Latina/o literature—with regard to race, class, gender, sexuality, ability, migration, citizenship, language politics and cultural mestizaje" (10)—with the traditional themes of the Latin American dictatorship novel. Vargas sees the fundamental message of these novels as the imagining of a better future in the wake of an authoritarian oppressive past.

The numerous critics who have focused on dictatorship narrative have attempted to extract some common major themes and motifs present in these works. According to Harford Vargas, who offers the best summary,

> Some typical themes and tropes associated with the Latin American novels include the monopolization of power and authority, supernatural or messianic power, omnipotence, megalomania, and egocentrism, cruelty, barbarism, repression (censorship terror, jail, torture, death, disappearance), paranoia, dependency on the United States, the dictator's lack of class and education, the dictator as a bastard child, the dictator's solitude (e.g., lack of friendship and of love), the dictator's double or doppelgänger, the dictator's homosocial acolytes, the dictator as archetype or myth, the failing body of the dictator, the demise of the dictator. (196)

Harford Vargas blends the terms "tropes" (motifs) and themes, but these are obviously different entities. Eugene H. Falk (*Types of Thematic Structure* [1967]) distinguishes between three key concepts: motifs, themes, and messages:

> The term "theme" may also be assigned to the ideas that emerge from the particular structure of such textual elements as actions, statements revealing state of mind or feelings, gestures, or meaningful environmental settings. Such textual elements I designate by the term "motif," the idea that emerges from motifs by means of an abstraction, I call the theme.... Sometimes the message a work is intended or supposed to convey is considered to be the theme. A message, however, is the result of reflections in which motifs are not under immediate consideration. The theme is a reflection upon a previous conception gained by abstraction from the motifs themselves. A message is thus a "second intention"; and when we confuse a message with a theme, we do so at the risk of assuming wrongly that a work is preconceived embodiment of a "philosophy." (2–3)

Falk's distinctions here are important ones to consider when analyzing dictatorship narratives. It is fairly obvious that most dictatorship novels are a criticism of authoritarian rule, and consequently their message is to learn from the past and avoid dictatorship in the future. Moreover, most of these novels share common themes such as abuse of power and the effects of repression based on common motifs such as torture and disappearance. However, despite these similarities, I would argue that these novels convey other central messages (or "secondary intentions") based on these common themes that go beyond the universal criticism of dictatorship and that can vary considerably between novels or groups of novels.

As this book lays out, a large group of works within the Chilean dictatorship novel (particularly those that are postmemory works, as opposed to early novels about the dictatorship) strongly emphasize the feelings and emotions of their characters and forcefully engage reader empathy. Although it certainly can be argued that all literature depicts the emotional states of characters and appeals to those of the reader, it is also true that often these emotions constitute a motif or evolve into a theme but are not the ultimate message of the work. A good example is Mario Vargas Llosa's *La fiesta del chivo* (2000; The Feast of the Goat) based on the dictatorship of Rafael Leonidas Trujillo in the Dominican Republic. The novel portrays the feelings of the protagonist Urania Cabral, who was raped by the dictator when she was only fourteen. We see her hate for her father, who was the one who offered her to the dictator to regain his favor after he had fallen into disgrace, as well as the devastating effects of her past on her psychological well-being and her future relationships. It is impossible for the reader not to feel empathy for Urania, as well as for the dictator's assassins, each of whom has a good reason for hating Trujillo. Nonetheless, these emotions do not constitute the central message of Vargas Llosa's novel. Instead, the novel ultimately conveys the message that the Dominican people were psychologically so traumatized by the dictator that as a society they became paralyzed to oppose him when the occasion arose. The novel is a study in social psychology and the psychological effects of dictatorship on a populace.[1]

In contrast, as I have argued here, the Chilean dictatorship novel does not employ emotions as a tangential motif or theme used to constitute a different message. Rather, emotions are part of the central message itself. According to Pacheco, the imperative the dictatorship novel has embraced to reexamine the past is part of a general movement of "revisionismo histórico" (historical revisionism). I would like to argue that the Chilean dictatorship novel, instead of filling in historical gaps as do novels such as *Yo el Supremo* (which shows a side of Dr. Francia left out by the historians who fashion a "black legend" around the figure), fills in the memory gaps of the past created by the political environments of the Pinochet dictatorship and Concertación governments. As the introduction makes clear, attempts either to forget the past during the dictatorship or to eliminate the emotional component of suffering in the postdictatorship era have created lacunae in the historical memory that have outlasted the Pinochet dictatorship. The message behind the emotions studied in this volume: loss and abandonment (ch. 2), despair (ch. 3), melancholy (ch. 4), abjection (ch. 5), and shock, disgust, and empathy (ch. 6) is that the emotional sequelae of the dictatorship matter greatly and need to be reconstituted to understand what dictatorship exacted and how to avoid its repetition. Without understanding what people felt under Pinochet, comprehension is impossible.

As Gerald Prince has pointed out, literary messages are variable depending upon what aspects of the text the receiver chooses to focus on (531). Readers (receivers) study a narrative's main features—the actions of characters, goals, situational changes, and motivations—to arrive at a text's message (530). Obviously, no single message exists in any text. Thus, what I am proposing here is that when we look at the Chilean novels as a group; indeed their preponderance of emphasis on affect and emotion across these texts suggests that returning feeling to memory is a central message (if not *the* central message) of the Chilean dictatorship novel.

To highlight the Chilean dictatorship novel's emphasis on emotion, I would like to compare Chile's novelistic production with that of the other countries of the Southern Cone, particularly, Argentina, whose historical trajectory most closely resembles that of Chile. Chile, Argentina, and Uruguay all suffered military coups in the 1970s. In 1973, the Uruguayan president Juan María Bordaberry, aided by the military, authored a coup d'etat (Ros 135). The dictatorship lasted until 1985. According to Ana Ros,

> In 1985, a plebiscite confirmed and legitimized the military amnesty, and the chief executives in the following fifteen years resorted to

> this vote to undermine victims' and human rights organization's demands for truth and justice.... In this context, 25 years after the first referendum about the law, the population again voted in favour of the amnesty for the military in 2009.... The historian Eugenia Allier observes that until 2006, Uruguay was the only country in the Southern Cone in which no military and police personnel had been prosecuted or extradited. The historical context helps understand the unique character of the Uruguayan post-dictatorship period. (159)

Ros goes on to explain that the military, instead of torturing and disappearing Uruguayan citizens, resorted to massive imprisonment, close to six thousand in a population of three million, making Uruguay the country with the highest percentage of prisoners per capita. The rest of the population was classified according to public "threat levels," which affected their ability to find employment and engage in other activities (161). Ros attributes the severe lack of cultural production on the topic of the dictatorship to the continued vote for military amnesty and the widespread effects of political profiling and imprisonment, which led to a powerful desire to forget the past in Uruguay and to a general culture of forgetting. One can only find a few isolated novels on the topic. These include *Las cartas que no llegaron* (2000; The Letters that Never Arrived) by Mauricio Rosencof; *El furgón de los locos* (2001; Truck of Fools) by Carlos Liscano; *Las cinco puntas del lucero* (2002; The Five Points of the Star) by Tessa Bridal; and *Acero y piel* (2006; Steel and Skin) by Tony Carro, as well as the novels published in English by Uruguay-American writer Carolina de Robertis: *Cantoras* (2017) and *The Invisible Mountain* (2010).

Las cartas is an excellent example of the difference I am positing here between the Chilean corpus of dictatorship novels and those from other countries. Its primary narrator is a man who is imprisoned during the Uruguayan dictatorship. He recalls his family members as well as letters that his extended family wrote in Poland during World War II (the latter died in the concentration camps). Rosencof's novel exudes feelings of nostalgia experienced by the protagonist in his cell as he reflects on his youth and family, particularly his father. However, the emotions felt by the protagonist are a motif, rather than the message. The nostalgia motif is used to construct the importance of memory above all else, and ultimately this constitutes the novel's principal message to the reader. This can be seen in the following montage of citations from *Las cartas*:

Viejo, en alguno de los escalones que conducen al monumento del gueto, las deposité [las piedras], como en un ritual, pensando cada paso, pensando cada piedra, cada resistencia que fue y que es papá, para siempre. (62)

. . .

La casa, en la memoria, no es tan grande. Ninguna casa cabe en la memoria. Se reducen. (73)

. . .

Todas las palabras tienen sortilegio, algunas, misterio. Son las que esconden una llave-cita que acciona sobre la memoria cuando escapan del cerco de los dientes. (78)

. . .

¿Cómo es el tiempo de la memoria en el perro? Yo me pregunto, un perro, ¿Cuánto tiempo tarda en olvidar?" (88)
La memoria es como una hoguera. . . . El tótem es básicamente la remisión del acto memorable. (93).

Old man, on one of the steps that lead to the ghetto monument, I deposited them [the stones] as in a ritual, thinking each step, thinking each stone, each resistance that was, and is, poppa, forever.

. . .

The house, in one's memory, is not so big. No house fits in one's memory. They are reduced in size.

. . . .

All words have their spell, some a mystery. Those are the ones that hide a key-citation that acts on memory when they escape the fence of the teeth.

. . .

What is time like in a dog's memory. I wonder, how long does it take a dog to forget?

. . .

Memory is like a bonfire. . . . The totem is basically the reference to the memorable act.

The first citation in the montage refers to the Jewish tradition of placing a stone on the tombstone of a loved one when one visits the cemetery. This is an important act of remembrance. All the other citations explicitly evoke the act of remembering and clearly illustrate the novel's topical focus.

Uruguay is a small country so that one would not expect to have the same quantity of works that Chile and Argentina produce; however, the small number of works do not constitute a corpus in the same way as they do in the other two countries, which means that, in the end, Uruguay does not provide a good point of comparison. Nonetheless, we can see when considering *Las cartas* as part of the genre of Latin American dictatorship novels that it prioritizes the importance of memory as its central message.

Paraguay, also a Southern Cone nation, did not suffer a military coup in the 1970s but was under the dictatorship of Alfredo Stroessner from 1954 to 1989. Paraguay, like Uruguay, is a small country that has not produced a genuine body of dictatorship novels, other than a few titles. Augusto Roa Bastos's novel *El fiscal* (1993; The Prosecutor) is about the Stroessner dictatorship; his earlier masterpiece, *Yo el Supremo* (1974), though centered on the nineteenth-century dictatorship of Dr. José Gaspar Rodríguez de Francia, also reflects on the Stroessner dictatorship through his portrayal of Dr. Francia. The small corpus of Paraguayan dictatorship novels also includes: *El invierno de Gunter* (1987; Gunter's Winter) by Juan Manuel Marcos; *Gustavo Presidente* (1990; President Gustavo) by Santiago Trias Coll; *El rector* (1991; The Dean) by Guido Rodríguez Alcalá; and, more recent, *La pasión de Lucrecia* (2013; Lucrecia's Passion) by Carlos Mateo Balmelli.

The two dictatorship novels written by Roa Bastos, Paraguay's most important writer, illustrate well the different directions that the dictatorship novel usually takes instead of focusing on emotions. The narrator of *Yo el Supremo* is the nineteenth-century dictator José Gaspar Rodríguez de Francia, who throughout the novel, analyzes the achievements and failures of his government, listing them in an accounting book. Historical texts, many of which perpetuated a black legend surrounding the dictator, are cited throughout the novel. These texts are counterposed to the fictional Dr. Francia's words and thoughts, Revisionist historians, such as Julio César Chaves, have questioned this entirely dark portrait of Dr. Francia. At the novel's end, the dictator concludes that he has done one good thing: he has preserved Paraguay's independence. Thus, the focus of the novel is the reassessment of a historical government by which its dictator is humanized, benefits from some positive traits, and earns credit for parts of his work. The message about an important figure in Paraguayan history is that nobody, not even a dictator, is completely negative. Ultimately, the novel conveys the concept of how difficult it is to judge any historical figure.²

Roa Bastos's second dictatorship novel, *El fiscal*, is based on the twentieth-century dictator Alfredo Stroessner. The protagonist, Félix Moral, is a Paraguayan exile in France. Moral seizes the opportunity to return to Paraguay for a scholarly conference, but his real intent is to assassinate the dictator and thus free his country from tyranny. The novel establishes parallels between Moral's actions and those of President Francisco Solano López, who governed Paraguay in the late nineteenth century during the Triple Alliance War (1864–1870). López led his people to defeat against Argentina, Brazil, and Uruguay in a war doomed to failure. Whether his efforts made him a hero or a martyr are questioned throughout the novel. Moral is like López in that his status as hero or martyr is debatable. Although emotions are important to the novel, especially Moral's love for and possible betrayal of Jimena, they constitute a secondary theme about the value of love and fidelity. The novel's message centers on the question of heroism or martyrdom, with a strong emphasis on Paraguay's history.³

Argentina suffered a military coup in 1976, very similar to the one that occurred in Chile, headed by army commander Jorge Videla. Videla, like Pinochet, began a "dirty war" against leftist militants and intellectuals, leading to an estimated thirty thousand disappearances as well as wide-scale torture. In 1983, democracy returned to Argentina with the election of Raúl Alfonsín. Although the members of the military Junta were prosecuted in 1985 after the testimonies of the Conadep report, also known as "Nunca más," in 1989 President Carlos Menem issued military pardons so that they did not have to serve their sentences. Videla did not go to jail until 2010. Moreover, the Ley de Obediencia Debida decreed in 1987 that lower-level military personnel could not be prosecuted. Thus Argentina went down a similar path of forgetting as did Chile, even though human rights groups continued to fight for justice and the importance of remembering (Paz-Mackay 49).

Although an analysis of the Argentine dictatorship novel would require a book unto itself, it is illustrative to examine what critics have already said about these Argentine literary works. In contrast to Chile, where the only comprehensive book written on the dictatorship novel is Grínor Rojo's *Las novelas de la dictadura y la postdictadura chilena*, several Argentine books have studied at least some dictatorship novels, often combined with a discussion of films, documentaries, photography, and monuments. These include works written both during and after the dictatorship.

María Soledad Paz-Mackay studies four Argentine postdictatorship novels in her book *Historia, memoria y novela en la Argentina de la posdictadura: Dos veces junio* (2002; Two Times June) by Martín Kohan; *Ni muerto has perdido tu nombre* (2014; Not Even Dead Have You Lost Your Name) and *Villa* (2009) by Luis Gusmán; and *El secreto y las voces* (2002; The Secret and The Voices) by Carlos Gamerro. Paz-Mackay identifies history versus memory as a key theme in these novels, which articulate two central messages: the extension of responsibility to the entire citizenry who often ignored what was happening and the important role of memory in the formation of identity (46). Similarly, Geoffrey Maguire in *The Politics of Postmemory* (2017) suggests that the major theme of the works that he studies in it is history versus memory and that the message behind this theme is the need to discover the truth so that future generations can reimagine and reclaim their identity and political agency. Maguire limits himself to the postmemory works of children whose parents were actively involved in resistance against the dictatorship or who actually disappeared. The two novels he examines are *Soy un bravo piloto de la nueva China* (2011; I Am a Brave Pilot from the New China) by Ernesto Semán; and *El espíritu de mis padres sigue subiendo en la lluvia* (2011; My Father's Ghost is Climbing in the Rain) by Patricio Pron. Although Maguire refers to the role of affect in these novels, it appears more as a motif than a message and is often used as a synonym for "personal" or for "personalizing" the experience of the dictatorship since the writers' parents were directly involved (58–65).

Silvia R. Tandeciarz's *Citizens of Memory* (2017) mostly focuses on films, documentaries, and photography (the single literary work she analyzes is Tomás Eloy Martínez's *Purgatorio* [2008]). She does, however, discuss what she terms affective transactions, namely, those that have a traumatic affect (intro.). In other words, she focuses exclusively on how a work generates feeling in the viewer/reader, yet she does not parse character affect or emotions in her analysis of *Purgatorio*. Its message, told from an exilic perspective, she contends, concerns the importance of invention in creating alternate realities (ch. 4).

Finally, Patricia Rotger's *Memoria sin tiempo* (2014) focuses on the dictatorship novels of women writers. Rotger analyzes *Conversación al sur*

(1981; Conversation in the South) by Marta Traba; *Pasos bajo el agua* (1987; Steps Beneath the Water) by Alicia Kozameh; *El dock* (1992; The Dock) by Matilde Sánchez; *El fin de la historia* (1996; The End of the Story) by Liliana Heker; *Soy paciente* (1996; The Patient) by Ana María Shua; *A veinte años, Luz* (1999; In Twenty Years, Light) by Elsa Osorio; *Un secreto para Julia* (2000; A Secret for Julia) by Patricia Sagastizábal; and *Memorias del río inmóvil* (2002; Memories of an Immobile River) by Claudia Feijóo. Rotger's hypothesis is that the message of these novels is how memory/the search for truth leads to the reconstitution of identity (cf. Paz-Mackay and Maguire).

The absence of a discussion of character emotions in these studies is a good indicator that Argentine fictions about dictatorship are not the same as the Chilean novel (to be sure, Argentine novels exist that do focus on emotions). To highlight the message of the Chilean novels, I would like to examine four case studies of Argentine texts that resemble Chilean novels in terms of plotlines—but that also transport their stories in a totally different direction. With these sets of comparisons, I hope to show how novels with the same themes and motifs can suggest different central messages to the reader.

The first pair of novels is Fontaine's *La vida* (see ch. 5) and Heker's *El fin*. As discussed in 5, Lorena, the protagonist of *La vida*, is a person who loathes herself for her betrayal and whose abjection haunts her throughout the novel. *El fin*, like *La vida*, is a tale of a left-wing militant, Leonora, who, like Lorena, betrays her comrades and ends up working for the government. These novels are also similar because each protagonist becomes the subject of a novel. In *La vida*, we learn toward the end that Lorena is telling her story to a novelist, while in *El fin*, the entire book is about Leonora's friend, Diana Glass, who is attempting to write a novel about her. Diana cannot find the right "fin de la historia" (ending of the story) because she fears her friend is dead. When she finally learns of her friend's betrayal, moreover, she cannot write the novel at all. However, her mentor, Hertha Bechofen, ultimately takes over the novel, interviews Leonora, and writes her story. Despite the remarkably similar plots, these novels have totally different messages.

As chapter 5 explains, Lorena does not attempt to justify her behavior. She feels base and hates herself to the point that she inflicts self-punishment by alienating the man in Stockholm, her home in exile, who loves her. In contrast, Leonora in *El fin* constantly attempts to justify her behavior. Although she turns her own husband in to the authorities (thus saving her daughter), her conscience is clear:

> La prisionera le reza cada mañana y cada noche, y Él la redime de todo sufrimiento, la protege de los gritos de horror que se escuchan en el ático, qué podría hacer ella (le dice por los que gritan, que podría hacer por el hombre del pecho acribillado que la mira [her husband Fernando] Dios la ha absuelto, ella puede vivir en paz. La única verdad es la vida. (*El fin* 155)

> The prisoner prays to Him every morning and every night, and He redeems her of all suffering, He protects her from the screams of horror that she hears in the attic. What could she do (He asks her) for those who are screaming, what could she do for the man with the bullet-riddled chest who is staring at her [her husband Fernando], who still stares at her? God has absolved her; she can live in peace. The only truth is life. (End 116)

Leonora tries to justify her betrayal through her religious beliefs, her love of life, and her inability to help the other prisoners, but the narrator's ironic tone undermines her possible justification. While Lorena might elicit some empathy because of her self-loathing and self-punishment, Leonora does not engage reader empathy at all. Indeed, the story actively seeks to condemn Leonora for her actions, by contrasting her lack of guilt to the self-condemnation of a fellow traitor, Chango:

> —Pero al menos yo los odio. Y a veces también me odio.—
> —Que hazaña. Te revolvés por dentro cada vez que los servís y eso te debe hacer sentir heroico.—
> —No me siento heroico, me siento una rata.—
> —Pero igual los servís. Yo, en cambio, no los sirvo.—
> —Sois una jefa.—
> —Trato de tener mi autoridad. Y creo de verdad en lo que estoy haciendo. Me digo: esto tiene que ser así y así y me esfuerzo por hacerlo de la mejor manera posible. Eso me hace sentir en paz conmigo misma.—

>   —Sos lo que se llama una persona feliz.—
>   —Soy feliz, si. Estoy viva. Y recuperé a mi hija.—
>   —¿A que precio?—
>   —Al precio que vale una hija, ¿te gusta así?— (*El fin* 203–04)

> "But I, at least, hate them. And sometimes I hate myself."
> "What a great feat. Your guts get knotted up every time you work for them, and that must make you feel like a hero."
> "I don't feel like a hero; I feel like a rat."
> "But you work for them, regardless. I, on the other hand, don't work for them."
> "You're a leader."
> "I try to exercise my authority. And I really believe in what I'm doing. I tell myself: it has to be like this and like that, and I try to do it the best possible way. It makes me feel at peace with myself."
> "You're what's known as a happy person."
> "I'm happy, yes. I'm alive. And I've got my daughter back."
> "At what price?"
> "At the price a daughter is worth. How do you like that? (*End* 152–53)

While *La vida* is almost entirely focused on the theme of betrayal, the concept of Stockholm syndrome, and the feelings of abjection that these cause, *El fin* contains important ancillary themes that detract from the focus on Stockholm syndrome and betrayal, as well as any feelings that might be associated with it. Although in both novels the protagonist becomes the subject of a novel, in *La vida*, other than for a brief interview with the novelist, no other reference to the writing process occurs. In contrast, *El fin* is as much centered on the writing process itself as it is on the story it tells of Leonora; Diana Glass's struggles with her story and her multiple interactions with other writers (Hertha, Garita) in a writer's workshop lead the reader away from feelings experienced by the characters (such as Leonora's love of life, Diana's feelings of survivor guilt), and engage the reader with elements surrounding the storytelling process. Diana's narrative about Leonora is, in addition, embedded within Hertha Bechofen's story about both Leonora and Diana. The frequent interpolations of Diana's fragmented discourse in italics, of her inability to put a beginning or end to her story, of an unidentified "I" who is assumed to be Bechofen at the narrative's end, all call upon the reader to focus more on the process of narration than on the characters' emotions.

As this brief analysis illustrates, although *La vida* and *El fin* revolve around highly similar plots with common themes and motifs, their messages diverge. *La vida* communicates the importance of Lorena's emotions, how dictatorship can lead to abject feelings and thus destroy lives, while *El fin* focuses on the effects of selfishness and betrayal on others and the difficulty of capturing these and other themes through the act of writing.

The second set of similar novels is Fernández's *La dimensión* (see ch. 6) and Pron's *El espíritu*. I have grouped these two novels together because each is based on documentary sources. *La dimensión*, as chapter 6 details, is based on a 1985 article appearing in *Cauce* that recounts how a torturer, Andrés Antonio Valenzuela Morales, renounces his activities and confesses his actions and those of other government officials to a journalist at the magazine. Pron's novel employs elements from several newspaper articles published in *El Trébol Digital* and *La Capital* regarding the disappearance of a man named Alberto Burdisso. The novel is about Pron's father, who belonged to a pro-Peronist group called La Guardia de Hierro (The Iron Guard). The protagonist's discovery of his father's search for Burdisso leads to the revelation of who his father was and why the unnamed protagonist sought to squelch his memories through sleeping pills and amnesia-inducing medications.

Fernández and Pron use their documentary sources quite differently. While Fernández extracts characters (both the torturer and his victims] from the *Cauce* article, though she does not directly cite it, Pron's novel repeats almost verbatim fragments of newspaper articles. Although much of what is narrated in *La dimensión* is true (with remembering a major theme), Fernández does not use this material solely for its historical value. Rather, she dedicates most of the novel to imagining what these characters (including the torturer) thought and felt, which causes the reader to identify with the emotions of the tortured and disappeared (see ch. 6). The parallels created with *Twilight Zone* television episodes are designed to create shock and surprise in the reader, and thus to attune the reader more finely to the emotions felt by the protagonists and thereby engender empathy.

In contrast, Pron's employment of newspaper fragments serves an entirely different purpose in *El espíritu*. Although Pron alters the dates of the appearance of some of these articles and the titles of the sources, most of the information taken from them is accurate and often reproduced verbatim. He disperses these newspaper fragments in a series of chapters or episodes in his novel, as he traces his protagonist's efforts to learn what his father was doing prior to falling ill. This activity is undertaken with the intent of learning more about his father and who he was, now that he thinks his father is dying. The search for the truth about Alberto Burdisso parallels the protagonist's search for his father's identity. The two fuse in the novel when it turns out his father was a militant who was also friends with the militant Alicia Burdisso, Alberto's sister, who disappeared during the Argentine dirty war:

> Era como si mi padre hubiera deseado descomponer el crimen en un puñado de datos insignificantes, en un montón de documentos notariales ... cuya acumulación le hiciera olvidar por un instante que la suma de todos ellos conducía a un hecho trágico ... y que eso iba a hacerle pensar en la simetría entre la muerte de ese hombre y la de su hermana y a generar otra simetría, también involuntaria y de la que mi padre no iba a saber nada nunca: mi padre procurando colaborar con la búsqueda de Burdisso y yo intentando buscar y hallar a mi padre en sus últimos pensamientos antes de que todo lo que había sucedido sucediera. (*El espíritu* 121)

> It was as if my father had wanted to deconstruct the crime into a handful of insignificant facts, a pile of notarized documents ... whose accumulation made him forget for a moment that they all added up to a tragic event ... which would make him think about the symmetry between the man's death and his sister's, also tragic about which my father was never going to know anything. This was my father's attempt to collaborate in the search for Burdisso and my attempt to search for and find my father in his last thoughts before everything that had happened happened. (Ghost 127)

As Maguire indicates in his study, the search for the truth/memory is necessary for the reconstitution of identity, and this is true for both the son and the father in the novel.

Although both novels rely on documentary sources, Fernández employs the historical veracity of her tale to enhance reader empathy, while Pron uses the sources to create a structure similar to that of detective fiction, in which the reality of his father's past slowly unfolds. Pron's novel undoubtedly conveys feelings, particularly that of fear felt by his family during the military dictatorship. The protagonist's fear is so severe that he spent years on drugs trying to forget it. However, this fear serves as a motif to develop the novel's main message, which does not concern fear itself but the dangerous spell it can cast through forgetting. The need to seek the truth and remember constitutes the novel's message. It is only through truth and memory that the protagonist is able to reconnect with his father and move on with his life.

While Fernández uses novelistic invention to fill in the gaps of what people felt when they were being tortured, Pron invents historical sources that are added to the authentic historical sources to create a collective dimension that parallels the concerns of the Argentine second generation (children of trauma survivors). This can be seen in the largely invented passage in which the townspeople of El Trébol organize a march to protest the slow-moving investigation of Alberto Burdisso's disappearance:

> También, el desaparecido dejaba de ser el motivo de preocupación de los habitantes de la ciudad, y en su lugar . . . lo que emergía era un temor colectivo, el temor a una repetición y, en cierta forma, el temor a la pérdida de la tranquilidad casi proverbial de El Trébol. En ese punto, si se quiere, se producía el tránsito inevitable de la víctima individual a la víctima colectiva, como testimonia el siguiente artículo: "Los amigos de Alberto Burdisso, el ciudadano desapareció misteriosamente hace 11 días, organizaron una marcha a la plaza San Martín para pedir el esclarecimiento del caso que es . . . todo un misterio para todos los trebolenses." (*El espíritu* 75–76)

At this point the missing man himself ceased to be a cause for concern among the town's inhabitants and, in his place, what emerged was a collective fear, the fear of a recurrence and the fear of losing the almost proverbial tranquility of El Trébol. At this point, to put it another way, the inevitable shift occurred from individual victim to collective victim, as witnessed by the following article: The friends of Alberto Burdisso, the citizen mysteriously disappeared 11 days ago, organized a march to the Plaza San Martín to call for the resolution of the case . . . a complete mystery to all Trebolenses.] (Ghost 74)

The fact that the citizens experience a collective fear and worry about a repetition of disappearances suggests a parallel with the second generation, who write with the goal of avoiding any future repetition of disappearances and dictatorship of the sort their parents lived through. This also catapults the narration back to the dilemmas of the second generation after the dictatorship. Pron addresses this connection with his generation in several passages toward the end of the novel that emphasize the work to be done by his generation:

> Me pregunté qué podía ofrecer mi generación que pudiera ponerse a la altura . . . del afán de justicia de la generación . . . de nuestros padres. . . .
>   Y me pregunté si todo aquello no era también una tarea política, una de las pocas que podía tener relevancia para mi propia generación, que había creído en el proyecto liberal que arrojara a la miseria a buena parte de los argentinos durante la década de 1990. . . . y pensé que una buena forma era escribiendo algún día acerca de todo lo que nos había sucedido a mis padres y a mí y esperando que alguien se sintiera interpelado y comenzase también sus pesquisas acerca de un tiempo que no parecía haber acabado para algunos de nosotros. (*El espíritu* 179; 184–86)

> I wondered what my generation could offer that could match . . . the thirst for justice of the generation of . . . our parents. . . .
>   My father had started to search for his lost friend and I, without meaning to, had also started shortly afterward to search for my father. This was our lot as Argentines. And I wondered whether this could also be a political task, one of the few with relevance for my own generation, which had believed in the liberal project that led a large portion of the Argentine people into poverty in the 1990s. . . . I thought a good way would be to one day write about everything that had happened to my parents and me and hope that others would feel compelled to start

their own inquiries into a time that still hasn't ended for some of us. (Ghost 191; 196–97)

As these citations illustrate, Pron's text contains an explicit message about his generation's mission.

But while Pron's text emphasizes learning the truth, as Maguire signals, for reasons of identity and political agency, Fernández's text invites us to remember what people felt so that she can bring emotion back into Chile's "memory box" in the hope of avoiding similar suffering in the future. The literary techniques may be similar, and the focus on the future is the same, but the messages are different because in *La dimensión*, justice is achieved through the emphasis on what people felt and suffered, while in Pron's novel it is achieved through the discovery of the truth regarding past events, a process that subordinates emotions. Fear about the past and sadness over the protagonist's father's illness become tangential motifs because detection (search and discovery) supersede all else—learning the truth is more important than emotional connections that might stop historical recurrence.

The third set of books I would like to compare are Dorfman's *La última* (see ch. 4) and Ricardo Piglia's *Respiración artificial* (1980; Artificial Respiration). These novels are both allegorical and were written about the same time at the beginning of each dictatorship. The protagonist of Dorfman's novel and symbol of Salvador Allende, Manuel Sendero, ends up disappeared and murdered by the military government. The legend regarding his song, which he allegedly sang right before his death, and whose memory is a source of inspiration for future generations, is symbolic of his humanitarianism, socialist politics, and positive philosophy for future Chileans. The memory of Manuel Sendero, who is mythologized and idealized as a Christlike figure, creates a strong feeling of nostalgia that permeates the novel, yet that message of nostalgia does not focus on Manuel Sendero exclusively. In the alternating sections that turn out to be fragments of a soap opera, the character David, who is in exile from dictatorial Chile, experiences an overwhelming nostalgia for his country. Dorfman employs allegory throughout to emphasize a revolutionary nostalgia that fuels and inspires future generations to create a better world because of Manuel Sendero's life philosophy.

In contrast, Piglia's *Respiración* employs allegory to transmit a message documenting the disappearances and tortures that occurred in Argentina during the dirty war and to connect them to those that occurred in Nazi Germany. Indeed, the novel is famous for speaking about the Argentine dictatorship without ever directly mentioning it, subscribing to its comment that: "En literatura... lo más importante nunca debe ser nombrado" ([*Respiración* 179–80] In literature... the most important thing should never be named [Respiration 142]).

In fact, the first paragraph of the novel establishes a connection between the Nazi genocide and the Argentine *Proceso*. The narrator, Emilio Renzi, describes the following photograph:

> Si hay una historia empieza hace tres años. En abril de 1976, cuando se publica mi primer libro, él [his uncle Marcelo Maggi] me manda una carta. Con la carta viene una foto donde me tiene en brazos... La foto es de 1941: atrás él había escrito la fecha y después, como si buscara orientarme, transcribió las dos líneas del poema inglés que ahora sirve de epígrafe a este relato [which is "We had the experience but missed the meaning, and approach to the meaning restores the experience."] (*Respiración* 13)

> If there is a story it begins three years ago. In April 1976, when my first book is published, he [his uncle Marcelo Maggi] sends me a letter. The letter arrives with a photo in which he is holding me in his armas... The photo is from 1941; on the back he had written the date and then, as if trying to guide me, had copied the two lines from the English poem that now serve as an epigraph to this story. (Respiration 11)

The beginning of the novel not only establishes a parallel between the two genocidal events by linking the two dates 1979 (three years after the Argentine military coup in 1976) and 1941 (three years after the start of WWII in 1939) but also suggests that the earlier event is key to understanding the later; linking the two is the photograph.

Another key aspect of the allegory put forward by *Respiración* is the futuristic novel written by Enrique Ossorio, who lived during the nineteenth-century Rosas dictatorship in Argentina and was the grandfather of Senator Ossorio, a character in the novel's present. We learn that the grandfather

Conclusion

Ossorio, late in the nineteenth century, writes an epistolary novel titled *1979* (a clear parody of Orwell's *1984*). In it, protagonists received letters from the future that censors intercept in the present (whether real letters or novelistic equivalents is unclear). In any event, the letters point to exiles, disappearances, and tortures, such as the one Angélica Inés Echevarne writes to the governor:

> Sucede lo siguiente, señor intendente: me han hecho una incisión y me colocaron un aparato transmisor disimulado entre las arborescencias del corazón. . . . Yo lo veo todo por ese aparatito. . . . Y está el Polaco. Polonia. Yo vi las fotografías: mataban a los judíos con alambre de enfardar. Los hornos crematorios están en Belén, Palestina. Al Norte, bien al Norte, en Belén, provincia de Catamarca. Los pájaros vuelan sobre las cenizas. (*Respiración* 98)

> What is occurring is the following, Mr. Mayor: they made an inicision and hid a transmitter among the branching veins and arteries around my heart. . . . I see everything through the device they installed in me. . . . And there is the Pole. Poland. I saw the photographs: they killed the Jews with bailing wire. The crematoria are in Bethlehem, Palestine. In the north, way up north, in Bethlehem, in the province of Catamarca. (Respiration 79–80)

In Angélica's letter, the crematoria of Nazi Germany overlap with the concentration camps in Argentina, given that she locates the ovens in Catamarca, an Argentine province. Once again, the connection between Nazism and the Argentine *Proceso* is incontrovertible, the one portending the other.

Marcelo Maggi, the narrator Renzi's uncle, is one of novel's main characters, even though we only hear his voice through the letters he writes to Renzi. When Renzi travels to meet him in Concordia, he has already vanished from the town, his disappearance, at that moment, widens into an allegory for the disappeared people of Argentina. In his stead, the character Tardewski, a Polish refugee who came to Argentina at the outbreak of World War II, entertains Renzi in the hope that Maggi will return before Renzi's return to Buenos Aires. A former philosopher, Tardewski recounts his disenchantment with and alienation from philosophy, due largely to Martin Heidegger's joining the Nazi

Party. Their discussion reinforces the novel's message about the roots of the Argentine dirty war in Nazism.

Even this brief comparison points to differences. Although *La última* and *Respiración* both adopt an allegorical structure, Dorfman's novel employs it to emphasize the emotions of those who were Allende's followers; whereas, *Respiración* engages allegory to speak covertly about the horrors of the dictatorship and its Nazi-inspired origins. The novel is more concerned with comprehending how such a phenomenon as dictatorship could occur in Argentina than it is with the emotions experienced by victims of the dirty war.

The final two novels I would like to compare are Franz's *El desierto* (see ch. 5) and Sagastizábal's *Un secreto*. Their plotlines are amazingly similar. In *El desierto*, the protagonist Laura is a judge during the dictatorship who finds herself incapable of defending justice. When lieutenant Cáceres tortures and rapes her, she reveals the whereabouts of the fugitive under her protection. To compensate for this betrayal, she agrees to repeat this scene to ensure the freedom of other prisoners, only to learn later that Cáceres has freed no one. All of this past information gets aired in a long letter Laura writes to her daughter Claudia, the product of her rape by Cáceres, who asks her where she was when all these horrible things were happening in Chile. Laura, as we know, had fled to Germany where she raised Claudia who believes her father to be Laura's ex-husband. Similarly, the protagonist of *Un secreto*, Mercedes Beecham, is a victim of torture and rape during the Argentine *Proceso* military dictatorship. She is eventually freed and exiled to England where she learns she is pregnant. She raises her daughter Julia in England, but despite her daughter's constant inquiries, she never reveals the truth to her about her father until the end of the novel. In both novels, the protagonists contemplate abortion but are so horrified by the thought that they decide to give birth to their daughters.

Although both novels center on the revelation of the truth to a daughter who is the product of rape and their protagonists give birth in exile, the focus of each novel is completely different. *El desierto* underscores Laura's feelings of abjection because of her betrayal of the fugitive and her inability to protect the political prisoners from injustice. Although the novel shares the same slow revelation of the truth that we find in *Un secreto*, truth as value forgoes the kind of specialized emphasis the Argentine novel accords it. Instead, Laura's troubled feelings and the justice needed to quell them constitute the focal points of the novel.

Conclusion

In contrast, as the commentary on *Un secreto* contends, Mercedes cannot free herself from the trauma she has suffered without catharsis: she must confess to her daughter the truth about her birth. As Patricia Rotger maintains in *Memoria sin tiempo*:

> No solo le ofrece su verdad a la hija, su secreto y su relato ... sino que de esta forma cierra la novela; ya no queda nada más por contar. El relato se abre con la posibilidad de decir como promesa y de la verdad como horizonte y se cierra con la actualización de dicha promesa lo que no escapa de cierto tono feliz sobre el final. ... La verdad supone al mismo tiempo la oposición a la mentira como la negación del olvido ya que es conocimiento y memoria. Porque la revelación de la verdad aparece como una forma de combatir el olvido y solo en su celebración es posible la memoria como demuestra el final de la novela. (96)

> [S]he not only offers the truth to her daughter, her secret and her story ... but also closes the novel in this way; there is nothing left to tell. The story opens with the possibility of telling as a promise and of truth as a horizon and closes with the actualization of said promise, which does not shrink from a certain happy tone at the end. ... Truth supposes, at the same time, the opposition to lies as a negation of forgetting since it is knowledge and memory. Because revelation of the truth appears as a way of fighting forgetfulness, only [then] in its celebration is memory possible as the ending of the novel illustrates.

Similarly, Ana María Zubieta groups Sagastizábal's novel with a series of other Argentine novels that deal with memory and personal secrets: "*Villa* (1995) ... *Ni muerto has perdido tu nombre* (2002) ambos de Luis Gusmán; *El fin de la historia* de Liliana Heker (1996) y *Un secreto para Julia* de Patricia Sagastizábal (2000); con esta novela se cierra un modo de narrar, ese que podríamos llamar el ciclo del secreto personal" ([194] *Villa* (1995) ... *Ni muerto has perdido tu nombre* (2002) both by Luis Gusmán; *El fin de la historia* by Liliana Heker and *Un secreto para Julia* by Patricia Sagastizábal; with this last novel a way of narrating closes, that which we could call the cycle of the personal secret). This is not to say that feelings and emotions are of a lesser concern in *Un secreto*. Indeed, the novel constantly emphasizes Mercedes's feelings, particularly those of emptiness, fear, ambivalence toward her daughter, and nostalgia for Argentina. Nonetheless, these feelings, though important motifs, do not constitute the central message of the novel. Whereas *El desierto* calls upon the reader to comprehend how torture victims were made to feel abject and how these feelings need to be remembered, Sagastizábal's novel uses the feelings to communicate the message that the only way to move beyond trauma is through confronting the truth of what happened. As soon as Mercedes tells Julia who her father is, she is able to put her fear behind her. At that moment, she recognizes that she belongs in London, not Argentina:

> Poco a poco, se fueron disipando las sombras de ese infierno. Y aun dudosa y titubeante, comencé gradualmente a armar la grafía de mi historia, y por ende, la de Julia. No fue fácil, y no fue grato, pero volteé el parapeto y encontré otras palabras, nuevos artificios para contarle a mi hija la trama oculta. Sentí que un cierto consuelo entraba en mi corazón.... Quizás una de las conclusiones más acabadas es que ya no estoy de tránsito, no estoy por irme en cualquier momento. De hecho, aquí nació mi hija en esta tierra se me dio la oportunidad de ser libre.... En eso estoy ahora, convencida de que este es mi lugar en el mundo, porque ya no soy la misma y eso es inmutable. (*Un secreto* 202–25)

> The shadows of that hell were fading away, little by little. Still dubious and hesitant, I gradually began to put together the building blocks of my history and, ultimately, Julia's. It was difficult and unpleasant, but I sought beyond the barricade and discovered other words, new devices for revealing the hidden plot to my daughter. I felt a consolation of sorts entering my spirit.... Perhaps one of the most definitive conclusions is that I am no longer in transit, never again on the point of having to leave at a moment's notice. In fact, my daughter was born here, and in this land I was given the opportunity to be free.... That is what occupies my thoughts now, convinced that this is my place in the world because I am no longer the same, and that is immutable. (Secret 217–43)

It is important to note that *El desierto* contains a central theme that is completely absent from *Un secreto*: that of the protagonist's betrayal. Mercedes, unlike Laura, did not betray anyone under torture. This explains why in *El desierto*, the novel veers away from the theme of the truth to that of justice, ending with the possible trampling of Cáceres by the crowd, an act engineered by Laura. Furthermore, this theme also explains to some degree the focus on feeling (those of guilt and abjection), which points to what constituted a relatively common situation under the dictatorship: that of victims confessing under torture and the subsequent feelings with which they had to live as survivors. While Sagastizábal's novel tells the reader about the significance of confronting the truth, Franz's communicates the self-loathing evoked through betrayal.

Although both the Chilean and Argentine dictatorship novels share an intellectual tradition rooted in postmodern techniques (intertextuality, historical subjectivism, the use of popular genres, and so forth), the comparison of these sets of novels illustrates how Chilean novels tends to emphasize the emotive aspects of the dictatorship, while the Argentine novels tend to emphasize matters such as truth, memory, origins of dictatorship, and comprehensibility through writing. Although emotions are undoubtedly present in the Argentine novel, they often constitute a theme or motif, rather the main message. That is not so in the Chilean novels.

As this chapter illustrates, the Chilean dictatorship novel inserts itself within a larger context of the Latin American dictatorship novel. Nonetheless, the specificity of its historical context is significant for comprehending the central messages of these novels. To some degree, the novels studied here constitute a circle: emotions appear as a motif (such as disappearance or torture), then develop into a theme (such as betrayal, Stockholm syndrome, or trauma), and finally leads us back to a central message about emotions. For example, in chapter 3, we discussed Marín's *Palacio*, in which the protagonist visited the ruins of the Villa Grimaldi torture site and reflected on its evolution from his friend's family estate to a camp for political prisoners. We observed how architectural elements such as void, patinas, ruins, and the like are employed to evoke feelings of despair. These feelings constitute a repetitive motif. Reflection upon this motif leads the reader to extract the theme of the effects of torture on the country, which in turn leads the reader to reflect on the question of the memory of torture. The lack of memory of torture, the country's desire to move on from the past and forget what occurred, to destroy the evidence of Villa Grimaldi, now in ruins, leads the protagonist back to feelings of despair in the present. Thus the need to remember the despair caused by torture, to recall the suffering and emotions of the populace, constitute the novel's ultimate message. Feelings need to be returned to the Chilean memory box and this has been accomplished through the Chilean dictatorship novel.

Notes

Chapter 1

1. I point out here that "postmemory" has been used in both a limited (to refer only to the second generation) and broader (to refer to all subsequent generations) sense. For the purposes of this book, I use "postmemory" in its second, extended meaning. In that regard, it is central to this study.
2. Aylwin, as we previously saw in his emotional address to the Chilean people after the results of the Rettig Commission were revealed, is to a certain degree an exception with regard to the approach taken by the Concertación governments toward memory.
3. All translations of *Voyager* are mine.
4. The term affect is used by some as a synonym for emotions, whereas others, such as Silvan Tomkins, distinguish affect as a physiological firing of neurons from the emotions that are associated with this neuronal stimulation. I discuss Tomkins's theory at length in chapter 6.
5. Guezzar cites Iser's *The Implied Reader* (1978), as well as Rosenblatt's books *Literature as an Exploration* (1937) and *The reader, the text, the poem* (1978).
6. Although this book is exclusively dedicated to examining affect and emotion in Chilean literature, it is important to mention here the extensive corpus of films, particularly documentaries, that focus on emotion and memory. These include the many documentaries by Patricio Guzmán (*The Battle of Chile*, *Memoria obstinada*, *La nostalgia de la luz*, among others); see also Carmen Castillo's *Calle Santa Fe*, Francisco López Balló's *La mujer metralleta*, Paula Rodríguez's *Volver a vernos*, and Andrés Wood's *Machuca*, to name a few. See the following studies for a more in-depth analysis of Chile's cinema on this topic: Alessandro Fornazzari, *Speculative Fictions*, 63–86; Kaitlin M. Murphy, *Mapping Memory*, 56–90; and Ana Ros, *The Post-Dictatorship Generation*, 120–35.
7. Silvan Tomkins coins the term "dissmell" to refer to an infant's reaction to a foul smell.

Chapter 2

1. The focus on the presence of mothers versus the absence of fathers in the three novels examined in this chapter suggests the importance of motherhood in nation-building and points to the viability of a feminist analysis of these texts. Such an analysis is outside the scope of this book but would undoubtedly be a fruitful object for future study.
2. All translations in this chapter, unless otherwise noted, are mine.
3. For more information on the role of ghosts, see Cardone and Trostel.
4. The photo does not show significant details of the trip. The narrator recalls that a boy who looked a lot like her helped her up when she fell, which is the accident that caused the nosebleed. She then asks her mother who the boy was, and she tells her that it must have been her brother. The narrator who was about ten at the time never knew that she had siblings. The photograph thus only tells part of the story of what happened that day and requires contextualization and explanation not self-contained in the picture.
5. Within the invented narrative about Fuenzalida, the first historical episode is about the man who throws himself under a bus. This episode is also discussed in Fernández's novel *La dimensión desconocida*. Carlos Contreras Maluaje, a man who is detained and tortured, tells the authorities that he has an appointment to meet another communist whom they can arrest if they let him free for a few hours. When they agree, Maluaje throws himself under a bus. In *Fuenzalida*, the character is referred to as Ríos, but this episode is likely based on the story of Maluaje, who appears in *La dimensión* with his historical name. In *Fuenzalida*, the episode is the catalyst for Fuenzalida's run-in with the dictatorship that characterizes him as a hero and a good father.
6. Note that Lorena Amaro Castro also mentions the contrast between Fuenzalida and Sebastián (109).
7. Fernández inserts various "clues" to the fictitious nature of Fuenzalida's heroic adventure during the dictatorship, which the reader may or may not pick up on. These include the following: the narrator says her father had a gold chain with a bull hanging from it (63), whereas in the invented story Fuenzalida is wearing a chain with a silver dragon hanging from it; in the invented story Ernesto Fuenzalida is twelve years old, exactly the same age as his half-sister (the narrator) when Fuenzalida abandons her; the unwaxed tiles that cause Fuenzalida's rupture with the narrator and her mother reappear in the invented story as the shining tiles of

the patio of his studio (72); Fuenzalida's dog in the invented story is named Marlén, which is the name of the narrator's ex-husband's new wife; the photo of Fuenzalida inscribed on the back by the narrator when she was a child reappears as a photo of Fuenzalida's enemy, Fuentes Castro, also inscribed by his daughter, in Fuenzalida's gym in the invented tale; finally, the narrator contemplates writing a soap-opera script in which Fuenzalida would be the hero who saves women and children (80).
8. It is worth noting here that Fuentes Castro is also described as having trained in martial arts, which serves to enhance the idea that he is a "gray zone" character, viz., if we associate martial arts with moral virtue. This also enables him to combat with Fuenzalida at the end of the invented narrative. Other critics, such as Macarena García-Avello, however, have interpreted the description of Fuentes Castro as largely ironic, as a man who imitates the official rhetoric of the military dictatorship (254).
9. Booth defines the implied reader as a "second self" to the author who is constructed by the reader through textual cues.

Chapter 3

1. The CNI (Centro Nacional de Información, or National Information Center) was the intelligence body and political police force under the Pinochet dictatorship in Chile.
2. Grínor Rojo notes: "nos debiera conducir a nosotros sus lectores hasta el encuentro con Mónica, cancela esa posibilidad cambiando al objeto del deseo por un *doppelgänger* grotesco, cuando se transa la figura de Mónica por la de María del Carmen Posadas" ([145] he should lead we the readers to his encounter with Mónica, he cancels this possibility exchanging the object of desire for a grotesque doppelgänger, when he cheats us with María del Carmen Posadas instead of the figure of Mónica).
3. The name Mañungo Vera brings to mind another indecisive protagonist with a similar name, Miguel Vera, from Augusto Roa Bastos's novel *Hijo de hombre* (1960). Miguel, just like Mañungo, vacillates in his commitment to the revolution, which he accidentally betrays when he gets drunk. The parallel is significant and suggests a possible intertextual connection between the two works.
4. The "peñas" were informal gatherings of folk artists during the 1960s and 1970s, usually presided over by a specific artist, for example, Violeta Parra or her children.
5. Trotsky speaks of "art with a tendency" as art put at the service of the revolution, and not merely art for art's sake.

6. In all other cases, I have used the translation of *La desesperanza* by Alfred J. MacAdam. However, I believe there is a mistake in his translation of this passage. He writes: "Mañungo was soft, he was saying, decadent, petit-bourgeois, a delusion" (*Curfew* 66). Since the Spanish text reads "desilusión" and not "delusión," I believe that the word was mistranslated and should read "disappointment" instead of "delusion."
7. See Friedman (13–24) and Morel (87–97).
8. According to Jelic and StaniCic, "that cognition is enactive is to say that the mind is enacted or brought forth through continuous reciprocal interactions of the brain, the body and the world . . . . [T]his is termed a process of sense-making which transforms the world into a place of meaning" (190).

Chapter 4

1. Estadio Chile was one of the stadiums used to torture prisoners right after the military coup on September 11, 1973.
2. The first part of this translation, preceding "Manuel before he compressed time," is from the translation by Dorfman and Shivers (352). Since the translators radically changed the content of the second half of the citation, as indicated, the words are mine.
3. Carl Barks is the name of a real cartoonist who worked for Walt Disney. Dorfman plays on the similitude between the names Carl Barks and Karl Marx in the dialogue between Felipe and David. Barks's name is a constant reminder of the context of Chilean socialism and its subsequent eradication by the dictatorship. Barks becomes the victim and pawn of the government who wants to use his imaginative abilities for the creation of a docile race of people.
4. It is important to note that Eduardo frequently expresses his skepticism by using the expression "hasta cuando." This may be another point of contact with Eltit's novel, in which the male protagonist also asks, "how much longer," albeit only once (*Jamás* 26; *Never* 13).
5. Although a song is not a tangible object as is a book or photograph, a song is still tangible in the sense that its lyrics and music constitute a unique and identifiable entity. In this way, the song becomes "concrete" for the purposes of memory and nostalgia.
6. Note that the translation up until the word "hoping" is from Dorfman's "Last" (115). The rest of the translation is mine, since in rewriting the book in an English translation, Dorfman omitted these words.

7. See Díaz, "Allegorical Specters"; also "Hacia una teoría,"; Auli Leskinen, "La novela"; and Olivera-Williams, "La década."
8. See where Eduardo tells his history class that he participated in the movement that destroyed the dictator (60); where the grandfather tells his grandchildren that the dictatorship is now only a memory (148); and where the footnote from 30,000 years in the future speaks of the barbarous practices of the past (169).
9. I use Hahn's translation of *Jamás* (Never).
10. See also 84, 108.

Chapter 5

1. DINA refers to La Dirección de Inteligencia Nacional, Chile's secret police under the Pinochet Dictatorship. DINA was dissolved in 1977 and reconstituted as the CNI (Centro Nacional de Informaciones).
2. I am referring here to the Comisión Nacional de Verdad y de Reconciliación, which is commonly known as the Rettig Comission and was authorized by President Patricio Alywin.
3. Occasionally, a "we," later identified with Mario, Laura's ex-husband, is injected into this third-person narration.
4. Note that the last part of the translation, beginning with "it was terrible," is mine because the published translation omits this line.
5. All translations of *Almuerzo* are mine.

Chapter 6

1. The *Cauce* article never tells why Flores turned informant, which is part of Fernández's inventive representation of the character in the novel.
2. Fernández's narrator refers to at least two other *Twilight Zone* episodes. When she is watching the documentary on the Vicaría de la Solidaridad, her feelings are likened to those of Barbara Jean Trenton, the main character in the episode titled "The Sixteen Millimeter Shrine." The narrator also refers to another purported *Twilight Zone* episode in which a man finds a book that forbids its reading because whoever reads it will die (207). I have been unable to find any *Twilight Zone* episode that corresponds to this plot, but Fernández's narrator uses it to create a parallel with an episode that involves a friend of a *Cauce* journalist This friend is supposed to

bring a copy of the article to the *Washington Post* but breaks his promise not to read it, which leads to a chain of events resulting in the deaths of several individuals in Chile. Perhaps it was inspired by the episode "The Library," which also deals with forbidden reading, though is also quite different in its development.

3. All translations of Parra's poetry are my own.

4. I am using the term allegorical according to the definition of allegory provided by Angus Fletcher and discussed at length here. Even though allegory is an extended metaphor that can often point to political situations, *La resta* also employs symbolic associations within the allegory of the Pinochet era. In contrast to Van Alphen's use of the term "allegorical" to mean a literal reading, I am employing allegory in the more traditional sense.

5. Two characters in *La dimensión* elicit negative empathy: the former torturer, Andrés Antonio Valenzuela Morales, and, to a lesser degree, Carol Flores, who betrayed his colleagues to save his brothers. All the other characters elicit positive empathy.

6. Although negative empathy might occasionally elicit in the reader feelings similar to those of abjection discussed both here and in ch. 5, negative empathy is a distinct concept from abjection as it does not necessarily elicit such feelings; instead, it reduces the amount of empathy one would normally feel for a character due to the perceived negative characteristics attributed to the character.

7. I have chosen to include Trabucco Zerán's novel here and not in the chapter on allegory because of its different emotional focus from *La última* and *Jamás*. Although all three use allegory, the latter two link allegory to melancholy; whereas in *La resta*, allegory is connected to affect and violence.

8. According to Fletcher, the five characteristics of allegory are: daemonic agency (a character who is identified with a single obsessive idea); the use of a cosmic image (kosmos) for both decorative purposes and also to evoke an intense emotional response; a journey or battle; a suspension of disbelief in magic often associated with accidental events that suggest supernatural intervention; and symmetrical plots or dualistic themes.

9. Felipe acts oddly on numerous occasions: killing his parrot to find internally the organic source of its voice (53), feeding sleeping pills to the chickens (80–81), undressing in public (147), and swallowing the cow's eye that the students were given to dissect during science class (205).

10. Note that the description of the volcanic ash storm raining down on Santiago may be another symbol of the tragic occurrences during the Pinochet dictatorship.

11. All translations of *Carne* are mine.

Chapter 7

1. For more on how *La fiesta del chivo* explores social psychology, see Weldt-Basson, "La fiesta."
2. For the image and question of a more balanced portrait of Dr. Francia, see Weldt-Basson, *Augusto Roa Bastos's I The Supreme*.
3. See my introduction to *The Prosecutor* for a more detailed analysis of the heroism/martyrdom dichotomy in *El fiscal*.

Works Cited

Alzate, Sergio. "El pasado es una hoja de ruta para el futuro." https://www.eltiempo.com/lecturas-dominicales/entrevista-a-la-escritora-chilena-nona-fernandez-216714.

Amaro Castro, Lorena. "Formas de salir de casa, o cómo escapar del Ogro: Relatos de filiación en la literatura chilena reciente." *Literatura y Lingüística*, vol. 29, 2014, pp. 109–29.

Arce, Luz. *The Inferno*. Translated by Stacey Alba Skar. U of Wisconsin P, 2004.

———. *El infierno*. Tajamar Ediciones, 2017.

Areco, Magdalena, et al. *Cartografías de la novela chilena reciente: Realismos, experimentalismos, hibridaciones y subgéneros (ensayos)*. Ceibo Ediciones, 2015.

Argentieri, Simona. "Incest Yesterday and Today: from Conflict to Ambiguity." *On Incest: Psychoanalytic Perspectives*, edited by Giovanna Ambrosio, Routledge, 2005, pp. 17–49.

Armillas-Tiseyra, Magalí. *The Dictator Novel: Writers and Politics in the Global South*. Northwestern UP, 2019.

Arya, Rina. *Abjection and Representation: An Exploration of Abjection in the Visual Arts, Film, and Literature*. Palgrave/Macmillan, 2014.

Auerbach, Nina. *Our Vampires, Ourselves*. U of Chicago P, 1995. EPUB.

Avelar, Idelber. *The Untimely Present: Postdictatorial Latin American Fiction and the Task of Mourning*. Duke UP, 1999.

Bakhtin, Mikhail. *Problems of Dostoevsky's Poetics*. Edited and translated by Caryl Emerson. U of Minnesota P, 1984.

———. *Rabelais and his World*. Translated by Helen Iswolsky. Indiana UP, 2009.

Barr, Lois Baer. *Isaac Unbound: Patriarchal Traditions in the Latin American Jewish Novel*. Arizona State University Center for Latin American Studies, 1995.

Bennett, Jill. *Empathic Vision: Affect, Trauma, and Contemporary Art*. Stanford UP, 2005.

Bernard, Andreas. *Lifted: A Cultural History of the Elevator*. Translated by David Dollenmayer. New York UP, 2014. EPUB.

Bhabha, Homi. *The Location of Culture*. 2nd edition. Routledge, 2004.

Bilbija, Ksenija. "Transacciones y facturas neoliberales: El valor de la pena desde Luz Arce a Arturo Fontaine." *Senderos de violencia: Latinoamérica y sus narrativas armadas*, edited by Oswaldo Estrada, Albatros, 2015, pp. 289–307.

Bisama, Álvaro. *Dead Stars*. Translated by Megan McDowell. Ox and Pigeon, 2014. EPUB.

———. *El brujo*. Alfaguara, 2016.

———. *Estrellas muertas*. Alfaguara, 2010. EPUB.

Booth, Wayne C. *The Rhetoric of Fiction*. 2nd edition. U of Chicago P, 1983.

Bowring, Jacky. *Melancholy and the Landscape: Locating Sadness, Memory and Reflection in the Landscape*. Routledge, 2018.

Braun, Lucille V. "Narrative Strategies in *La última canción de Manuel Sendero*." *Revista Canadiense de Estudios Hispánicos*, vol. 20, no. 3, 1996, 409–32.

Brintrup, Lilianet. "Desde el abismo del horror: El lenguaje como represión, perversión and violencia en Muñeca brava de Lucía Guerra y Carne de perra de Fátima Sime." *Donde no habite el olvido: Herencia y transmisión del testimonio en Chile*, edited by Laura Scarabelli and Serena Cappellini, Universitá degli Studi di Milano Ledizioni, 2017, pp. 127–45.

Caballero Vázquez, Miguel. "Museo de la Memoria y los Derechos Humanos de Santiago de Chile: crisis de memoriales y lógicas urbanísticas del Mercado." *Revista Canadiense de Estudios Hispánicos*, vol. 40, no. 3, 2016, pp. 509–33.

Cardone, Resha S. "Nona Fernández's Mapocho: Spirits in a Material Wasteland." *Studies in Twentieth & Twenty-First Century Literature*, vol. 39, no. 2, 2015, pp. 1–17.

Carreño, Rubí. "Historias de amor en *Jamás el fuego nunca*." *Taller de letras*, vol. 43, 2008, pp. 189–96.

Caruth, Cathy. *Literature in the Ashes of History*. Johns Hopkins UP, 2013. EPUB.

Chossudovsky, Michel. "Chile September 11, 1973: The Ingredients of a Military Coup. The Imposition of a Neoliberal Agenda." https://www.globalresearch.ca/chile-september-11-1973-the-ingredients-of-a-military-coup-the-imposition-of-a-neoliberal-agenda/5545251.

Collyer, Jaime. "Narrativa que resurge de las cenizas." *Inti: Revista de Literatura Hispánica*, vol. 69–70, 2009, pp. 99–114.

Connelly, Frances S. *The Grotesque in Western Art and Culture: The Image at Play*. Cambridge UP, 2012.

Coplan, Amy. "Understanding Empathy: Its Features and Effects." *Empathy: Philosophical and Psychological Perspectives*, edited by Amy Coplan and Peter Goldie, Oxford UP, 2011.

Corral, Will H., Juan E. De Castro, and Nicholas Birns, eds. *The Contemporary Spanish-American Novel: Bolaño and After*. Bloomsbury, 2013.

Coyne, André. "César Vallejo, vida y obra." *César Vallejo: El escritor y la crítica*, 2nd ed., edited by Julio Ortega, Taurus, 1981.

Cummings, Peter M. M. "Democracy and Student Discontent: Chilean Student Protest in the Post-Pinochet Era." *Journal of Politics in Latin America*, vol. 7, no. 3, 2015, pp. 49–84.

Densmore, Francis. *Chippewa Customs*. Minnesota Historical Society Press, 1979.

De Toro, Alfonso. "Lo indecible, lo irrepresentable: Topografías: terror e intertextualidad *El desierto* de Carlos Franz/*La vida doble* de Arturo Fontaine." *Iberomania: Zeitschrift fur die iberomanischen Sprachen und Amerika/Revista Dedicada a las Lenguas y Literaturas iberománicas de Europa y América*, no. 83, 2016, pp. 35–55.

Díaz, Carolina. "Allegorical Specters and the Rhetorics of Mourning in Diamela Eltit's *Jamás el fuego nunca*." *Journal of Latin American Cultural Studies*, vol. 23, no. 3, 2014, pp. 251–66.

———. "Hacia una teoría afectiva de la paranoia en *Jamás el fuego nunca* de Diamela Eltit." *Revista Iberoamericana*, vol. 84, no. 262, 2018, pp. 181–201.

Dion, Lisa. *Aggression in Play Therapy: A Neurobiological Approach for Integrating Intensity*. W. W. Norton, 2018.

Donoso, José. *Curfew*. Translated by Alfred MacAdam. Widenfeld and Nicolson, 1988.

———. *La desesperanza*. Alfaguara, 1986.

Dorfman, Ariel. *The Last Song of Manuel Sendero*. Translated by Ariel Dorfman and George R. Shivers. Penguin, 1987.

———. *La última canción de Manuel Sendero*. Planeta, 1990.

Eltit, Diamela. *Jamás el fuego nunca*. Editorial Periférica, 2012.

———. *Never Did the Fire*. Translated by Daniel Hahn. Charco Press, 2021.

Engels, Frederick. *The Housing Question*. International Publishers, n.d.

Ercolino, Stefano. "Negative Empathy: History, Theory, Criticism." *Orbis Litterarum: International Review of Literary Studies*, vol. 73, no. 3, 2018, pp. 242–62.

"El escritor Álvaro Bisama nos habla de su nueva novela *El brujo*." https://video.search.yahoo.com/search/video?fr=mcafee&ei=UTF-8&p=Alvaro+Bisama+on+El+brujo&type=E211US105G91649#id=1&vid=e1623a7ee4532ea71a7107ddc5bc0542&action=click.

Eyerman, Ron. *Cultural Trauma: Slavery and the Formation of African American Identity*. Cambridge UP, 2001.

Falk, Eugene H. *Types of Thematic Structure: The Nature and Function of Motifs in Gide, Camus, and Sartre*. U of Chicago P, 1967.

Fernández, Nona. *La dimensión desconocida*. Random House, 2016.

———. *Fuenzalida*. Mondadori, 2012. EPUB.

———. *Mapocho*. Planeta, 2002.

———. *The Twilight Zone*. Translated by Natasha Wimmer. Graywolf Press, 2021.

———. *Voyager*. New York, Literatura Random House, 2020.

Fletcher, Angus. *Allegory: The Theory of a Symbolic Mode*. Princeton UP, 2012.

Flores-Rodríguez, Daynali. "Familial Longings: Trans-Caribbean Narratives of Dictatorship and the Latin American Imaginary." *Small Axe: A Caribbean Journal of Criticism*, vol. 60, 2019, pp. 69–85.

Fontaine, Arturo. *La vida doble*. Tusquets Ediciones, 2010. EPUB.

———. *La vida doble: A Novel*. Translated by Megan McDowell. Yale UP, 2013.

Fornazzari, Alessandro. *Speculative Fictions: Chilean Culture, Economics, and the Neoliberal Transition*. U of Pittsburgh P, 2013.

"The Four of Us are Dying." *The Twilight Zone*, season 1, episode 13, CBS, 1 January 1960.

Frank, Adam J. and Elizabeth A. Wilson. *A Silvan Tomkins Handbook: Foundations for Affect Theory*. U of Minnesota P, 2020. EPUB.

Franken Osorio, María Angélica. "Memorias e imaginarios de formación de los hijos en la narrativa chilena reciente." *Revista Chilena de Literatura*, vol. 96, 2017, pp. 187–208.

Franz, Carlos. *The Absent Sea*. Translated by Leland H. Chambers. McPherson, 2005.

———. *Almuerzo de vampiros*. Alfaguara, 2007.

———. *El desierto*. Editorial Sudamericana, 2005.

———. *Santiago Cero*. Debosillo, 2019. EPUB.

Friedman, Mary Lusky. "The Artistry of *La desesperanza*." *Hispania*, vol. 78, no. 5, 1995, pp. 13–25.

Fritz Roa, Sergio. *La recta provincia: Una cofradía de brujos en el sur de Chile*. Editorial Bajo los Hielos, 2015. EPUB.

Frosh, Stephen. *Those Who Come After: Postmemory, Acknowledgement and Forgiveness*. Palgrave/Macmillan, 2019. EPUB.

Galeano, Eduardo. *Memoria del fuego. Los nacimientos*, vol. 1. Siglo XXI Editores, 2014. EPUB.

García-Avello, Macarena. "Inventa un cuento que te sirva de memoria: Narración del vacío de *Fuenzalida* de Nona Fernández." *Chasqui: Revista de Literatura Latinoamericana*, vol. 45, no. 2, 2016, pp. 249–60.

García-Corales, Guillermo. *El debate cultural y la literatura chilena actual: un diálogo con cinco generaciones de escritores*. Edwin Mellen, 2007.

Gernsbacher, Morton Ann. "Activating Knowledge of Characters' Emotional States." *Discourse Comprehension: Essays in Honor of Walter Kintsch*, edited by Charles A. Weaver, Suzanne Mannes, and Charles R. Fletcher, Eribaum, 1995, pp. 141–54.

Gómez-Barris, Macarena. "Witness Citizenship: The Place of Villa Grimaldi in Chilean Memory." *Sociological Forum*, vol. 25, no. 1, 2010, pp. 27–46.

Guezzar, Terri Pullen. "Mental Imagery and Literature: Centers and Vectors in Students' Visual and Verbal Responses." *Language and Image in Reading-Writing Classroom: Teaching Vision*, edited by Kristie S. Fleckenstein, Linda T. Calendrill and Demetrice A. Worley. Lawrence Erlbaum, 2002, pp. 47–58.

Gürsel, Zeynep Devrim. "Framing Zarqawi: Afterimages, Headshots, and Body Politics in a Digital Age." *Double Exposure: Memory & Photography*, edited by Olga Shevchenko, Routledge, 2014, pp. 65-89.

Harford Vargas, Jennifer. *Forms of Dictatorship: Power, Narrative, and Authoritarianism in the Latina/o Novel*. Oxford UP, 2018. EPUB.

Harpham, Geoffrey. *On the Grotesque: Strategies of Contradiction in Art and Literature*. Davies Group, 2007.

Hart, Bjorn t., et al. "Tracking Affective Language Comprehension: Simulating and Evaluating Character Affect in Morally Loaded Narratives." *Frontiers in Psychology*, vol. 10, no. 3339, 2019, pp. 1–14.

Heker, Liliana. *The End of the Story*. Translated by Andrea G. Labinger. Biblioasis, 2012.

———. *El fin de la historia*. Alfaguara, 1996.

Henríquez, Florencia C. "Álvaro Bisama." *The Contemporary Spanish-American Novel: Bolaño and After*, edited by Will H. Corral, Juan E. De Castro, and Nicholas Birns, Bloomsbury, 2013, pp. 295-300.

Hirsch, Marianne. *The Generation of Postmemory: Writing and Visual Culture After the Holocaust*. Columbia UP, 2012.

Hoffman, Eva. *After Such Knowledge: Memory, History, and the Legacy of the Holocaust*. Public Affairs, 2004.

Hogan, Patrick Colm. *Affective Narratology: The Emotional Structure of Stories*. U of Nebraska P, 2011. EPUB.

Iacoboni, Marco. *Mirroring People: The Science of Empathy and How We Connect with Others*. Picador, 2009.

Iser, Wolfgang. *The Implied Reader: Patterns of Communication in Prose Fiction from Bunyan to Beckett*. Johns Hopkins UP, 1978.

Jaén, Isabel. "Fascism, Torture, and Affect in Postwar Spain: Memoria Histórica Narratives and Audience Empathy." *The Palgrave Handbook of Affect Studies and Textual Criticism*, edited by Donald R. Wehrs and Thomas Blake. Palgrave/Macmillan, 2017, pp. 803–26.

Jelić, Andrea and Aleksandar Stančić. "The Memory in Bodily and Architectural Making: Reflections from Embodied Cognitive Science." *Affective Architectures: More-Than-Representational Geographies of Heritage*, edited by Jacque Miceli-Voutsinas and Angela M. Person, Routledge, 2021, pp. 187–203. EPUB.

Jelin, Elizabeth. *Los trabajos de la memoria*. Fondo de cultura económica, 2021. EPUB.

Johnson, Gary. *The Vitality of Allegory: Figural Narrative in Modern and Contemporary Fiction*. Ohio State UP, 2020.

Jukes, Jacqueline A. and Jeffrey H. Goldstein. "Preference for Aggressive Toys." *International Play Journal*, vol. 1, 1993, pp. 81–91.

Justo, Liborio. *Así se murió en Chile: Reformismo y revolución en la trágica experiencia de la Unidad Popular*. Cienflores, 2018. EPUB.

Kaplan, E. Ann. "Empathy and Trauma Culture: Imaging Catastrophe." *Empathy: Philosophical and Psychological Perspectives*, edited by Amy Coplan and Peter Goldie, Oxford UP, 2011, pp. 255–76.

Karr-Conejo, Katherine. "Imagined Worlds and the Gendered City in Chilean Historical Fiction." *Cincinnati Romance Review*, vol. 44, 2018, pp. 1–18.

Kim, Euisuk. *Una reconstrucción alternativa del pretérito: Una aproximación psicoanalítica a la obra de Ariel Dorfman*. University Press of the South, 2003.

Kohut, Karl. "Más allá de la barbarie y del horror: La literatura argentina de la dictadura." *Texto social: Estudios pragmáticos sobre literatura y cine*, edited by Annette Paatz and Burkhard Pohl, Tranvía-Verlag, 2003, pp. 169–87.

Kristeva, Julia. *Powers of Horror: An Essay on Abjection*. Translated by Leon S. Roudiez. Columbia UP, 1982.

Krueger, Richard B., et. al. "Proposals for Paraphilic Disorders in the International Classification of Diseases and Related Health Problems, Eleventh Revision." *Archives of Sexual Behavior*, vol. 46, no. 5, 2017, pp. 1529–45.

Landkildehus, Søren. "Taxonymy of the Double: Struggles of Cognition in the Works of Vita Sackville-West and Walter de la Mare." *The Poetics of Shadows: The Double in Literature and Philosophy*, Ibedem-Verlag, 2008, pp. 65–88.

Lazzara, Michael J. *Chile in Transition: The Poetics and Politics of Memory*. U Press of Florida, 2006.

———. "Diamela Eltit." *The Contemporary Spanish-American Novel: Bolaño and After*, edited by Will Corral, et al., Bloomsbury, 2013, pp. 320–27.

———, ed. *Luz Arce and Pinochet's Chile: Testimony in the Aftermath of State Violence*. Palgrave/Macmillan, 2011.

Leskinen, Auli. "La novela del nuevo milenio: *Jamás el fuego nunca* de Diamela Eltit, alegoría del cuerpo moribundo de la utopía revolucionaria de América Latina." *Debate Feminista*, vol. 37, 2008, pp. 249–54.

Levi, Primo. *The Drowned and the Saved*. Simon and Schuster, 2017.

Longo, Mariano. *Emotions through Literature: Fictional Narratives, Society and the Emotional Self*. Routledge, 2020. EPUB.

Lozoya, Johanna. "Dwellers of Silence: Conflict and Affective Borderlands of the Estadio Nacional, Santiago de Chile." *Affective Architectures: More-Than-Representational Geographies of Heritage*, edited by Jacques Micieli-Voutsinas and Angela M. Person, Routledge, 2021, pp. 55–66. EPUB.

Lynch, Joseph J. "Plato and the Shaolin Monks Square Off." *Martial Arts and Philosophy: Beating and Nothingness*, edited by Graham Priest and Damon Young, Open Court, 2010, pp. 35-46..

Lyndon, Donlon. "The Place of Memory." *Spatial Recall: Architecture and Landscape*, edited by Marc Treib, Routledge, 2009, pp. 62–85.

MacCarthy, Brendan. "Counterpoints." *On Incest: Psychoanalytic Perspectives*, edited by Giovanna Ambrosio, Routledge, 2005, pp. 115–20.

Maguire, Geoffrey. *The Politics of Postmemory: Violence and Victimhood in Contemporary Argentine Culture*. Palgrave Macmillan, 2017. EPUB.

Maier, Gonzalo. "Bruce Lee en Chile: Ironía y parodia en *Fuenzalida* de Nona Fernández." *Symposium: A Quarterly Journal in Modern Literatures*, vol. 71, no.1, 2017, pp. 38–49.

Marín, Germán. *El palacio de la risa*. Ediciones Universidad Diego Portales, 1995.

McClennen, Sophia A. *Ariel Dorfman: An Aesthetics of Hope*. Duke UP, 2010.

Merriam-Webster Online Dictionary. https://www.merriam-webster.com.

Micieli-Voutsinas and Angela M. Person, eds. *Affective Architectures: More-Than-Representational Geographies of Heritage*. Routledge, 2021. EPUB.

Miller, William Ian. *The Anatomy of Disgust*. Harvard UP, 1997. EPUB.

Montes Capó, Cristián. "'Carne de perra' de Fátima Sime: La persistencia de lo urgente." *Iberoamericana: América Latina-España-Portugal*, vol. 11, no. 44, 2011, pp. 63–78.

Mulián, Tomás. *Chile actual: Anatomía de un mito*. LOM-Arcis, 1997.

Murphy, Kaitlin M. *Mapping Memory: Visuality, Affect, and Embodied Politics in the Americas*. Fordham UP, 2019.

Ngai, Sianne. *Ugly Feelings*. Harvard UP, 2005. EPUB.

"Nightmare at 20,000 Feet." *The Twilight Zone*, season 5, episode 123, CBS, 11 October 1963.

Olick, Jeffrey K. "Willy Brandt in Warsaw: Event or Image?" *Double Exposure: Memory & Photography*, edited by Olga Shevchenko, Routledge, 2014, pp. 21-40.

Olivera-Williams, María Rosa. "La década del 70 en el Cono Sur: Discursos nostálgicos que recuerdan la revolución y escriben la historia." *Romance Quarterly*, vol. 57, no.1, 2010, pp. 43–62.

Oxford Advanced American Dictionary. https://www.oxfordlearnersdictionaries.com.

Oxford Online Dictionary. https://www.lexico.com/en.

Pacheco, Carlos. *Narrativa de la dictadura y crítica literaria*. Fundación Centro de Estudios Latinoamericanos, 1987.

Pallasmaa, Juhani. "Space, Place, Memory, and Imagination: The Temporal Dimension of Existential Space." *Spatial Recall: Architecture and Landscape*, edited by Marc Treib, Routledge, 2009, pp. 16–41.

Palmer Bonte, Eleanor and Mary Musgrove. "Influences of War as Evidenced in Children's Play." *Child Development*, vol. 14, no. 4, 1943, pp. 179–200.

Parra, Nicanor. "Noticiero 1957." *Antipoemas: Antología (1944–1969)*, edited by José Miguel Ibáñez-Langlois, Seix Barral, 1981, pp. 164-67.

Paz-Mackay, María Soledad. *Historia, memoria y novela en la Argentina de la posdictadura: La cuestión de la responsabilidad extendida*. Editorial Biblos, 2017.

"Periodismo de oposición: 1979–1989." http://www.memoriachilena.gob.cl/602/w3-article-96758.html.

Petremen, David. "The Chilean Ghost Ship: The Caleuche." *Into the Mainstream: Essays on Spanish American and Latino Literature and Culture*, edited by Jorge Febles, Cambridge Scholars, 2006, pp. 202–14.

Phelan, James. "Voice, Tone, and the Rhetoric of Narrative Communication." *Language and Literature: Journal of the Poetics and Linguistics Association*, vol. 23, no.1, 2014, pp. 49–60.

Piglia, Ricardo. *Artificial Respiration*. Translated by Daniel Balderston. Duke UP, 1994.

———. *Respiración artificial*. Editorial Pomaire, 1980. EPUB.

Plotnik, Viviana. "La figura de la colaboradora en la narrativa chilena: El síndrome de Estocolmo y la zona gris en *La vida doble* de Arturo Fontaine y *Carne de perra* de Fátima Sime." *Chasqui*, vol. 46, no. 2, 2017, pp. 82–95.

Poblete, Juan. "The Memory of the National and the National as Memory." *Latin American Perspectives*, vol. 42, no. 3, 2015, pp. 92–106.

Prince, Gerald. "Narrative Pragmatics, Message, and Point." *Poetics: Journal of Empirical Research on Culture, the Media, and the Arts*, vol. 12, no. 6, 1983, pp. 527–36.

"Probe 7, Over and Out." *The Twilight Zone*, season 5, episode 129, CBS, 29 November 1963.

Pron, Patricio. *El espíritu de mis padres sigue subiendo en la lluvia*. Vintage Español, 2011.

———. *My Father's Ghost is Climbing in the Rain*. Translated by Mara Faye Lethem. Borzoi, 2013.

"The Renaissance of the Train in Chile." https://chiletoday.cl/the-renaissance-of-the-train-in-chile.

Richard, Nelly. *Cultural Residues: Chile in Transition*. Translated by Alan West-Durán and Theodore Quester. U of Minnesota P, 2004.

———. *Eruptions of Memory: The Critique of Memory in Chile, 1990–2015*. Polity, 2019.

Rimmon, Shlomith. *The Concept of Ambiguity—the Example of James*. U of Chicago P, 1977.

Rodríguez Freire, Raúl. "Carlos Franz." *The Contemporary Spanish-American Novel: Bolaño and After*, edited by Will H. Corral, Juan E. De Castro, and Nicholas Birns, Bloomsbury, 2013, pp. 335–38.

Rojas, Eric. "Los muertos vivientes y el destierro de un pasado olvidado en *Almuerzo de vampiros* de Carlos Franz." *A Contracorriente: Una revista de estudios latinoamericanos*, vol. 18, no. 3, 2021, pp. 253–76.

Rojo Grínor. "Germán Marín está de visita en *El palacio de la risa*." *Las novelas de la dictadura y la postdictadura chilena: Quince ensayos críticos*, edited by Grínor Rojo, vol. 4, LOM Ediciones, 2016, pp. 131–50.

———. *Las novelas de la dictadura y la postdictadura chilena: ¿Qué y Cómo Leer?* vol. 1, LOM Ediciones, 2016.

———, ed. *Las novelas de la dictadura y la postdictadura chilena: Quince ensayos críticos*, vol. 2. LOM Ediciones, 2016.

Romero, Ivana. "Nona Fernández: Cuando escribo, soy." https://eternacadencia.com.ar/nota/nona-fernandez-quot-cuando-escribo-soy-quot-/1718

Ros, Ana. *The Post-Dictatorship Generation in Argentina, Chile, and Uruguay: Collective Memory and Cultural Production*. Palgrave/Macmillan, 2012.

Rosenblatt, Louise. *The Reader, the Text, the Poem: The Transactional Theory of the Literary Work*. Southern Illinois UP, 1978.

Rosencof, Mauricio. *Las cartas que no llegaron*. Alcalá La Real Alcalá, 2014.

Rotger, Patricia. *Memoria sin tiempo: Prácticas narrativas de la memoria en escritoras argentinas de la posdictadura*. Comunicarte, 2014.

Rothlisberger, Silvia. "Author Interview: *The Remainder* by Alia Trabucco Zerán." *Literary South*. https://literarysouth.org/2019/03/25/author-interview-the-remainder-by-alia-trabucco-zeran.

Sagastizábal, Patricia. *A Secret for Julia*. Translated by Asa Zatz. W. W. Norton, 2001.

———. *Un secreto para Julia*. Editorial Sudamericana, 2000.

Scarry, Elaine. *The Body in Pain: The Making and Unmaking of the World*. Oxford UP, 1985. EPUB.

Schevchenko, Olga. "Memory and Photography: An Introduction." *Double Exposure: Memory & Photography*, edited by Olga Schevchenko, Routledge, 2014, pp. 1–17.

Schlickers, Sabine. *La narración perturbadora: un nuevo concepto narratológico transmedial*. Ediciones Iberoamericana/Vervuert, 2017. EPUB.

———. "Perturbatory Narration in Literature and Film." *Frontiers of Narrative Studies*, vol. 3, no. 2, 2017, pp. 206–23.

Senio Blair, Laura. "The Recurring Theme of Incest in Contemporary Chilean Women's Narrative." *Letras Femeninas*, vol. 36, no. 2. 2010, pp. 183–98.

Sharman, Adam, et al. *Memo/Sur/Memo-South: Memory, Commemoration and Trauma in Post-Dictatorship Argentina and Chile*. Critical, Cultural and Communications Press, 2017.

Sime, Fátima. *Carne de perra*. LOM Ediciones, 2009. EPUB.

Singer, Tania and Claus Lamm. "The Social Neuroscience of Empathy." *Annals of the New York Academy of Sciences*, vol. 1156, no. 1, 2009, pp. 81–96.

"The Sixteen Millimeter Shrine." *The Twilight Zone*, season 1, episode 4, CBS, 23 October 1959.

Sklar, Howard. "Empathy's Neglected Cousin: How Narratives Shape Our Sympathy." *The Palgrave Handbook of Affect Studies and Textual Criticism*, edited by Donald R. Wehrs and Thomas Blake, Palgrave/Macmillan, 2017, pp. 451–80.

Soja, Edward W. *Seeking Spatial Justice*. U of Minnesota P, 2010.
Sontag, Susan. *Illness as Metaphor and AIDS and Its Metaphors*. Picador, 1990.
Steiner, George. *Nostalgia for the Absolute*. House of Anansi P, 1974. EPUB.
Stern, Steve J. *Battling for Hearts and Minds: Memory Struggles in Pinochet's Chile, 1973–1988*. Duke UP, 2006.
———. *Reckoning with Pinochet: The Memory Question in Democratic Chile, 1989–2006*. Duke UP, 2010.
———. *Remembering Pinochet's Chile: On the Eve of London 1998*. Duke UP, 2006.
Tandeciarz, Silvia R. *Citizens of Memory: Affect, Representation and Human Rights in Postdictatorship Argentina*. Bucknell UP, 2017. EPUB.
Taylor, Craig. "Literature, Moral Reflection, and Ambiguity." *Philosophy*, vol. 86, no. 335, 2011, pp. 75–93.
Taylor, Diana. "Memory and the Archive." *Feeling Photography*, edited by Elspeth H. Brown and Thy Phu, Duke UP, 2014, pp. 239–51. EPUB.
Thomas, Nigel. "Are Theories of Imagery Theories of the Imagination? An Active Perception Approach to Conscious Mental Content." *Cognitive Science*, vol. 23, no. 2, 1999, pp. 207–45.
Tierney-Tello, Mary Beth. *Allegories of Transgression and Transformation: Experimental Fiction by Women Writing Under Dictatorship*. SUNY P, 1996.
Todorov, Tzvetan. *Symbolism and Interpretation*. Translated by Catherine Porter. Cornell UP, 1982.
Tomkins, Silvan. *Affect, Imagery, Consciousness: The Negative Affects: Anger and Fear*. Vol. 3, Springer, 1991.
———. *Affect, Imagery, Consciousness: The Positive Affects*. Vol. 1, Springer, 1991.
Trabucco Zerán, Alia. *The Remainder*. Translated by Sophie Hughes. Coffee House P, 2019.
———. *La resta*. Editorial Demipage, 2014.
Traverso, Enzo. *Left-Wing Melancholia: Marxism, History and Memory*. Columbia UP, 2021.
Treib, Marc. "Yes, Now I Remember: An Introduction." *Spatial Recall: Architecture and Landscape*, edited by Marc Treib, Routledge, 2009, pp. x–xiv.
Trostel, Katharine. "City of (Post) Memory: Memory Mapping in Nona Fernández's 2002 *Mapocho*." *Arizona Quarterly*, vol. 74, no. 21, 2018, pp. 119–43.
Trotsky, Leon. *Art & Revolution: Writings on Literature, Politics, and Culture*. Pathfinder, 1970.

Tuszewicka, Monika. "The Land of Childhood. Nostalgia and Myth of Poland's Recent Past." *Polish Journal of the Arts and Culture*, vol. 15, no. 3, 2005, pp. 167–81.

Urzúa Opazo, Macarena. "Electrodomésticos, *El frío muerto* y *Estrellas muertas*: Recorridos por la memoria de las ruinas en el paisaje chileno actual." *Revista Iberoamericana*, vol. 83, no. 258, 2017, pp. 207–25.

Vallejo, César. *The Complete Poetry: A Bilingual Edition*. Translated by Clayton Eshleman. U of California P, 2009.

Vallejo, César. "Los nueve monstruos." *Poemas humanos. Obras Completas*. Editorial Laia, 1977, pp. 34–36.

———. "El pan nuestro." *Los heraldos negros*. Editorial Losada, 1961, pp. 72–73.

Van Alphen, Ernst. "Affective Operations of Art and Literature." *RES: Anthropology and Aesthetics*, no. 53–54, 2008, pp. 20–30.

Vergara Perucich, Francisco. *Urban Design Under Neoliberalism: Theorising from Santiago, Chile*. Routledge, 2019.

"Yo torturé," *Cauce*, semana del 23 al 29 de julio de 1985. https://vivachilemierdathefilm.files.wordpress.com/2014/06/valenzuelacauce.pdf.

Weldt-Basson, Helene Carol. *Augusto Roa Bastos's I The Supreme: A Dialogic Perspective*. U of Missouri P, 1993.

———. "Mario Vargas Llosa's *La fiesta del chivo*: History, Fiction, or Social Psychology?" *Hispanófila*, 156, 2009, pp. 113–31.

———. *Masquerade and Social Justice in Contemporary Latin American Fiction*. U of New Mexico P, 2017.

———. "Introduction." *The Prosecutor* by Augusto Roa Bastos. Translated by Helene Carol Weldt-Basson. Farleigh Dickinson UP, 2018.

Zheng, Nan. "El huacharaje como subdivisión y la paradoja del incesto en *Mapocho* de Nona Fernández y "Árbol genealógico" de Andrea Jeftanovic." *Chasqui*, vol. 48, no. 2, 2019, pp. 142–56.

Zubieta, Ana María. "La tela de Penélope." *De memoria: Tramas literarias y políticas: el pasado en cuestión*, edited by Ana María Zubieta, Eudeba, 2011. EPUB.

Index

abandonment, 14, 20, 23–25, 29–30, 34–36, 38, 41, 42–50, 60, 196
abduction, 4, 40, 47, 56, 161, 164
abjection, 21, 128, 130–31, 133–34, 136–43, 145, 147–57, 166, 173, 183, 196, 202, 204, 205, 212, 214 215, 222n6
abortion, 107, 109, 212
absence, 24, 37, 44, 51, 52, 60, 87, 172, 202, 218n1
Acevedo Becerra, Sebastián, 41, 42, 43, 44, 47
Adentro, 101, 104, 106, 108, 111, 112, 113
aesthetics, 13, 172–74, 192
affect, 10, 12, 16, 17, 21, 61, 62, 79–80, 82, 84, 88–89, 94, 112, 160, 165, 166, 167, 176, 177, 201; startle, 22, 87, 157–60, 163, 172, 177–78, 180, 182–83, 185, 187, 191
afterimage, 55–57
Afuera, 102, 105, 110, 111, 112, 114
Alfonsín, Raúl, 200
allegory, 21, 35, 74, 85, 95, 97–98, 99, 101, 102, 103, 106, 107, 116, 117, 118, 119, 120, 121, 122, 123–27, 160, 172, 175, 176, 177, 178, 182, 209–12, 222n4; embedded, 98, 102, 104–5, 204; strong, 21, 98, 102, 105, 116; weak, 21, 116, 125
Allende Gossens, Salvador, 3, 21, 31, 63, 76, 96, 100–103, 106, 109, 111, 113–14, 122, 128, 139, 145, 152, 170, 209, 212
Almuerzo de los vampiros, 21, 63, 128, 129, 145–56, 221n5
Álvarez, Julia, 193
Alywin, Patricio, 170, 22n21

Alzate, Sergio, 168
Amalia, 192
Amaro Castro, Lorena, 218n6
ambiguity, 20, 30, 48, 50–51, 54, 149, 190
ambivalence, 32, 39, 91, 130, 149, 214
Americo Vespucio, 31
Amheim, Rudolf, 18
amnesia, 89, 115, 205
amnesty, 5, 7, 9, 196–97
Apollonian, 139, 143–44
Arce, Luz, 128, 129, 130, 131, 132, 133, 134, 137, 138, 139
architecture, 1, 20–21, 62, 79–82, 84–85, 87–88, 91, 93, 134
Argentieri, Simona, 29
Argentina, 22, 101, 192–93, 196, 199, 200–202, 206–15
Arrabal, Felipe, 102, 174–82, 220n3, 222n9
Artaza, Flaco, 134–36, 138
artist, 38, 58, 71, 75–77, 148, 172, 219n4
arts, martial, 39, 40, 43, 44, 45, 219n8; creative, 34, 58, 78, 148–50, 219n5
Arya, Rina, 128–30
audience, 22, 58, 61, 112, 158
Aue, Maximillien, 173
Auerbach, Nina, 154
Auschwitz, 58
authoritarianism, 168, 194–95
Avelar, Idelber, 85
Aylwin, Patricio, 4, 7, 8, 12, 119, 170, 217n2

Bachelet, Michele, 12
Baensch, Otto, 61

236

Index

Bakhtin, Mikhail, 21, 130, 148–49, 151, 156
Balmelli, Carlos Mateo, 199
Barks, Carl, 106, 114, 220n3
Barks, Sarah, 114
Barr, Lois Baer, 114
Bechofen, Hertha, 202, 204–5
Beecham, Mercedes, 212–15
Bellavista, 33
Bennett, Jill, 57
Bernard, Andreas, 104
betrayal, 64, 109, 128–29, 131–35, 137, 139, 141, 143, 145, 147, 149, 151, 153–56, 163, 164, 174, 179, 200, 202–5, 212, 215, 219n3, 222n5
Bhabha, Homi, 32
Bianchi, Edwin Dimter, 183
Bilbija, Ksenija, 138
birds, 26, 51, 53, 181
Bisama, Álvaro, 20, 23, 47, 48, 59, 61, 66, 70
blockade, 3
bodies, 27, 33, 35, 48–49, 50, 117, 122, 128, 134, 176, 180, 182. *See also* corpses
Bolivia, 193
Bonte, Eleanor Palmer, 179
Booth, Wayne C., 52, 219n9
Bordaberry, Juan María, 196
Boric, Gabriel, 1–2
bourgeoisie, 77–78, 122–24, 220n6
Bowring, Jacky, 21, 79, 85–88, 90–92
brain, 13–14, 17–19, 220n8
Brandt, Willy, 56
Brasil. *See* Brazil
Braun, Lucille V., 102, 104, 106, 108, 113–14
Brazil, 193, 200
Bridal, Tessa, 197
Brintrup, Lilianet, 190
brujo, El, 20, 23, 47–60, 68
Buenos Aires, 72, 211
buildings, 33, 71, 80–82, 103, 104
Burdisso, Alberto, 205, 206, 207–8
Burdisso, Alicia, 206

Caballero, El, 103, 104, 107, 108, 109, 111, 114
Caballero Vázquez, Miguel, 170
Cabral, Urania, 195
Cáceres, 139–42, 144, 145, 212, 215
CADA (Art Actions Collective), 116
cadaver, 7, 67, 91, 175–77, 180, 182
Café Hesperia, 66, 70
Caleuche, El, 78–79, 89, 90
camera, 49, 53, 56
cancer, 137, 190
canción, 21, 27, 95, 109–10, 126. *See also* song
Cal y Canto bridge, 24, 33, 36
capitalism, 1–2, 30, 103, 124
Montes Capó, Cristián, 183, 190
Caravan of Death, 9, 139
Cardone, Resha S., 30, 33, 218
Cardoso, Fernando, 99
Carpentier, Alejo, 192
Carne de perra, 22, 157, 159, 183, 187, 191, 222n11
carnivalesque, 149
Carpentier, Alejo, 192
Carreño, Rubí, 116
Carro, Tony, 197
Cartas que no llegaron, Las, 197, 199
Caruth, Cathy, 14
Cauce, 160, 161, 205, 221n2
cells, revolutionary, 120, 122–23, 125–26
cemetery, 34, 36, 88, 92, 95, 198
censorship, 12, 21, 194, 211
cerebellum, 17. *See also* brain
Chacón, Dulce, 169
Chango, 203
Chapulín Colorado, El, 171
Chaves, Julio César, 199
Guevara, Che, 100
childhood, 36, 84, 105, 140, 174, 175, 177, 179
children, 10, 20, 22, 24, 25, 26, 27, 29, 41, 42, 43, 47, 68, 96, 106, 110, 111, 115, 164, 165, 174, 178–80, 182, 201, 207, 219n8, 219n4

Chilóe, 48–50, 59, 75, 78–79, 89–91
Chimba, La, 24, 33, 35, 38
Chossudovsky, Michel, 170
CIA, 3
cities, 31, 85, 103
ciudad, 46, 83, 90, 93, 105, 121, 207. *See also* cities
Claudia, 140, 212
CNI (*Central Nacional de Inteligencia*), 66, 67, 128, 219n1, 221n1
Cobain, Kurt, 69
cognition, 16, 87, 220n8
cold, 80–81, 95, 96, 103, 104, 118, 124–25. *See also frío*
colonialism, 32, 56, 117
communism, 4, 76, 122–23, 132, 134, 138, 218n5
Conadep, 200
Concepción, 40, 42
Concertación, La, 1, 3, 4, 8, 12, 47, 69, 118–19, 123, 144, 155, 170, 196, 217n2
Conejo, 135
confession, 52, 131, 138, 160, 189
Connelly, Frances, 149, 150, 156
Conquest, 24, 32, 37, 46
Conrad, Joseph, 50
consensus, 1, 3, 12, 116
conservatives, 30
Constitution, 5, 7
contradiction, 95, 97, 107, 109, 116, 119–20, 127, 129, 138
Contreras, Manuel, 12, 133, 138
Contreras Maluaje, Carlos, 161–62, 218n5
Convivencia, 7, 19, 119
Copito, 51, 53
Coplan, Amy, 16, 225
corpses, 114, 130, 180, 182. *See also* bodies
Corral, Wilfrido, 117
cortex, 17. *See also* brain
Cortázar, Julio, 74
Cosme, 41–42
coup, 4, 9, 13, 22, 75, 101, 103, 104, 113, 124, 141, 145, 170–71, 196, 199, 200, 210, 220n1
Coyne, André, 95
Cuartel Villanova, 71
Cuba, 3, 76
culpability, 117, 137, 140, 190 *See also* guilt
Cummings, Peter M. M., 2–3

daemonic, 175–76, 222
David, 78, 102, 105–6, 110–15, 209, 220n3
Decoty, Jean, 167
degradation, 73, 128, 135–36, 148, 152
Dehesa, La, 40, 46–47
Delbo, Charlotte, 58
democracy, 1–4, 7, 12, 31, 63, 71, 95, 117, 118, 119, 144, 145, 160, 168–70, 200
Densmore, Francis, 33
desesperanza, La, 20, 61, 62, 65, 75–79, 89–94, 220n6
desierto, El, 21, 63, 72, 80, 128, 129, 130, 139–45, 156, 212, 214–15
Díaz, Carolina, 116–17, 125, 221n7
Díaz, Junot, 193
dictatorship, 1–7, 9, 11, 13, 14, 15, 19, 20–24, 30, 31, 32, 34–36, 38, 40–44, 47–48, 50, 52, 54, 56, 57, 59, 60, 62–75, 77–79, 82, 84, 90, 94–97, 99, 101–2, 104, 106, 116–18, 120, 124, 127–28, 131, 139, 144, 145, 146, 148, 150, 152, 154, 155, 157–58, 160, 162, 168, 169–71, 175, 176, 177, 178, 179–80, 182, 189–97, 199, 200, 201, 202, 205, 207–10, 212, 215–16, 218n5, 218n7, 219n8, 219n1, 220n3, 221n8, 221n1, 222n10
dimensión desconocida, La, 22, 23, 132, 157, 158, 160–72, 183, 205, 209, 218n5, 222n5
disorder, paraphilic, 184–85
DINA (*Dirección de Inteligencia Nacional*), 128, 134, 221n1
Dion, Lisa, 178–79
Dionysian, 139, 143–45

Index 239

disappearance, 4, 6, 9, 27, 30, 35, 42, 52, 69, 88, 91, 110, 116, 126, 127, 145, 160, 162, 164, 165, 171, 172, 176, 194, 195, 200, 205, 207, 208–9, 211, 215
Disney, Walt, 220n3
dissmell, 22, 157, 183, 185, 187, 191, 217n7
Dominican Republic, 193, 195
Donoso, José, 61, 62, 63, 66, 74–75, 78, 79, 89
Donoso (*Estrellas muertas*), 67–69, 82
doppelgänger, 194, 219n2. *See also* double
double, 146–47, 152, 156. *See also* doppelgänger
Doralisa, 103, 108
Dorfman, Ariel, 21, 95–97, 100–102, 104, 106, 108, 113–16, 118, 126–27, 209, 212, 220n2, 220n3, 220n6
Dracula, 155
dragon, 106, 110–12, 218n7
Dylan, Bob, 63

Echevarne, Angélica Inés, 211
Ecuador, 193
Edensor, Tim, 88
Eduardo, 107, 111, 112, 220n4, 221n8
Scarry, Elaine, 189
election, 1–3, 4, 200
elevator, 103–4, 114, 115
Elliot, Jorge, 171
Eloy Martínez, Tomás, 201
Eltit Diamela, 21, 95, 96, 97, 98, 115, 116–17, 118, 124–27, 175, 220n4
embargo, 63, 134, 150, 161
emotions, 1, 3, 8, 10–20, 22, 24, 30, 34, 49, 51, 56, 58, 61–62, 75, 78–80, 82, 84, 87–88, 105, 118, 140, 157–61, 166–67, 176–77, 183, 187, 195–97, 199–202, 205, 209, 212–13, 215–17, 222n7
empathy, 1, 3, 11, 14–19, 22, 57, 157–59, 161, 163, 165–67, 169, 171–75, 177, 181–83, 187, 189, 191, 195–96, 203, 205, 207, 222n5, 222n6

empuzzlement, 54
Engels, Frederick, 103–4
England, 212
Ercolino, Stefano, 22, 172–74
Ernesto, 40, 43, 201, 218n7
Estadio, Chile, 102, 183, 220n1; Nacional de Santiago, 30
Estrellas muertas, 20, 47, 61, 66–71, 74, 82–84
exile, 4, 21, 35, 43, 62, 71, 73, 74, 78, 89, 90, 99, 101, 106, 113, 115, 116, 145, 183, 189, 200–202, 209, 211–12
Eyerman, Ron, 10–11

Falk, Eugene H., 194–95
fascism, 35, 53–54, 168
Fausta, 77
Fausto, 24–31
fear, 2, 3, 12, 14, 18, 20, 22, 23, 30, 44, 57, 58, 59, 99, 119, 142, 143, 156, 157, 158, 161, 166, 207–9, 214
feelings, 11, 19, 20, 21, 23, 25, 29, 30, 34, 35, 36, 40, 41, 44, 47, 54, 56, 57, 58, 59, 60–61, 67, 70, 74, 80, 93, 97, 98, 112, 120, 125, 127, 130, 131, 140, 152, 153, 156, 161, 166, 167, 171, 172, 174, 189, 190, 191, 194, 195, 197, 204, 205, 207, 212, 213, 214, 215, 216, 221n2, 222n6
Feijóo, Claudia, 202
Felipe (*La última canción*), 105–6, 110–11, 113–14
feminist, 61, 218n1
Fernández, Nona, 13–14, 20, 23, 28, 32, 35, 38, 40, 42, 43, 157, 158, 160–61, 163, 165, 166, 168–69, 170–71, 172, 182, 205, 207, 209, 218n7, 221n2
fetishism, 22, 32, 184
fiction, perturbatory, 20, 54
Fin de la historia, El, 202, 213
fiscal, El, 199, 200, 223n3
Flaquísimo, El, 112
Fletcher, Angus, 175, 176, 178, 182, 222
Flores, Carol, 163–64, 221n1, 222n5

Flores-Rodríguez, Daynali, 193
fMRI, 18
Fontaine, Arturo, 21, 128, 129, 131–33, 138, 202
forgetfulness, 30, 213
forgiveness, 118, 132, 138
Fornazzari, Alessandro, 217n6
Francia, Dr. José Gaspar Rodríguez de, 196, 199
Franco, Francisco, 117–18
Frank, Adam J., 158
Franz, Carlos 20, 21, 61, 63, 128, 129, 139–41, 145, 150, 152, 212, 215
Freddy, 77
Frei, Eduardo, 8, 12, 69
Frei Montalva, Eduardo, 31, 183
Freud, Sigmund, 14, 29, 85, 86
Friedman, Mary Lusky, 78
frío, El, 80, 88, 96, 104, 124. *See also* cold
Fritz Roa, Sergio, 59
Frosh, Stephen, 10
Fuentes, Carlos, 74
Fuentes Castro, Raúl Emilio, 41, 43, 44, 45, 219n7, 219n8
Fuenzalida, 20, 23, 38–47, 55, 60, 218, n5, 218n6, 218n7, 219n8
funas, 8

Gahona, Alonso, 171
Galeano, Eduardo, 26–28, 36–37
Gamerro, Carlos, 201
García-Avello, Macarena, 39, 219n8
García Barría, Narciso, 79
García-Corales, Guillermo, 169
García, 51–53, 57, 60
García Márquez, Gabriel, 74, 192
genocide, 4, 186, 210
Gernsbacher, Morton Ann, 159, 161
ghosts, 10, 24, 26, 28, 33, 34, 36–38, 124, 201, 218n3
Glass, Diana, 202, 204–5
goals, happiness, 62–63, 66, 70, 75, 76
Goldstein, Jeffrey, 179

Gómez-Barris, Magdalena, 71
grotesque, 21, 129, 147, 148, 149–52, 154, 156, 219n2
Guardia de Hierro, 205
Guatemala, 193
Guevara, Che, 100
Guezzar, Terri Pullen, 18, 217n5
guilt, 62, 73, 140, 142, 203–4, 215. *See also* culpability
Gürsel, Zeynep Devrim, 55
Gusmán, Luis, 201, 213
gustatory, 187
Guzmán, Patricio, 217n6
Guzmán, Juan, 9

Hahn, Daniel, 221n9
Haiti, 19
hands, 114–15
Harpham, Geoffrey, 149
haunting, 7, 10, 36, 39, 84, 125, 129, 169, 202
Heidegger, Martin, 211
Heker, Liliana, 202, 213
Henríquez Silva, Raúl, 6
hero, 44, 62, 64, 111, 182, 200, 203–4, 218n5, 219n7, 223n3
Hirsch, Marianne, 10, 13
historical, 2–5, 8, 9, 11, 12, 22, 24, 25, 32–33, 34–35, 36, 40, 42–43, 59, 97, 99, 102, 106, 122–23, 126, 149, 161, 163, 166, 167, 169–71, 173, 176, 193, 196, 197, 199–200, 205, 207, 209, 215, 218n5
Hoffman, Eva, 12
Hogan, Patrick Colm, 21, 62–63, 66, 73
Holocaust, 4, 10, 11, 13, 56, 99, 173
Honduras, 193
hopelessness, 21, 69–70, 74, 81, 129
horse, 139–42
Hueso, El, 134, 138

Iacoboni, Marco, 17
Ibáñez, Carlos, 24, 34

ideology, 23, 95, 127, 169
imperialism, 20, 117
incest, 23–25, 28–29
indeterminacy, 20–21, 54, 60, 98, 116, 118, 120, 125
Indians, 37, 171
Indigenous, 1, 26, 32–33, 35
Indio, El, 24–25, 26, 29, 32, 34, 35, 36, 37, 38
infierno, El, 128–29, 130–32, 133, 136, 137, 138–39, 156, 214
Ingrid, 174, 180, 182
injustice, 36, 43, 47, 96, 143, 212; spatial, 20, 24, 31–36, 46–47
insula, 17, 18
intertextuality, 20, 25, 60, 77, 104, 108, 130–31, 139, 215, 219n3
Iquela, 174–75, 176, 177–78, 179, 180–81, 182
irony, 41, 62, 92, 93, 203, 219n8
Iser, Wolfgang, 18, 217

Jamás el fuego nunca, 21, 68, 95, 96, 97, 98, 115, 116–27, 220n4, 221n9, 222n7
Jara, Víctor, 102–3, 114, 183
Jarpa, Sergio Onofre, 160
Javiera, 66–68, 82
Jaén, Isabel, 167, 169
Jelić, Andrea, 87, 220n8
Jelin, Elizabeth, 5
Jiménez-Polli, Víctor, 147–48, 150, 152, 154, 156
Johnson, Gary, 21, 97
Jota, La, 78
Jukes, Jaqueline, 179
junta, 71, 200
Justo, Liborio, 122

Kaplan, E. Ann, 15
Karr-Cornejo, Katherine, 33
Kast, José Antonio, 1–2
Keller, Carlos, 59
Kintsch, Walter, 159
Kohan, Matin, 201

Kohut, Karl, 192–93
kosmos, 222n8
Kozameh, Alicia, 20
Krank, Emilio, 183–91, 210
Kristeva, Julia, 21, 129, 130, 133, 134, 137, 139–40
Krueger, Richard, 184–85

Labanyi, Jo, 169
Lagos, Ricardo, 9, 11–12
Lamm, Claus, 16–17, 19
Landkildehus, Søren, 146–47, 156
Larco, Laura, 139–45, 212, 215, 221n3
Lautaro, 24, 32–33, 35, 36
Lazzara, Michael J., 116–17, 128, 134, 171
Lee, Bruce, 41
leftist, 6, 30, 77, 128, 183, 200
legend, 3, 32, 90, 106, 108, 110–12, 132, 196, 199, 209
Leonora, 202–4
Leskinen, Auli, 221n7
Levi, Primo, 22
Ley de Obediencia Debida, 200
limbic, 18–19
liminality, 86, 91–92
Lipps, Theodor, 172–73
Liscano, Carlos, 197
Littell, Jonathan, 173
Lolo, 110
Longo, Mariano, 15
Lonquen, 7
Lopito, 76, 77, 93, 94
López-Balló, Francisco, 217n6
López Rega, José, 192
Lord Jim, 50
Lorena, 129, 132–38, 139, 145, 202, 203, 205, 218n6
Lozoya, Johanna, 30
Lucio, 148, 152–53
Lyndon, Donlon, 84
Ludwig II, 82
Lynch, Joseph J., 43
Lyndon, Donlon, 84

MacAdam, Alfred, 220n6
MacCarthy, Brendan, 29
Maddrell, Avril, 79
maestrito, el, 147–54, 156
Maggi, Marcelo, 210–11
Maguire, Geoffrey, 201–2, 206, 209
Maier, Gonzalo, 41
Manzur, Yolita, 80–81
Mapocho, 20, 23–38, 46, 47
Mapocho River, 175–76
Mapuche, 78
Marcos, Juan Manuel, 199
María Rosa, 22, 183–91
Mario, 221n3
Marlén, 219n7
Mármol, Jorge, 192
Marras, 115
martyrdom, 100, 110, 200, 223n3
Martínez-Roth, 144
Marx, Karl, 220n3
Marxism, 6, 61, 95–96, 100–101, 127, 174
Marín, Germán, 20, 61, 71, 84, 215
Max, 41
McClennen, Sophia A., 111
melancholy, 21, 85–86, 92, 95, 96, 98–101, 102, 106, 107, 108, 112, 114, 115, 116, 118, 120, 122, 126, 127, 166, 196, 222n7
Memorias del fuego, 26
memories, 1, 5–6, 10, 26, 28, 33, 36, 40, 46, 63, 69, 72, 84–85, 91, 112, 114–16, 125, 140–41, 155, 168, 170, 174–79, 198, 201, 202, 205, 213, 217n2, 217n6
Mendoza, 180–81, 182
Menem, Carlos, 200
messianic, 100–101, 194
metaphor, 6, 18, 55, 100, 102, 115, 118, 137, 155, 222
Mexico, 113–14
Miguel, José Luis de, 131
Milanés, Pablo, 76
military, 46, 141, 93, 165, 168, 171, 193
Moira, 143
Moneda, La, 100–101

Moral, Félix, 200
morality, 18–19, 50, 52–53, 130, 137, 159, 170, 174, 187, 191
Morel, Hortensia, 78, 220n7
Morton, Adam, 172
motif, 36, 95, 113–14, 118, 143, 194, 195, 197, 201–2, 205, 207, 209, 214–15
Moulián, Tomás, 1
Murphy, Kaitlin, M., 217n6
Museo de la memoria, 11, 170
Musgrove, Mary, 179
myth, 21, 23, 26–28, 37, 59, 78, 89, 100–101, 105–6, 108–12, 127, 194
Myyry, Lisa, 166
Máscara, 114–15
Mónica, 54, 57–59, 72–74, 219n2
Musgrove, Mary, 179

National Intelligence Directorate, 171
nausea, 186–87
navel, 36–38
Nazi, 4, 84, 113, 173, 210, 211–12
Neal, Arthur, 11
neoliberalism, 1–2, 20, 23, 30–36, 46–47, 96, 97, 103, 117, 119, 124, 126–27, 169–70
Neruda, Matilde, 75–76, 78, 92
Neruda, Pablo, 75, 77, 176
neural, 17, 157–58, 178
neurobiology, 178–79
neurons, 13–14, 17–19, 187, 217n4
neuroscience, 16–17
Neuschwanstein, 82
Ngai, Sianne, 21, 61, 62, 94, 97, 174
Nicaragua, 193
Noddings, Nel, 166
Nora, 50, 52
nostalgia, 75, 96–102, 106–15, 118, 120–22, 197, 209, 214, 217, 220; reflexive, 125–27

O'Higgins, Bernardo, 24
olfactory, 144, 187

Index

Olick, Jeffrey, 56
Olivera-Williams, María Rosa 116, 124, 125–26, 127, 221
Ordóñez, El doctor, 144–45
orphan, 23–24, 30, 43, 145
Orwell, George, 211
Osorio, Elsa, 202
Ossorio, Enrique, 210–11

Pacheco, Carlos, 192–93, 196
Palacio de la risa, El, 20, 61, 71–74, 84–88, 215
Pallasmaa, Juhani, 79, 82, 85
Paloma, 174–76, 180–82
Pamela, 109, 111
Pampa Hundida, 139, 142, 144
Paraguay, 193, 199–200
parody, 41, 110, 170–71, 211
Parra, Nicanor, 170–71, 222n3
Parra, Violeta, 219n4
patina, 21, 86, 215
Rozin, Paul, 186
Rodríguez, Paula, 217n6
Paz-Mackay, María Soledad, 200–203
Perón, Isabel, 192
Peronist, 205. *See also* Perón, Juan
Peru, 95, 193
Perón, Juan, 192. *See also* Peronist
Petremen, David, 78
peñas, 76, 219n4
perceptions, sensory, 183, 188
Pérez Yoma, Edmundo, 8
Phelan, James, 61, 97, 112, 126
photographs, 6, 39–40, 47, 50, 55–57, 59, 70, 102, 121–22, 172, 210–11, 218n4, 220n5. *See also* photography
photography, 13, 18, 20, 23, 39–40, 42, 47–49, 52–53, 55–56, 58, 121, 201, 211. *See also* photographs
physiological, 157, 159, 166, 177, 179–80, 182, 183, 186, 187, 217n4
Piglia, Ricardo, 209
Pinchot, 106, 110–12

Pinochet, Augusto, 1–9, 11–13, 19, 20, 23, 25, 30–31, 35, 38, 40, 41, 43, 47–48, 52, 59, 60, 62–63, 66, 69, 71, 74, 79, 83, 95, 101, 103–4, 106, 111, 113, 116, 120, 124, 128, 131–32, 139, 158, 160, 168–70, 174, 176–77, 178, 179, 191–92, 196, 200, 219n1, 221n1, 222n4
Plato, 44
plebiscite, 4, 180, 196
Plotnik, Viviana, 138
Poblete, Juan, 2
Poland, 197, 211
Polli, Víctor, 147–48, 150, 152–54, 156
Posadas, María del Carmen, 73, 219n2
postcolonial, 61
postdictatorship, 2, 3, 6, 11, 21, 22, 66, 70, 85, 95–97, 101, 124, 127, 154–55, 169, 175, 193, 196, 201
postmemory, 1, 3, 5, 9, 10, 11, 12, 13, 19, 20, 47, 62, 193, 195, 201, 217n1
postmodern, 5, 215
Prague Spring, 101
Prats, Carlos, 171
primacy effects, 164
Prince, Gerald, 196
privatization, 32, 46, 127
Probe Seven, 161
Proceso de Reorganización Nacional, El, 192, 210–12
Pron, Patricio, 201, 205–9

queerness, 180
Quiruvilca, 95

Rafa, 134
Raquel, 64–66, 80–82
reactions, 15, 17, 22, 157–59, 167, 178, 182–83, 185–87, 217n7
rebellion, fetal, 96, 101, 109
recency effects, 164
reconciliation, 7, 12
remainder, 174, 176, 182
remembrance, 23, 101, 118, 199

Renzi, Emilio, 210–11
reparation, 8, 12, 62, 71
República Dominicana, La, 193
Respiración artificial, 209–12
Resta, La, 22, 157–58, 172–83, 191, 222n4
Rettig Commission, 7, 217n2, 221n2
Richard, Nelly, 12, 174–75
Rimmon Kenan, Schlomith, 54
Roa Bastos, Augusto, 59, 192, 199–200, 219n3, 223n2
Robertis, Carolina de, 197
Roberto, 137
Rodolfo, 174
Rodríguez, Paula 217n6
Rodríguez Alcalá, Guido, 199
Rojas, Eric, 155
Rojo, Grínor, 11, 73–74, 200, 219n2
romance plots, 21, 61, 62–76, 94
Romanticism, 192
Romero, Ivana, 168
Ros, Ana, 196–97, 217n6
Rosas, Juan Manuel, 210
Rosenblatt, Louise, 18, 217n5
Rosencof, Mauricio, 197
Rotger, Patricia, 201–2, 213
Rothlisberger, Silvia, 180
Rozin, Paul, 186
Rucia, 24–26, 28–29, 32–38
Ruskin, John, 150
rust, 86–87

sadism, 178, 186
sadness, 18, 30, 85, 92, 99, 125, 126, 209
SAG, (*Servicio Agrícola y Ganadero*), 53, 54
Sagastizábal, Patricia, 202, 212–15
Sánchez, Matilde, 202
Santiago, 8, 20, 23–24, 26, 28, 30–31, 33, 34–36, 38, 42, 46–49, 54, 56, 59, 61, 63, 65–66, 74, 80–84, 93, 146, 148, 154, 156, 170, 177, 181–82, 199, 222n10
Santiago Cero, 20, 61, 63–66, 80–82, 83–84
satire, 148, 170

Sattelzeit, 126–27
Scarry, Elaine, 189–90
Schvchenco, Olga, 39
Schlickers, Sabine, 20, 54
Sebastián, 64–66, 80–82
Secreto para Julia, Un, 202, 212–15
Semán, Ernesto, 201
Senderito, 96, 101, 106, 107–9, 111–12, 114
Sendero, Manuel, 21, 95–97, 101–12, 124, 126, 209
Senio Blair, Laura, 25
Shevchenko, Olga, 39
Shivers, George R., 220n2
shortage, 3, 103, 104
Shua, Ana María, 202
silence, 21, 86–88, 92
Sime, Fátima, 157, 159, 183
simulation theory, 16, 19
Singer, Tania, 16–17, 19
Sklar, Howard, 164, 166, 167
skyscraper 30–31, 34, 36
soccer stadium, 24, 30, 34, 36
socialism, 1–3, 21, 76, 95, 96, 98–100, 103, 106, 113, 115, 118, 122–23, 126, 209, 220n3
Soja, Edward W., 20, 31–32
Solano López, Francisco, 200
song, 97, 108–10, 112, 209, 220n5. *See also* canción
Sontag, Susan, 137
Southern Cone, 196–97, 199
Soviet Union, 96, 122
Spain, 32, 74
stadium, 24, 30, 34, 36, 171, 220n1
Stančić, Aleksander, 87, 220n8
Steiner, George, 100–101
Stern, Steve J., 3–4, 6, 7–9, 11–12, 42, 118–19
Sternberg, Meir, 164
Stockholm, 137, 189, 202; syndrome, 132, 139, 183, 187, 191, 204, 215
Stoker, Bram, 155
Stroessner, Alfredo, 199–200

students, 2–3, 64, 81–82, 143–44, 145, 148, 153, 222n9
suicide, 24, 38, 47, 69, 83, 100
survivors, 71, 99, 154–56, 204, 207, 215
symbolism, 7, 21, 29, 30, 32–33, 34, 38, 64, 73, 78, 89, 97, 104, 105, 109, 113–14, 118, 124–25, 144, 151, 154–55, 182, 209, 222n4, 222n10
sympathy, 166–67
syntagmatic indices, 97, 116, 120

Tandeciarz, Silvia R., 201
Tardewski, 211
Taylor, Diana, 58
terror, 70, 117, 123, 157, 190, 194
testimony, 39, 52, 64, 109, 116, 128, 129, 130, 131, 133, 138, 144, 200, 207
theme, 20, 22, 24, 32, 42, 45, 75, 77–79, 97, 98, 115–16, 126, 129, 131, 139, 144–45, 154–55, 176, 192–95, 200–202, 204–5, 215, 222n8
Thomas, Nigel, 18
Todorov, Tzvetan, 97, 116, 120
Tomkins, Silvan, 22, 157, 158, 178, 191, 217n4, 217n7
tone, 21, 61–62, 79, 92, 94–97, 105–6, 112, 126, 203, 213
Toro, Alfonso de, 131
Torre, Judit, 75–77, 92–93
torture, 4, 7, 8, 9, 20, 21, 22, 23, 30, 42, 48, 50–51, 52, 56, 58, 67–68, 71, 72, 73, 84, 85, 90, 102, 114, 120, 128, 130, 131, 132, 133, 134, 137, 138, 139, 141, 145, 156, 160–61, 162, 163–64, 165, 171, 172, 178, 182, 183, 184–90, 191, 194, 195, 197, 200, 205, 207, 209, 211, 212, 214, 215–16, 218n5, 220n1, 222n5
Traba, Marta, 202
Trabucco Zerán, Alia, 157, 158, 172, 174–75, 177, 180, 222n7
trauma, 4–7, 10–15, 15, 33, 48, 50–51, 57–58, 68, 86, 115, 149, 169, 179, 187, 189, 195, 201, 207, 213, 214, 215

Traverso, Enzo, 21, 98–100, 114, 126
Treib, Marc, 84
Trenton, Barbara Jean, 221n2
Trias Coll, Santiago, 199
Triple Alliance War, 200
Trostel, Katherine, 33, 218n3
Trotsky, Leon, 77, 219n5
Trujillo, Rafael Leonidas, 195
Tuszewicka, Monika, 96–97, 106
Twilight Zone (TV series), 22, 160, 161–64, 205, 221n6

Última canción de Manuel Sendero, La, 21, 95–116, 117, 126, 209, 212, 222n7
Unidad Popular, La, 76, 122, 170
urbanization, 33, 46
Urbina, 51–53, 57, 60
Urqueta, Genovena, 45
Uruguay, 193, 196–97, 199, 200
Urzúa Opazo, Macarena, 82
utopía, 21, 99, 107, 126–27

Valdivia, Pedro, 24, 32
Valech Commission, 9
Valenzuela, Luisa, 165, 205
Valenzuela Morales, Antonio, 165, 205, 222n6
Vallejo, César, 93, 95–96, 104–5, 108, 118, 124, 199
Valparaíso, 47, 66, 82, 84
vampire, 21, 63, 128–29, 145, 154–56
Van Alphen, Ernst, 160, 165–66, 222n4
Vanesa, 152–53
Vargas, Jennifer Harford, 193–94
Vargas Llosa, Mario, 74, 195
Velasco, Professor, 143–44
Vera, Mañungo, 75–79, 89–92, 219n3, 220n6
Vera, Miguel, 219n3
Vergara, Perucich, Francisco, 30–31
verticalization, 30
Vicaría de la Solidaridad, 6, 221n2
Víctor (*La resta*), 174

Vida doble, La, 21, 128, 129, 130–39
Videla Jorge, 200
Vignemont, Frédérique de, 16
Villa Grimaldi, 11, 71–74, 84–86, 88–89, 215–16
violence, 10, 25, 43, 48–49, 50, 52, 54, 55, 56, 57, 58, 68, 77, 96, 101, 108, 114, 119, 127, 132, 174, 175, 178–79, 183, 222n8
void, 86–87
Voyager, 13, 217n3

warlocks, 59–60, 78
weathering, 21, 86–87
Weibel Barahona, José, 164–65
Weibel, María Teresa, 165
Weldt-Basson, Helene Carol, 223n1, 223n2
Wenderoth, Rolf, 139
witches, 59, 78, 79
World War II, 210

Ximena, 125

Zheng, Nan, 23, 25
Zillmann, Dolf, 179
Zubieta, Ana María, 213
Zósima, 146, 155–56

www.ingramcontent.com/pod-product-compliance
Lightning Source LLC
Chambersburg PA
CBHW020945230426
43666CB00005B/172